Reflective Clinical Supervision in Speech and Language Therapy

This book de-mystifies supervision in speech and language therapy, focusing on the practicalities and pitfalls. Clinicians are encouraged to reflect on their individual style as a supervisor and the tools they utilise to make a successful supervisory relationship.

Drawing on previous experience, Howes offers a combination of reflective, solution-focused, and strengths-based approaches, covering topics such as:

- The importance of the supervisory conversation
- Ways to ensure conversations are reflective and appreciative, supportive yet challenging
- The training needed to be effective supervisors and 'good supervisees'
- The functions of supervision and how these change over time for each clinician, from learning new clinical skills to support in time and energy management
- Practical resources for busy clinicians, making it a manual of insights and support for supervision in SLT

Reflective Clinical Supervision in Speech and Language Therapy will be an invaluable guide for all speech and language therapists who are either experienced or newly established supervisors supporting others with the complexities of casework and the stress of relationships in every busy working day.

Ruth Howes worked for 34 years in the NHS with various SLT roles including clinical lead for complex developmental needs and autistic spectrum disorder. She was a specialist adviser to RCSLT for much of her time in the NHS and was lead author for the RCSLT Assistant Practitioners project (2022). Ruth is now in independent practice, Communicology SLT Consultancy, working primarily with families of children with autistic spectrum disorder. She also separately runs ARC Supervision, offering both supervision and training in supervision.

Professional Development in Speech and Language Therapy

This series centres on the speech and language therapist and provides practical resources to help the professional grow in confidence and learn new skills allowing them to improve their practice.

Often the busy therapist is consumed with their caseload and their own personal development is put on the back burner. This series provides the reader with practical, accessible resources which allow the reader to focus on themselves, rather than their client. Tailored specifically for the Speech and Language Therapist these books are suitable for newly qualified therapists as well as seasoned professionals who want to add more to their toolkit in a specific area.

Reflective Clinical Supervision in Speech and Language Therapy
Strengthening Supervision Skills
Ruth Howes

Reflective Clinical Supervision in Speech and Language Therapy

Strengthening Supervision Skills

Ruth Howes

Routledge
Taylor & Francis Group

LONDON AND NEW YORK

Cover image: © Getty Images

First published 2023
by Routledge
4 Park Square, Milton Park, Abingdon, Oxon OX14 4RN

and by Routledge
605 Third Avenue, New York, NY 10158

Routledge is an imprint of the Taylor & Francis Group, an informa business

© 2023 Ruth Howes

British Library Cataloguing-in-Publication Data
A catalogue record for this book is available from the British Library

Library of Congress Cataloging-in-Publication Data
A catalog record has been requested for this book

ISBN: 978-1-032-12902-0 (hbk)
ISBN: 978-1-032-12901-3 (pbk)
ISBN: 978-1-003-22677-2 (ebk)

DOI: 10.4324/9781003226772

Typeset in Galliard
by Deanta Global Publishing Services, Chennai, India

Contents

Contents

Introduction

"Every adventure requires a first step. Trite, but true, even here."
Cheshire Cat, *Alice's Adventures in Wonderland*

Opening Reflections

Why has this book been so difficult to write? I wrote the proposal and signed the contract with confidence. Time passed. It was several years since I'd undertaken a reflective supervision project as part fulfilment of a master's degree; so I'd gone back to the literature to ensure I was aware of the latest thinking around reflective practice and its application in clinical supervision.

Finally, a reflective conversation with someone made me realise it was a case of 'getting this on paper' and 'just writing' (thank you Tina). In effect I needed a supervisory conversation to boost confidence and make this book happen. It is built upon my clinical and management/leadership experience over 35 years in the NHS and more recently in independent practice. Most of all it is about knowing speech and language therapy and working alongside my colleagues who are therapists, assistant practitioners, and managers. We are all leaders in different ways. I certainly had to lead myself into writing this book.

In the end it was knowing that this is not an academic work, but a practical guide to clinical supervision in the professional arena of speech and language therapy, sharing my journey into becoming a reflective practitioner and flourishing in my work (on a good day). Ours is a profession with a heavy weight of both decision making and navigating interpersonal relationships with clients and colleagues. Every day we encounter clinical situations which are slightly different to ones we have experienced before. We navigate through and draw on evidence using our own experience and networking with colleagues. It is easy to carry work round with us and potentially dwell

DOI: 10.4324/9781003226772-1

on issues and decisions. This book is about tools to increase resilience and job satisfaction.

I find metaphor valuable in making sense of concepts and events. You will find quotations from *Alice's Adventures in Wonderland* and *Alice through the Looking Glass* (Carroll 1865 & 1871) throughout this book. The imagery of a reflective looking glass, seeing things slightly differently from how they appear at first sight, fits. During NHS re-structuring with continual changes in direction I found standing back and thinking of painting the roses red, then painting the roses white, then red again humorous and helpful. I draw on other metaphors and imagery too and share my own model for viewing events in a freeze frame approach through reflective conversations. The aim has been to gather together approaches which are valuable in supervision, and present them for professional development and practical use by busy practitioners.

Dedications

This book is dedicated to all those I have supervised. I wince when I think about the early years when I had management training, but no training in the art and practice of supervision. Thanks go especially to my monthly online supervision group who encouraged me to continue when energy was flagging and time in scarce supply.

I must shine the spotlight on a retired colleague, Nicola Hughes, who was both manager, and supervisor when I was an overconfident, newly specialist paediatric clinician. Nicola created a community of practice at Keighley Health Centre in Airedale NHS Trust. We were a small team who, with Nicola's leadership, talked about our cases, shared our enthusiasm for therapy, and puzzled out the different factors in clinical situations which were troubling, or somehow just not going to plan. In this shared, sheltered learning environment I learnt from an expert practitioner with much clinical wisdom about personal constructs, tolerance, compassion, and barriers we face in daily practice and learnt through countless reflective conversations. Also, the importance of a supportive network of colleagues, a coffee break, and humour too. I went on to work in other roles and organisations but took away with me that with time and space to talk about our casework we are more successful and competent clinicians.

Reflective clinical supervision in speech and language therapy would never have been written without the endless positive support of my husband Nigel and daughter Hetta who had more belief in my ability to complete this book project than I had in myself.

Setting off

And so, an exploration of reflective clinical supervision in speech and language therapy begins. We each begin our supervisory journey in different ways as there is no specific pathway or training route. However, we do all have in common the fact that we begin as supervisees. Our first supervision may be informal or formal, mediocre or fantastic, but we begin by talking about our work with someone and realising that casework is rarely straight forward.

> *All in the golden afternoon*
> *Full leisurely we glide;*
> *For both our oars, with little skill,*
> *By little arms are plied,*
> *While little hands make vain pretence*
> *Our wanderings to guide.*
>
> Alice's Adventures in Wonderland

What Is Clinical Supervision?

"You learn something new every day.

Make a note of that, Marchy, it might come in useful."
Hatter, *Alice's Adventures in Wonderland*

Key Themes

- Ask four SLTs what is clinical supervision
- A brief history
- Visiting various definitions of supervision
- Why supervision?
- Peer or manager as supervisor?

Ask Four SLTs and They May All Say Different Things!

If you ask four speech and language therapists (SLT) or assistant practitioners "What is clinical supervision?," it is likely they will all say different things. There can still be confusion about the difference between management and clinical/professional supervision. The Royal College for Speech and Language Therapists (RCSLT) Guidelines for Supervision (2019) are very specific and clear, but nevertheless the busy clinician can still feel confused about specifics of 'what to take' to each type of supervision.

There is also still a proportion of practitioners who view clinical supervision as purely case-based supervision. This is certainly important, but clinical supervision covers far more than case-based support. Clinical supervision is part of continuing professional development through reflective learning.

DOI: 10.4324/9781003226772-2

Daily dilemmas and decisions are explored, as if through a lens, from a safe distance in a supervisory conversation. The lens gives a different perception of the wider situation, as if transforming from 2D into 3D vision, and not just reviewing the event, but the relationships, emotions, and practitioner's role within the situation. This is situational supervision: guided reflection leading to changed perspectives and learning.

History of Clinical Supervision and Reflective Practice – Briefly and Not Boringly!

It seems likely that the word 'clinical' was first used in supervision in the teaching profession in relation to the need to explore and analyse 'events' in the classroom and in so doing learn from experience. Events are 'clinically' examined using a reflective framework from a distance through a sharply focused lens. When training supervisors, I draw attention to this, as the assumption is, unsurprisingly, that clinical supervision is about 'clinical' work, when it started out as clinically analysing professional practice.

Clinical supervision took root in healthcare services including clinical psychology, counselling, and occupational therapy. Historically occupational therapists (OT) worked more closely with mental health services, and perhaps that is why some of the first allied health professional (AHP) literature comes from OT.

Underpinning clinical supervision are various approaches, with the strongest and most established being reflective practice. Reflective practice has a longer history than clinical supervision. Combining of the two has provided a positive and powerful tool for supporting learning and development in healthcare.

There is considerable literature focusing on supervision in healthcare professions, particularly from nursing. John Driscoll's *Practising Clinical Supervision: A Reflective Approach for Healthcare Professionals* (2006) has been revised and refreshed over time with several editions published. Della Fish and Sheila Twinn (1996) have written extensively about clinical supervision in healthcare and a "*principled approach*" to practice. The information tends to be well argued and thoughtful, but academic in style.

There is also a strong strand of reflective practice history in healthcare professions, for example, contributions from Tony Ghaye, Sue Lillyman, Christopher Johns, and Melanie Jasper. The Johns Model of Structured Reflection (2017) was developed for healthcare practitioners and has evolved over time since the first version in the 1990s.

In the chapters which follow, reflective practice, and its importance as a strategy for learning and developing professional practice, is examined with frameworks for exploring daily clinical events and experience. The ability to critically reflect on our work has become a required competency in all healthcare professions, including speech and language therapy.

Clinical Supervision in Speech and Language Therapy

There is little written specifically in connection with clinical supervision or reflective practice in relation to speech and language therapy.

Kathleen Williamson when devising a competency-based Model of Professional Practice for SLTs for RCSLT (2001), drew heavily upon Coles and Fish's work, *Developing Professional Judgement in Health Care: Learning Through the Critical Appreciation of Practice* (1997); this model was later extended to support practitioners (2002). Williamson puts the ability to make sound judgements and decisions at the heart of professional practice. How we make judgements is based on our knowledge, skills, and experience, as well as the values which underpin our practice. This is compared to an iceberg (Figure 1.1), and on the surface all we see is an SLT going through a busy day at work, making decision after decision. Underneath a competent therapist is using high-level reasoning skills, analysing the many relevant factors and perspectives involved to identify the best option.

In making a decision the practitioner has worked out the best course of action for that day and that particular set of circumstances.

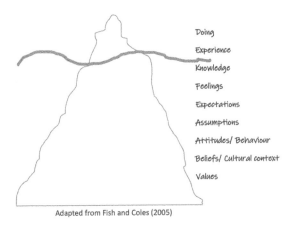

Doing
Experience
Knowledge
Feelings
Expectations
Assumptions
Attitudes/ Behaviour
Beliefs/ Cultural context
Values

Adapted from Fish and Coles (2005)

Figure 1.1

Speech and language therapy professional practice is

far greater than the ability to deliver a service through a predetermined care plan or pathway. A therapist is constantly facing unique situations and practice dilemmas, not just in relation to individual clients, but also in relation to managing caseload demands and all the unexpected happenings.

(RCSLT 2002)

Practice is complex; it is impossible to absolutely pin down and predict professional actions.

The RCSLT guidelines state

Judgement and decision-making emerge not only as the least visible yet most important aspects of practice, but also as the hardest aspects to quantify and measure. In addition, it follows that developing expertise with a given client group relates not just to the development of knowledge and practical skills, but to the making of increasingly fine-tuned, appropriate, accurate and speedy judgements and decisions.

Quality of professional practice will be achieved and improved on primarily by individual professionals working with integrity in a critically reflective way. The fundamental requirement of therapists is that they should act from a position of commitment and care about the work they are engaged in. Flowing from this comes a desire to continually improve the quality of individual practice through a process of critical reflection and the integration of evidence from the "outsider" knowledge base.

(RCSLT 2002)

So, there is a need to be aware of the complexities and keep pausing and considering our decisions about our cases and workload priorities through reflection on practice. If we keep a reflective lens in our professional toolkit, then we are committing to continually learning from experience and strengthening our skills and commitment to safe and competent practice.

Looking at the various frameworks can seem daunting. There are few opportunities for short courses to develop skills outside of postgraduate courses. Practitioners are interested in strengthening their practice in these areas, but realistically have little time for trawling literature, comparing approaches, and applying them in their casework. There is a need for information to be drawn together and made easily accessible, relevant, and practically useable; an explanation of reflective practice in clinical supervision and when and how we should use it. It is, as with much in the profession, a case of finding an approach which fits with our learning preferences and our individual professional style.

That is the aspiration of this book, to share ideas and to strengthen professional development.

Different frameworks and models of reflective practice relevant to speech and language therapy, which can be used practically in clinical supervision, will be explored. Those new to supervision can access resources and information to extend their knowledge and skills. Experienced supervisors should find additional ideas to refresh and extend their practice in new directions.

Different Varieties of Supervision

The differences between the types of supervision, especially management and clinical supervision, can still be confusing.

Management supervision is concerned with oversight of performance, support, and development within the line management structure. It covers clinical governance, quality, team issues, dissatisfaction, or complaints plus overall wellbeing at work. The conversation may cover how a job is going, and how objectives, set in an individual's Personal Development Review (PDR), are progressing.

Clinical supervision, also known as *professional supervision*, is regular protected time for discussing caseworking. It is an opportunity for in-depth guided reflection on practice, enabling learning through experience. It is part of ongoing development, supporting quality in therapy provision.

Safeguarding supervision is different in that it blends aspects of both management and clinical supervision. Depending on the practitioner's level of experience there might be more directive guidance from a safeguarding supervisor due to management of risks and the need to assure safe and efficient practice.

Safeguarding supervision is concerned with the implementation of safeguarding practice. It gives practitioners support, on an agreed schedule for managing cases with a complex background. It is usually provided within an agreed organisational framework, combining advisory guidance alongside reflecting on a case from different perspectives. Cases with varying levels of concern ranging from identified high-risk cases to potential concerns are discussed. Underlying the supervision is a need for assurance that the approach to cases is consistent with safeguarding policies/procedures.

Professional support is about wider supportive networks and might include peer conversations with colleagues, expert practitioners, attendance at professional meetings, action learning sets, and Clinical Excellence Networks (CENs).

Visiting Various Definitions

Definitions of clinical supervision can vary in emphasis, but generally include common themes. A strong theme is that it is about more than discussing cases and obtaining advice. It is a structured opportunity to talk and reflect on casework and to support learning from experience, resilience and safety in practice.

Examples of definitions of clinical supervision include:

- *"Clinical Supervision is a formal, ongoing, collaborative relationship, whereby one person (the supervisor), assists the other (the supervisee) to attend to issues of clinical effectiveness and professional well-being, with the underlying intention of enhancing the quality of client/patient care."*

  Lawton 2000

- *"Regular protected time for facilitated in depth reflection on clinical practice aimed to enable the supervisee to achieve, sustain and creatively develop a high quality of practice through the means of focused support and development."*

  Bond and Holland 1998

- *"Stepping back from the immediate, intensive experience of hands-on work and taking the time to wonder what the experience really means."*

  Parlarkian 2001

- *"Supervision is a working alliance between supervisor and supervisee in which the worker can reflect on herself in her working situation by giving an account of her work and receiving feedback and where appropriate guidance and appraisal. The object of the alliance is to maximise the competence in a helping profession."*

  Inskipp and Proctor 1993

- *"A formal process of professional support and learning which enables individual practitioners to develop knowledge and competence, assume responsibility for their own practice and enhance consumer protection and safety of care in complex situations."*

  NHS Management Executive definition (1993)

The Development of Supervision in Speech and Language Therapy

So, clinical supervision is the formal arrangement that enables you to discuss your work regularly with someone who is experienced and qualified. Supervision is an essential component of a good quality speech and language therapy service and a tool to identify and reduce risk. This is the case for all SLTs, including those practising independently or employed in other contexts.

As a profession, on first appearances, it looks as though we came late to clinical supervision. There is certainly more literature in occupational therapy, nursing, and teaching professions. However, speech and language therapy has always been a uniquely different profession, especially in its early history. It blended science and arts, teaching and behavioural therapy. The spectrum of human communication disorder is vast, and students who train together will have vastly different career paths. Having qualified before clinical supervision was ever mentioned and discovering it as a vehicle for reflective practice around 15 years after I'd qualified, I was immediately aware of the strength of supervision and its benefits for individual practitioners and services.

However, I do believe there was a current of very successful reflective practice and professional support in our profession before clinical supervision began to be introduced across services from the late 1990s. As therapists we have always been inclined to seek out conversations with colleagues and check out our clinical decision making when working with a case where there are a number of different options. I was certainly involved in weekly case discussions in a multi-disciplinary team (MDT) for adults with learning disabilities which resembled formal clinical supervision. In our small speech and language therapy team in West Yorkshire we would talk about cases over coffee, over lunch, and in weekly meetings. I felt well supported by enthusiastic, experienced colleagues who were keen to share their knowledge and enthusiasm for therapy. In this supportive environment I made the transition to specialist and RCSLT Clinical Advisor. We would certainly talk, consider possibilities, and share experiences together. Perhaps there was more advice giving, but I certainly always felt 'listened to' in my early career days.

Clinical supervision gave a system and assurances to organisations that support was in place. Following various traumatic national enquiries, this became part of the clinical governance and standards agenda. The drive to expand nursing supervision combined with interest in strategies from clinical psychology and counselling gave new frameworks for speech and language therapy. I still think we tend to be busy practitioners, endlessly juggling workload, perhaps preferring being given advice and ideas. The essence of being a reflective practitioner is about engaging in casework, standing back from the decisions and dilemmas we make every day, processing when something 'isn't going quite as expected,' and pausing to consider 'what's happening' and whether we need to change anything. It is about learning at work, from experience, with the support of colleagues. My learning point was to confront my defensive tendency and reflect more on my role in clinical situations. Could it be that the way in which I'd introduced a plan might have led to some reaction or resistance in carers? Freeze frame, view the situation from a distance, and I could see that a different style of communication might have had a more positive outcome. The learning process was not without a little discomfort at times!

Many working in the field of speech and language therapy, therapists, assistants, managers, leaders, will have a strong network of professional support, and clinical supervision will be one strand of this support. There is probably still more time spent 'talking about cases' in snatched moments between visits or at the end of the working day than in formal supervision sessions and long may this continue. There may never be resources available for research into the effectiveness of this professional support; but there is strong practitioner consensus that it is invaluable for the effectiveness of therapy and wellbeing of practitioners. We know it has value. When practitioners find themselves in a more isolated role as sole practitioner, in a school or in independent practice, they realise the difference and tend to seek out ways of replicating a supportive network. I believe this ability to form strong, supportive networks is one of the strengths of the profession.

Alongside this is formal clinical supervision with a clear steer from the Health Care Professional Council (HCPC), RCSLT, and the Association of Speech and Language Therapists in Private Practice (ASLTIP) that engagement in supervision is expected. This is specific time outside of the hurried, coffee break chat. It is space and time away from busy, clinical days. It is an opportunity to have a reflective conversation about casework and any clinical dilemmas, or difficulties with relationships or communication. It is freeze framing events, viewing them in slow motion, and noticing aspects which we may have missed which give us insight into our next steps. This is not just clinical decision making, e.g. which assessment approach to take; it is about considering the whole situation, including our own role in that situation. It is work-based learning and continuing professional development (CPD).

There are frameworks available to help us to do this effectively, many of which are not widely known in speech and language therapy. The crucial component though is connection with a supervisor whom we trust and respect. From the literature we know the common denominator is always a supervisor who creates an environment of trust and respect in supervision sessions. When we feel safe with protected time to explore our practice in a guided conversation, then we are more likely to 'ease out' of our comfort zone, and this is reflective, work-based CPD.

Before considering reflective practice and clinical supervision in more depth I feel the need to explain that I had dilemmas around terminology for describing the increasingly complex landscape of our profession. The initiative of apprentices, transitioning from an assistant role to qualification as an SLT, adds another dimension. At one time I would have just written therapist; however alongside SLTs are assistant practitioners who also access clinical supervision. This is support around a delegated care plan, plus supervision for wider caseworking with potentially different decisions and dilemmas to those of the therapist, supporting clients and carers, training others in therapy approaches and sometimes dealing with the conflicting styles of therapists in a team. Increasingly experienced assistant practitioners may be offering supervisory support to colleagues. So, I will be using the term 'practitioner' to include both therapists and assistants and specifying therapist, assistant, student, apprentice, manager, or clinical leader when necessary.

RCSLT Guidance gives a helpful profession-specific definition:

Supervision is:

- *A specific type of professional development.*
- *A mutually agreed, formal, regular 1:1 or group-learning relationship.*
- *The formal arrangement that enables an SLT, or assistant practitioner, to discuss their work regularly with someone who is experienced and qualified.*
- *A process of practice development.*
- *A mechanism through which you can reflect on your learning and practice.*

This is helpful in pinpointing that supervision is professional development through a formal, mutually agreed relationship. The focus is on regularly talking about work with an experienced supervisor.

Supervision is defined as "*a process of practice development.*" We don't tend to use the term practice development as much as some other professions. It is an incredibly valuable term and concept which deserves to be used more in speech and language therapy. This is about our 'practice,' which is our approach to clients, carers, colleagues, values, and learning. It is about how we develop as practitioners in our own practice. It is a little more personal than CPD as it is about the person developing as an individual practitioner.

As with any supervisory relationship there will be an uneven distribution of power as the supervisor holds more of the control, but the supervisee should be involved in mutual decision making about how the supervision works in practice, what is discussed, and when and where it takes place.

Why Do We Need Supervision?

Supervision gives a formal 'mechanism' to reflect on our practice and learn from experience. It:

- Supports innovation in practice
- Creates a culture of ongoing professional development
- Acknowledges the stress of caring and avoiding 'burnout'
- Supports safe practice and reduces risk
- Assures accountability
- Supports expanding roles and practice
- Creates 'reflective practitioners'

There tends to be agreement that there are three main functions of clinical supervision in the model devised and developed by Brigid Proctor (1986). This model has stood the test of time and will be explored further in other chapters of this book.

Proctor identified three functions:

Formative: connected to learning and development
Restorative: support around emotional responses to the stress of work
Normative: standards, accountability, assuring safety and effective practice

Kadushin (1992) taking a social work perspective further considered Proctor's three functions and suggested slightly more accessible labels utilising educational, supportive, and administrative for the functions. We can identify with education and learning, support for the emotional load at work, and the administrative aspects of practice such as quality standards and governance.

Proctor's labels for different functions have been changed by others, but the functions are the same. Alternative names include:

Formative: developmental/learning

Restorative: supportive/resilient/emotional

Normative: norming/standards/administrative

Clinical supervision can be a combination of:

- *One-to-one supervision*; which can be face-to-face, by telephone, or by videoconference
- *Group supervision*; in which two or more practitioners discuss their work with a supervisor
- *Peer or co-supervision*; where practitioners discuss work with each other and share the role of supervisor
- A blend of one-to-one and group/peer supervision

Professional Values and the Self-Renewing Professional

I was incredibly lucky to have a supervisor for my postgraduate project who was a teacher, who had become a lecturer and had an interest in the concept of the 'self-renewing professional.' She also had an interest in power at work and how people 'cling to power' or 'throw it around' which has since given me many insights into difficult work situations! However, it was her enthusiasm for the concept of self-renewing through reflective practice which was an important 'take away' from this supervisory relationship. In any of the caring professions there is the possibility of overextending ourselves and veering towards burnout. Restorative resilient supervision (Wallbank 2010) is proven to be an antidote to this. With self-development through reflective practice and the ability to look at a wider professional horizon beyond the attritional pressures of the day job, the theory is that we reduce the risk of stress and burnout.

This leads into an RCSLT statement about responsibility to engage in professional development. There is also a weighty reminder of the consequences of not having effective supervisory arrangements affecting indemnity insurance:

It is your responsibility as a registered professional to keep your knowledge and skills up-to-date and relevant to your scope of practice through continuing professional development (HCPC, 2016, p. 7). The RCSLT considers that supervision is at the core of continuing professional development as it provides a pivotal opportunity for you to address and structure aspects of your learning. Failure to access appropriate supervision may affect the indemnity insurance that SLTs have as part of their RCSLT membership.

RCSLT November 2017

Benefits of Clinical Supervision – What's Not to Like?

There are clear benefits to clinical supervision. It is seen as *"critical to the delivery of a high-quality client service through accountable decision-making and clinical practice, the facilitation of learning and professional development and the promotion of staff wellbeing"* (RCSLT 2017). Supervision has been associated with higher levels of job satisfaction, improved retention, effectiveness, and reduced turnover.

What Are the Risks of Not Accessing Supervision?

Issues with effective supervision have been identified in major incident reviews in healthcare, for example:

- The final report of the Mid Staffordshire NHS Foundation Trust Public Inquiry (2013)
- The Department of Health's final report on Winterbourne View Hospital (2012)

How Much and How Often?

- RCSLT recommends at least one hour of professional supervision every four to six weeks
- Newly qualified professionals (NQP) must access supervision more frequently: one hour every week for three months, then every month

In addition to supervision, it is important that practitioners also access professional support, e.g. through colleagues, managers, RCSLT Advisers, CENs, and other peer groups and networks.

Clinical supervision and wider support networks are essential to keep practice sharp and focused. By engaging in supervision, where we are guided into reflecting on our day-to-day casework covering both clinical and wider interpersonal situations, in a reflective conversation we pause and take time to learn from our experiences (formative professional development through work-based learning). We can learn to deal with any residual emotional reactions (restorative for wellbeing at work and avoiding burnout). We are ensuring we are seen as practicing in an efficient, comparative way to colleagues in our organisation and out in the wider profession (normative function).

Whatever the specialist area we work in, whether in adult or children's services, in a health or educational setting, with a specialist clinical or preventative/universal approach, as a specialist therapist or assistant practitioner, these same functions of supervision are relevant. When we meet with our clinical supervisor we will all be reflecting on topics relating to these three areas:

- Practice development
- Resilience/wellbeing
- Quality/assurance/standards

Who Should Provide Clinical Supervision in Speech and Language Therapy?

RCSLT Guidelines suggest the following:

- Supervisors should have relevant knowledge and skills and experience in the area of practice required and be supported through their own professional supervision arrangements; increasingly this includes specific 'supervision for supervisors'
- Assistant practitioners should receive professional supervision from an experienced therapist
- NQPs should be supervised by an experienced SLT
- Experienced therapists may choose to access supervision from another professional working in the same area of specialism, perhaps within an MDT or to support a therapist in a specific management or leadership role

The recommendation is that managerial and professional supervision are offered by different people; however, this is never clear cut, and this will be covered in later chapters. There is recognition in the guidelines that there are situations where this is difficult in practice. There are reports of very positive dual supervisors, but there always needs to be clear role differentiation.

Peer/Manager as Supervisor

This is possibly one of the more controversial aspects of clinical supervision. The debate rages on. There are vastly differing opinions. Some feel this is a total 'no go' area. Others have a 'well it depends' perspective.

The important point is to differentiate between the two roles. If the service approach is to allocate supervisors rather than allow choice then it would be possible for some poor supervisee to end up with a management supervisor where the relationship 'isn't going well,' who also doubles up as their clinical supervisor. Ouch! Even the supervisor should realise this is giving no space to the supervisee and is not a positive and productive relationship.

I have had direct reports who asked me to be their clinical supervisor. It was necessary to have separate meetings, or at least to divide the time with a formal division. My approach, all credit to *Edward de Bono Six Thinking Hats* (1985) for swiping his idea, was to talk openly about changing hats and putting a supervision hat on.

On occasion I might specify, "that needs to be followed up in management supervision," or "I'm speaking as a manager now and I'm going to note that down and follow it up." The roles need to be clearly differentiated.

When attending supervision training with colleagues who were predominantly clinical psychologists this subject was discussed in depth. The consensus of attendees and the course lead was that this was not an exact science. Experiences of very positive, possibly their best supervisory relationships with a line manager were described, in comparison with dreadful supervision with someone 'outside of the line.' The literature agrees that it is respect and trust which are critically important. If the supervisee respects and trusts their manager, then a dual supervisory relationship can work well.

The key is

> *establishing a supervisory relationship based on trust and respect. Being able to develop and build a positive relationship, based on trust with the supervisor, was seen as very important to a wide range of professions.*
> Literature Review commissioned by HCPC (2019)

A Spectrum of Support, Supporting Practice Development

Alice laughed. "There's no use trying," she said: "one can't believe impossible things."

"I daresay you haven't had much practice," said the Queen. "When I was your age, I always did it for half-an-hour a day. Why, sometimes I've believed as many as six impossible things before breakfast."

Alice through the Looking Glass

Key Themes

- Tackling terminology
- A spectrum of support
- Statutory supervision
- Professional development through reflective practice

Tackling Terminology

In Chapter 1 the differences between management, professional, clinical, and safeguarding supervision were explored. In RCSLT Guidelines (2017) the term professional supervision is used for what is usually referred to in the literature, across healthcare professions, as clinical supervision. In this book these terms will be used interchangeably. The term most frequently used is clinical supervision as this is still the term most frequently used by practitioners and in the literature and evidence drawn upon for each chapter.

DOI: 10.4324/9781003226772-3

There is wider debate among different professions about the terminology. Driscoll (2006) suggested the term *"practice supervision"* as supervision is holistic, covering whole practice. As this term is widely used in student education it is unlikely to take off as an idea. In some ways RCSLT choosing the term professional supervision reinforces that supervision is about much more than considering clinical cases. The term clinical can be misunderstood to mean the supervision is solely about clinical issues when it is about wider casework and relationships at work. However, the term clinical supervision is used most often in the literature; by HCPC, Care Quality Commission (CQC); NHS documentation across all four nations; Health Education England's (HEE) Competency Projects; and by clinicians in other professions such as occupational therapy, nursing, and clinical psychology. The term is not perfect and may change in the future; but for now there is general consensus in healthcare professions about its use.

Part of one of the definitions used in Chapter 1 gives a simple cornerstone for clinical supervision. *"Clinical supervision is regular, protected time for facilitated, in-depth reflection on clinical practice"* (Bond and Holland 1998). It is something which needs regular commitment with space for reflection on practice, facilitated by a supervisor.

The Spectrum of Support

The idea of a Spectrum of Support ranging from daily ad hoc professional support to structured clinical supervision is incredibly important. There is a difference between giving advice over a snatched coffee or across desks in a shared office and encouraging in-depth reflection on events and recognising work-based learning. Both are essential but are very different within a Spectrum of Support.

Professional support is the over-arching, umbrella term used to refer to a wide range of learning opportunities. It is typically more ad hoc and informal than supervision. There is overlap, yes, but clinical supervision provides dedicated time and space for critical reflection on events.

There are other types of professional support in the Spectrum of Support in speech and language therapy including management supervision, coaching, mentorship, preceptorship, counselling, and advice giving. There are significant differences as well as overlaps between coaching, mentoring, and clinical supervision. As these differences still cause some confusion among practitioners the differences are explored here:

Clinical supervision (aka professional) provides an opportunity for the practitioner to discuss complex situations within work in a non-judgemental environment. It is a formal professional arrangement between a supervisor and one or more supervisees. It can be one-to-one or group supervision. It is delivered through an agreed schedule of regular meetings/sessions using a conversation-based framework for in-depth reflection focusing on the practice issues brought to that safe space by the supervisee.

Managerial supervision provides an opportunity to discuss clinical, service-related, and wider professional issues. It is carried out by a manager with authority and accountability for the supervisee – usually their line manager. This person may have a speech and language therapy background, but this is not essential. I have managed and learnt a lot from management of OTs, physiotherapists, and special school nurses.

Coaching focuses on supporting the achievement of specific goals related to job role, including personal development skills. Coaching can be integrated into clinical supervision. Coaching relates to moving forward in new directions through goal setting. It can be focused on a current job role or extending skills to allow for career progression to new roles.

Mentoring is a process of facilitating and assisting another person's development with a mentor sharing experience. It tends to focus on the wider career landscape and achieving career aspirations.

Clinical supervision and coaching focus on current job role and immediate pre-occupations and issues. Coaching also looks to the medium term with specific goal setting. Mentoring is often focused on a wider horizon and next steps in a career.

Advice giving is different again. It is more general professional support. Advice is given in supervision, but tends to be when a less experienced colleague is struggling with an issue and the direction seems clear and obvious to the supervisor.

In those cases, in order to support learning and development and promote client wellbeing, I might specifically say that I'm going to give some direct advice about next steps.

Preceptorship is a term used mostly in nursing for pre-registration training. This is very specific support about evolving into a professional role. It could be argued that NQPs in SLT continue with preceptorship until their RCSLT Competency Profile is completed.

Counselling is concerned with emotional support. Some of the tools and techniques we use in clinical supervision originated in counselling, such as active listening and summarising. Counselling is about the provision of professional assistance and guidance in resolving personal or psychological problems. There are times when someone is distressed in supervision and we use a counselling approach. However, where a colleague needs to access counselling for emotional support this is outside the remit of most SLTs. We should not be counselling our colleagues.

A useful definition from the British Association of Counselling and Psycotherapy (BACP) website focuses on practicalities, using the umbrella term of talking therapies.

Counselling and psychotherapy are umbrella terms that cover a range of talking therapies. They are delivered by trained practitioners who work with people over a short or long term to help them bring about effective change and/or enhance their wellbeing.

Sometimes, as supervisors, we realise that a supervisee needs more focused emotional support connected with life events, anxiety, stress levels at work, or potentially a depressive illness. Recognising this, and having a gentle conversation about accessing support via GP or, if available, an organisations occupational health service, should be explored with the supervisee.

There may be just one session with a high emotional load. There is divided opinion about whether to continue or end the session at a suitable point and suggest alternative support. My approach would be to listen and give time and space to a supervisee in this situation before broaching the need for more emotional support through counselling.

Statutory Supervision? What Are the Recommendations of National Bodies about Clinical Supervision? Is It Mandatory at a National Level?

HCPC

The HCPC standards of proficiency for speech and language therapy stipulate that registrants must *"understand the importance of participation in training, supervision and mentoring in order to be able to practice as an autonomous professional"* (HCPC 2014).

There is a curious situation regarding HCPC and clinical supervision. Clinical supervision is clearly advocated as a positive aspect of development. Excellent resources are available via HCPC, and the message is that this is 'a good thing' in which therapists should engage:

- *"Supervision helps develop skills and knowledge throughout a registrant's career and supports continuing fitness to practise"*
- *"Supervision can support a culture of openness and candour and can help registrants meet our expectations by providing the opportunity to reflect on their practise and discuss challenges, with the support and guidance of another professional"*

However clinical supervision is not mandatory for registered practitioners. This is not just the case with speech and language therapy but with other professions regulated by HCPC, some of which, such as clinical psychology or occupational therapy, have a longer history in relation to supervision. This seems a 'curious' situation. Clinical supervision may not be mandatory but if a therapist was the subject of a professional investigation then their support and supervision network would, no doubt, be explored in the context of the investigation. It is clearly advocated as good practice and guidance is given as to choices in style and implementation.

Although HCPC does not require clinical supervision there is recognition that supervision *"plays an important part in professional development and learning"*:

- *Supervision can also help you to reflect on your practice, which plays a key part in professional development and service improvement.*
- *Our Standards therefore support the case that registrants should be participating in supervision as part of their practise where possible.*
- *Effective supervision has multiple benefits for both the supervisee and supervisor. It can also have significant benefits for the wider service and service users.*

There is a 'where possible' here, but the expectation is that practitioners engage in clinical supervision unless there are exceptional reasons why this is not possible. With the advent of videoconferencing there will hopefully be fewer circumstances where isolated practitioners are unable to access supervision.

There are signs of increased focus on clinical supervision beginning with the commission of a literature review (HCPC 2019) to establish what makes clinical and peer supervision effective. The review also considered how *"systems of effective clinical or peer supervision may be implemented"* and to explore opportunities for the HCPC *"to engage and support stakeholders' support and supervision for registrants."*

RCSLT

The RCSLT Guidance gives an overview of the importance of all types of supervision and recommendations for how many supervisions should be undertaken.

RCSLT Guidance contains the following key points:

- *As an individual practitioner, you are legally responsible for meeting the HCPC standards and UK legislation related to supervision.*
- *If you are an employee, you are responsible for meeting your supervision requirements, as set out in your contract of employment*
- *If you are self-employed, you need to ensure that you maintain a robust supervision arrangement and system of professional support.*

(RCSLT 2017)

The RCSLT is placing clinical supervision at the core of continual professional development as a pivotal opportunity to engage in structured learning based on everyday practice. Practitioners are encouraged to be self-motivated in identifying gaps and learning and developing through experience.

Professional Development through Reflective Practice

Reflective practice is advocated as a tool for professional learning and development by both HCPC and RCSLT.

Reflection is a process which helps you gain insight into your professional practise by thinking analytically about the different elements. The insights which emerge, and lessons learned, *"can be applied to maintain good practice and can also lead to developments and improvements for both the professional and their service users"* (HCPC).

HCPC emphasises that meeting and talking with someone about a case becomes reflective when we think analytically about our casework, evaluate, and develop insights into our practice.

A skilled clinical supervisor will be able to use different models of reflective practice, alongside other models such as solution-focused and appreciative approaches and fine tune the approach depending on individual needs.

Clinical supervision is clearly strongly advocated by regulatory and professional bodies. It is incredibly important to have that strong strand of reflective practice integrated into clinical supervision. However, sometimes it is the informal conversation with a colleague about a situation in daily practice which makes the difference. In the Spectrum of Support both formal arrangements for clinical supervision and informal support from a colleague over a coffee are equally valuable.

 REFLECTIVE LEARNING

Support Network

Think about your own network of support. Mind map or jot down your network visually on paper or a document. Include informal ad hoc support alongside professional colleagues in speech and language therapy and other professionals you work with in your job role. Where do you get your clinical supervision?

Check You Know the Different Terms for Supervision and What They Mean

Management, safeguarding, coaching, mentoring, and preceptorship as well as professional/clinical supervision.

How Do You Log and Record Your Clinical Supervision?

Is there a system in your service? If you are a sole practitioner working independently how do you log your attendance at supervision?

Reflect on This Quote

> Clinical supervision is regular, protected time for facilitated, in-depth reflection on clinical practice.
>
> (Bond and Holland 1998)

Do you have this protected time for facilitated, in-depth consideration of your clinical caseworking in place? If not, then what are the barriers? Is it a lack of prioritisation? Is it a cost issue? If it is then maybe consider a shared time arrangement with a colleague. This might not provide the same level of reflective focus as a facilitated session with an experienced supervisor, but you have made a commitment to supervision

CAMEO – TOO BUSY TO ORGANISE CLINICAL SUPERVISION

Ann was busy. She had left the NHS and set up in independent practice. It was working well and she had several contracts with local schools. This meant she was able to be involved in the school-based therapy she enjoyed. She had received several enquiries from other schools about possible contracts and could see a time when she might be extending her business and recruiting an associate therapist or an assistant practitioner. Therapy life was good.

However she was not accessing any support from colleagues. She had previously been part of a large team and there had always been someone to talk to about a difficult session which hadn't quite gone to plan. She had intended to arrange clinical supervision, but she hadn't got round to it and months passed and it was still on her To Do list. As the end of term approached she felt more exhausted than usual and was losing her motivation. She was watching her teaching colleagues leaving for summer break, and her leave was not due for some weeks. She had a lot of administrative paperwork to complete.

Ann finally got round to contacting a supervisor who worked independently for a telephone chat about possibly setting up supervision. The supervisor listened and talked about her supervision needs, e.g. how often, style of supervision. Then she signposted Ann to a local group organised by the Association for Speech and Language Therapists in Independent Practice (ASLTIP) which met face to face or online. She also suggested an online forum for therapists interested in a similar clinical area. The supervisor suggested Ann considered her development needs and whether she had any continuing professional development (CPD) goals for the year ahead. The supervisor agreed to offer Ann some one-to-one supervision as a starting point with a view to offering her a place in an online group she facilitated when one became available. This would introduce her to colleagues and widen her support network.

After the call the supervisor worried that she had made too many suggestions for follow up. However Ann actually felt energised that she now had a supervisor and the beginnings of a support network. It had been difficult working in isolation and she had kept putting off organising clinical supervision and prioritising other priorities.

Scaffolding Supervision

"I learned that I may not be able to change history, but I can learn from it."

Alice, *Alice through the Looking Glass*

Key Themes

- Foundations of clinical supervision
- Supervision frameworks
- Guided conversation

Does Clinical Supervision 'Work'?

Clinical supervision is a new field of study. It was advocated as beneficial by both the NHS and professional bodies in the wake of the Beverly Allit and Harold Shipman cases. The days of practitioners governing themselves ended with the repercussions of these cases. However, there is little research on clinical supervision and even less on any positive effects on client outcomes.

One reason may be that funding streams for research are limited. The professional bodies do not have the funding to commission research studies, and this is not the remit of HCPC. There is possibly funding in academia, e.g. for patient safety, but it is not a high-profile research area. There are limited international studies. The UK and Australia are aligned in terms of models and approaches to supervision. The USA has a different approach with supervision being more directive, evaluative, and closer to a practice educator model.

Frameworks for supervision tend to derive from counselling and clinical psychology, which have a tradition of more frequent clinical supervision

DOI: 10.4324/9781003226772-4

than we expect to access in speech and language therapy. In nursing more academics have an interest in devising frameworks for reflection. There is activity in academia, but the focus is on reflective practice rather than clinical supervision. In summary *"there is insufficient research as to outcomes. It can only be hoped that a body of research based evidence about supervision will be available in the not too distant future"* (Lewis 2012).

There is a need for an overview of the most frequently used frameworks of clinical supervision in relation to speech and language therapy. The tools and techniques used within the frameworks also need to be explored – conversational tools like critical reflection, solution-focused questioning, Thinking Space, and appreciative inquiry are included as relevant to speech and language therapy.

This chapter considers three over-arching frameworks for clinical supervision.

- Proctor – Three Functions Model (2001)
- Hewson and Caroll – Different Rooms/Spaces Model (2019)
- Hawkins and Shohet – 7 Eyed Model and the Triangle (2012)

Proctor – Three Functions Model

Proctor's Three Functions of supervision (formative, restorative, and normative) is the most well-known framework. This framework is one I utilise when I deliver supervision training. These functions are referred to in the RCSLT Guidance (2017). In explaining these functions I have given them labels which are more accessible for SLTs.

Three Functions of Supervision:

Formative or Developmental
This is about learning/skills/abilities
An alternative SLT term: *practice development*
Normative or Administrative/Management
This is about standards/clinical Governance/safety/effectiveness/ competencies
An alternative SLT term: *standards and quality*
Restorative or Emotional
This is about resilience around the emotional stresses of the job
An alternative SLT term: *support and wellbeing*

So, alternative terms for speech and language therapy are:

- Practice development
- Standards and quality
- Support and wellbeing

Proctor's Three Functions of supervision can cover:

- The development of practice skills, knowledge, insights, and confidence
- Ensuring practice is at an appropriate standard and is safe and effective
- Giving emotional support and resilience

There is a chapter covering each of Proctor's functions of supervision.

> *The exact configuration of these different forms will depend on a number of factors, including the experience of the supervisee, the weight of their workload, their professional background and their work context.*
>
> (Care Quality Commission (CQC) 2013)

The functions also give a framework for considering how our needs in supervision change over time. *"Throughout your working life, as you progress in your skills, knowledge and experience, your supervision and professional support needs will change in terms of frequency, content and style"* (RCSLT). Early career SLTs will want more developmental supervision, and an experienced specialist may need restorative supervision when casework management is challenging. With an experienced clinical supervisor guiding the conversation those differing needs and styles can be considered.

Six Supervisory Spaces to Structure a Conversation

Daphne Hewson and Michael Caroll (2016) developed several visual, structured frameworks for supervision with the aim of giving practical tools to guide practitioners.

This model is a metaphor of a supervision session as a house with different rooms. Each room represents a different function and style of supervision. The conversation moves through some or all the rooms in a process which clarifies thinking and allows different perspectives.

The six rooms have different functions:

The office – a directive space, for advice, compliance with standards, safeguarding

The examination or consulting room – an analytical space where the supervisor is evaluating competence and capability

The lecture theatre – a large, passive space, where the supervisor responds to teaching needs, giving information and advice

The sitting room – a restorative space, with light and warmth and a comfortable settee ready for debriefing stories with offloading, sharing emotional reactions to events

The studio – an active space for considering solutions and shared action planning

The observatory – a glass-roofed reflective space, for exploring events and discovering new perspectives

For me, the metaphor is a detached house on a cliff top, facing the sea with the shiny glassed observatory giving a view out to the horizon. The observatory is the most important room as it is focused on reflection. It is important to visit several rooms in a session. Which rooms depends on the material brought to supervision.

On reflection, this seems a rather affluent metaphor. I don't know anyone with an observatory or a lecture theatre at their house, so I have adapted this to something resembling a more ordinary living space. Feel free to adapt the imagery; if gardens or parks are real and relevant for you then adapt the imagery. I enjoy gardening and so I have adapted the metaphor for garden and park landscape. Hewson's metaphor highlights the different types of supervisory conversation giving a structured visual framework to a session.

In the House

Desk – directive space/advice/compliance/standards

Dining table – analytical/evaluative

Bookcase/computer – teaching/information/advice

Settee – restorative space/comfortable settee ready for sharing emotional reactions

Kitchen – active/considering solutions/planning together

Big window/porch – reflective space – glass/open views

Garden/Outside the House

The garden path/straight line and not winding – directive/advice/
  compliance/standards
Under a tree/looking at patterns in branches/leaves – analytical/eval-
  uative space
The lawn – teaching/information/advice
A bench in the sunshine – restorative space
Garden table – active/considering solutions/planning together
Next to a pond with a reflective surface – reflective space

The Park

A map at the entrance – directive/advice/compliance/standards
Wooded walk area – analytical/evaluative conversation
Open grassy area – teaching/information/advice
Picnic area – restorative space/warm and comfortable seating for shar-
  ing emotional reactions
Café tables – active/considering solutions/planning together
Next to a duck pond or stream – reflective space

If solution-focused questions are used this will be in the studio area design-
ing solutions. The incisive questions from *Time to Think: Listening to Ignite
the Human Mind* (Nancy Kline 2002) will be up in the observatory. Active
listening for a supervisee who is emotionally drained will need the sitting
room.

The supervisor refers to the framework during the session with discussion and pauses to agree which room/space they are in at that point in the
conversation.

Triangle Talk

Hewson also devised the Triangle framework (2002). This visual Triangle is
a template of areas which are most often discussed in supervision (Figure 3.1
shows the Triangle adapted for speech and language therapy). The framework gives depth to the conversation covering wide ranging issues. Many
sessions focus on the client and their problems. If this is all that is discussed,
then supervision just becomes support for case management.

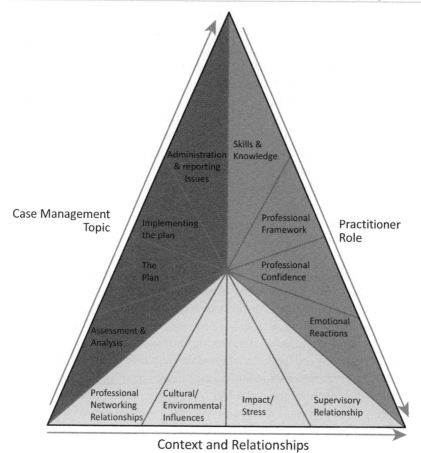

Case Management
Topic

Practitioner
Role

Skills &
Knowledge

Administration
& reporting
Issues

Implementing
the plan

Professional
Framework

The
Plan

Professional
Confidence

Assessment &
Analysis

Emotional
Reactions

Professional
Networking
Relationships

Cultural/
Environmental
Influences

Impact/
Stress

Supervisory
Relationship

Context and Relationships

Figure 3.1

My experience is that many practitioners still see clinical supervision as
case based. This is due to a lack of coherent literature and limited training
opportunities. Indeed, there are currently clinical supervisors who perceive
supervision as solely around case management. It's an ongoing issue in the
profession.

In Hewson's model each side of the Triangle focuses on different conversational areas. There is a topic (client or situation) and a practitioner-focused
side with the base being relationship/context-focused. The practitioner side
considers their role in the situation, including confidence and skill levels.
The client side is about the needs of client and carers and the implementation
of any plan. The base focuses on relationships and wider context.

Each side has specific 'cells' for different topics of conversation. The
supervisor uses these cells, moving around the edges of the Triangle to

guide the conversation. Not every conversation needs to include all the cells – this is an in-depth framework. Here the framework has been adapted to enable practical use in speech and language therapy. A detailed exploration of the Triangle and accompanying questions can be found in Hewson and Carroll's *The Reflective Supervision Toolkit* (2016).

The supervisor structures the session around the cells, beginning by moving up the topic side (client or wider situation) considering things like assessment/needs analysis, planning, and problems with implementing the plan. Then, after the apex, the conversation moves down the other side with the focus changing to the practitioner and whether they feel comfortable in the situation, does their skillset meet the demands, are there any gaps/learning and development needs, what strengths are they using. Issues like risk, legal, ethical factors, and duty of care fit here. The reality of any emotional reactions/feelings triggered by this situation is included on this side of the Triangle.

Finally along the base and the wider context of relationships including cultural and social factors. What is influencing decision making? Is there someone or something (such as pressure to reduce waiting times) impacting? Is collaborative working with other professionals going well or does there need to be some attention to networking? For speech and language therapy the parallel process cell has been adapted to focus on 'impact of the case' and whether the practitioner experiences any strong empathy for those involved or negative 'contagion' from the feelings/experiences of others. There is a cell focusing on the supervision and whether anything should be done differently in supervision.

Triangulating a Conversation

In this framework the supervisee always prepares a topic for supervision, bringing notes to share. The supervisor uses the Triangle as a visual reference point during the conversation.

Examples of questions linked to 'cells' on the Triangle are:

Topic Side (Client or Situation)

Assessment and Analysis

What is the topic/issue/presenting problem?
What methods have you used (will you use) to assess the situation?
Any other issues or problems?

What are the strengths and "non-problems"?
What are your thoughts/evaluation about what is happening?
Is there another way of looking at it?

Planning

What's the current plan?
If the client's family was here, what would they say about the plan?
Is the plan within a care pathway/routine approach or more individualised?

Implementation

What's happened?
Do you need to modify your plan?

Administration

Any admin issues?

Practitioner Side

Emotional Responses

In what ways is this work triggering emotions/impacting on you?
I noticed … What are the feelings behind that?
How does who you are affect what you notice?
Who does this client/carer remind you of?
Does this case/situation remind you of other cases/situations?

Professional Confidence

Have you confidence in delivering the plan?
How does it fit with your values as a practitioner?

Professional Framework

Exploring any legal, ethical, professional issues, e.g. duty of care
Considering risk (clinical or situational)

Skills and Knowledge

Do you have the skillset needed for this case/situation?
Have you any gaps/need opportunity to gain skills and knowledge?

Context/Relationships Side

Professional Relationships

Is networking in place, e.g. a multi-agency team approach?
Does anything need to happen to strengthen joint working?

Cultural/Environmental Influences

Consider the client's 'community'
Broaching cultural curiosity
Are there cultural needs?
Consider social/economic needs
Who is influencing this situation?
Is any influence helpful/not helpful?

Impact of Case

Are you experiencing any mental grime/'contagion' due to impact of
    behaviours/feelings of those involved?
Is there strong empathy/lack of empathy in this situation?

Supervisory Support

Is there anything the supervisor could do to support more?
Are there any wider support needs, e.g. expert clinical advice?

As with all these frameworks I find myself re-wording questions into a style with which I feel comfortable. Separated and set out in a framework, questions can seem stilted and distant. Each supervisor needs to personalise the questions in their own style.

Having the Triangle and the questions visible for reference does help guide the conversation in different directions, allowing an in-depth consideration of the topic as needed. I would be selective of cells covered. Hewson gives a mini-structure for each conversational cell. Initially there is information gathering and immediate reflections (this is the Mindful Stance). The next step is to analyse the material in more depth (the Consideration Stance).

There is a demonstration of a Triangle-based supervision session on you-tube.com. This is, of course, her gold standard application of her model, and the case discussed is not relevant to speech and language therapy. However, a glance at the video gives a chance to see Hewson using a very relaxed, supportive yet focused style.

Using a framework can give a new way of facilitating a session. Conversational style can be informal yet allow an in-depth consideration of the topic. Remember the key needs are for trust and respect, feeling comfortable, yet prepared to be stretched in thinking.

The Pleased Platform, *Reflective Supervision Toolkit* (2016), is another conversational approach developed by Hewson based on appreciative approaches. Hewson noticed that practitioners tended to bring problems and things which had gone wrong to supervision, "*They take what they do well for granted and don't recognise their strengths.*" This tool shifts the conversational focus from what the practitioner is concerned about to what's positive and they're pleased about.

7 Eyed Supervision Framework – Taking Different Viewpoints

Peter Hawkins and Robin Shohet devised the first version of this model in 1985. It was ahead of its time as it integrated relational and organisational aspects of supervision. The focus is on the relationships between client, therapist, and supervisor. It also considers the interplay between relationships and the wider context.

The model is called "*7 eyed*" because it focuses on seven different viewpoints which act as a framework for exploring the topics in supervision.

The model proposes seven different perspectives ("*eyes*") from which to look at the case and generate new awareness. Unless you are specifically interested in psychotherapy approaches my suggestion is to use this framework as a 5 Eyes, not 7 Eyes, missing out Eyes 5 and 6.

Eye 1: the perspective of **the client**. This is the client within a wider background of progress, ongoing objectives, pattern of therapy, and communication with the practitioner about the therapy. Hawkins believed that empathy is blocked when we see our clients in terms of problems and solving problems. He says the need is to focus on client, tuning in to needs, motivation, and choices, seeing the client with carers and not just the client on their own.

Eye 2: next is **interventions**, why we choose them, preferred approaches, and some gentle challenging. We may have a tendency to choose a particular approach which might not be the best fit for the client.

Eye 3: now the **client-practitioner relationship** and any rapport/dissatisfaction/relationship between client/carers and practitioner. The suggestion is to stand back and talk this through, bringing in metaphor to gain insights if that fits with your style.

Eye 4: this is the practitioner viewing their **own experience** in working this case and considering their responses to the case. Moment-by-moment thoughts, emotions, memories. The practitioner can also consider their body language and reactions when working with a client. This is also about identifying any gaps in learning/professional development.

Eye 5: the **supervisor-practitioner relationship** and any parallels between what is going on in the clinical session and during the supervision session; a concept used in mental health. It is not something we pick up on, and my suggestion is to focus on just noticing anything, e.g. any resistance to suggestions.

Eye 6: the **supervisor's viewpoint**. Again, this is something which is less relevant in speech and language therapy. It is about the supervisor's reflections during the supervision. Hawkins advocates supervisors share how they imagine the client and how they might interact with the client if they were a therapist.

Eye 7: the final eye is looking at a client's needs within a **wider context**, external influences, the current relationship, and history of the client's relationship with the practitioner/service.

Guiding the Conversation

A framework can help a supervisor structure a conversation. These frameworks are designed to facilitate a guided conversation where practitioners perceive different perspectives. The conversation covers multifaceted aspects of working with a complex caseload. This fits especially well in speech and language therapy where we focus on interactive communication, often with the knowledge that we can extend and enhance communicative competence but there may be an enduring impairment. Practitioners support complex human communication and eating and drinking needs. No clinical case is ever quite the same. We strive to draw upon and apply broad evidence-based techniques. That's incredibly important in modern practice. However, we do this knowing that each client is unique in both abilities and motivation to engage and in their background of family/carer support. Having a scaffolding structure to guide a conversation and facilitate different perspectives on a situation can strengthen supervision.

When I was a student, attending a series of lectures on aphasia, it was with a practitioner who was nearing retirement, but who talked in innovative terms about how a patient existed not only in an individual context or background but in an 'ecology.' The concept of an ecology reinforced that this was dynamic, and the patient interacted continually with and within the ecology. This struck a chord, and I have been surprised never to hear communication needs described in this way. There is something in it; it was ahead of its time as a way of viewing communication needs and deficits.

So, imagery and metaphors within a framework can be powerful tools, giving us different perspectives and insights into our casework. I choose the terms casework and caseworking specifically to emphasise that the work considered is wider than individual cases. Caseworking is the ability to organise and plan work, interact and support others, assess and analyse communication needs, and plan intervention to uphold and/or extend communication. The term caseload or workload seems rather static, and casework is more dynamic than considering individual cases – this is supervision around wider caseworking.

 **REFLECTIVE LEARNING**

Three Functions of Supervision:

Make sure that you know Proctor's Three Functions of supervision. Choose the labels you like best to describe formative, normative, and restorative functions. Mine were:

Practice development
Standards and quality
Support and wellbeing

Think back about the support and supervision you've received in the past. Which functions were most high profile and were these the right ones?

Reflect about whether the supervisor was focusing on norming your work into a specific care pathway when you really needed a listening ear and a restorative session. It's interesting to consider this from the point of view of both supervisor and supervisee.

Look ahead at any planned supervisions (as supervisor or supervisee) and what function of supervision is relevant to your needs now.

Supervisory Spaces:

Look again at the six supervisory spaces and my dreamed-up alternatives. Think of your own places for spaces. If you are a visual learner then choose some images, photos, or drawings to represent your spaces. If you are an auditory learner then some sounds or music. If you are a kinaesthetic learner imagine how it feels to be in the space.

In fact, stretch your learning style and imagine yourself in the space and what you see, what you hear, how hot or cold it is, what you smell and whether there is a cup of hot herbal tea or a cool drink waiting for you on a table, and so on. Make these supervisory spaces real and relevant to you.

Now, can you remember what function each space stands for? E.g. analytical, restorative, reflective?

If you have time and interest then set up your own crib sheet with the spaces and functions of supervision which you cover in your usual supervision. There will be frequent themes, and you may not want to include all six spaces in your version.

The Triangle:

What topics do you tend to take to supervision? Is it clients, relationships, wider situations, learning needs, concerns, confidence levels?

Should you change anything? What are you *not* taking to supervision?

Look at the Triangle again. Imagine a conversation while considering the cells on the Triangle's sides. What do you feel comfortable with and usually include? Are there any cells you never cover? Is this a gap? If not then identify the cells which are relevant to you and your job and your supervisions.

If you have time then scribble out your own Triangle … if you really have time then maybe use a different shape and build your own individual framework. If you are a supervisor then try it out in a session. If you are not a supervisor and have managed to develop your own framework, then well done and maybe you should consider being one in the future!

Hewson suggests the same mini-structure for each conversation. She suggests taking a mindful stance first and gathering the basic background and facts and reflecting on what's happened. Then it is time to stand back and take a consideration stance and analyse and consider solutions/ways forward. Try this mini-structure out one day when you are thinking about events and planning. Does taking a wider scope mindful stance before honing in on narrower analysis work for you? Do you do this already?

Caseworking:

Which words do you use to describe 'what you do'? Is it therapy, intervention, case management, caseworking? You probably have preferred terms. Do these preferred terms actually describe what you do?

There are several frameworks in this chapter. What's your 'top takeaway' from this chapter?

CAMEO – A TALKING TRIANGLE

Kristina was fairly experienced, working with children with complex needs and providing outreach support from a child development centre. She was competent with cases but tended to need a lot of support (and re-assurance) when working with the most complex cases. Jodie her supervisor was always happy to provide ad hoc support or formal supervision but was beginning to wonder why Kristina was not more self-sufficient and confident after receiving a high level of support. In simple terms Jodie felt her time was now needed for less experienced colleagues and Kristina should be coping well without an urgent need for ad hoc support most days.

Jodie approached this by considering what Kristina tended to bring to supervision (including the ad hoc). When she stood aside from it and considered it carefully, she could see a pattern. Kristina was most insecure if there was a possibility of challenge from a family. If there was any hint of dissatisfaction, then she usually worked to pass on the case as quickly as possible (to someone who had more experience). The difficulty was that when Jodie looked around their small team that meant just her. The others were early career practitioners at the early stages of building their experience.

This was a situation where Jodie had a dual role of supervisor and line manager for Kristina.

Once Jodie had identified the themes, she used Hewson's Triangle to jot down how this linked with Kristina's supervision needs. She chose this model as she wanted a structured framework to share with Kristina which would cover each case comprehensively and ensure that therapist, client/carers, and wider context were considered. She explained to

Kristina that she thought it could work to try out a different structure in supervision and it involved a little preparatory planning but would be valuable CPD through supervision. She also suggested they meet more often, fortnightly for a two-month period, and a series of supervisions were planned in a few weeks' time. (*Although we are considering Hewson's model here, notice that Jodie has moved into Proctor's developmental/learning function of supervision.*)

In preparation Jodie adapted the Triangle for their team, e.g. changed terminology in the questions and specified the colleagues who might be discussed in terms of networking. Kristina prepared information on two cases in preparation for the session. Jodie began the session by reading aloud Kristina's notes. She was positive and validated what was written and mentioned how this should work well with the new framework. She showed Kristina the Triangle and put it on the table as a reference throughout the session.

The conversation worked through the 'conversation cells'. It was helpful to pause and consider what the family might think about the plan. Had they been involved? What were their dreams and hopes for their child? What did Kristina think they would like in the plan? This wasn't possible yet, but it was helpful to talk about it and focus on family opinions. When they reached the practitioner side and were considering both skills and confidence in implementing the plan there was valuable reflection on difficulties dealing with the communication around working with families. Kristina was more comfortable from an expert stance and knew she was 'telling' families rather than 'involving' them in care planning. Kristina knew this already but had found it hard to talk about in supervision. By going through a structured framework, it was necessary to talk about style and confidence and begin to imagine how things might be in the future.

Jodie brought in questions about how to get to a place where Kristina felt confident working with families as partners. Kristina mentioned some possible training options and Jodi said that training needs could be discussed in their next management supervision meeting (when she would wear a different hat). In that management meeting a more specific Personal Development Plan was devised. Jodie also suggested that when the Triangle-based sessions were completed, she wondered if Kristina might take on clinical supervision of a less experienced colleague – and Kristina was keen to take on this role.

Freeze Frame, Reflective Practice in Action

"I don't see how he can ever finish, if he doesn't begin."
Alice, *Alice's Adventures in Wonderland.*

> ## Key Themes
>
> - How we develop as practitioners
> - The practitioner skillset
> - Swamp skills
> - Reflection

The reality of professional practice is filled with daily dilemmas. Even before the complications and pressures of modern healthcare in the 21st century Donald Schön (1984) wrote that *"practitioners are frequently embroiled in conflicts of values, goals, purposes and interests."* Hawkins and Shohet (2012) propose that supervision is *"a place where a living professional breathes and learns."* This is about time and space to think with structured models of reflection guided by a skilled clinical supervisor.

How We Develop as Practitioners – Skills and Competencies

There is a very useful concept which explains the way we develop as practitioners. It is about professional 'know how' and 'being' an SLT or assistant practitioner.'

This professional *"know how"* (Schön 1991) is more difficult to measure than the acquisition of specific competencies. It is how the practitioner

DOI: 10.4324/9781003226772-5

applies knowledge and acts in their daily work and so develops their competent practice. Ghaye and Lillyman (2007) come at this from an interesting angle and say that there is a point in our professional development where we begin to "*think like*" a lawyer, a teacher, or a speech and language therapist.

At the beginning of this process a practitioner acquires a set of competencies linked to their role. Indeed, for therapists and assistants this is formalised with the need to complete competency profiles to assure a level of knowledge and know-how on the job. After initial competencies are completed then the focus changes to how capable we are in actually doing the job and carrying out our professional role. Schön focused his ideas on how we gain expertise in our professions. What is the specific skillset of any profession which makes a successful practitioner?

What Is a Practitioner Skillset?

These skills are rarely highlighted or included in a university curriculum, though skills like listening and empathy may be covered in role play exercises. This is about the wider practical application of competencies. It involves factors like individual style, confidence, and the ability to make judgements and decisions in a work situation. Eventually practitioners reach a stage where the focus is on the intuitive application of their professional knowledge and skills in day-to-day work. Some actions become almost automatic, and it is the more complex dilemmas which require additional reflection time.

Sometimes we utilise observation and feedback by colleagues as tools to support our practice development. Certainly, the practitioner at this stage needs to be able to access an identified colleague as a supervisor with the opportunity to meet for reflective learning. At a basic level all practitioners need to have conversations about their experiences and 'unpick events.' Decision making in a session might be retrospectively explored with questions such as:

"What went well?"

"Would you have done anything differently?"

"Would you do the same again in a similar situation?"

A skilled, experienced colleague can guide the conversation through a reflective learning cycle and through this process jointly identify new learning points.

Schön's work set the scene for later research on the reflective practitioner in both education and healthcare. Through work-based learning, with support, we acquire our professional 'know how,' and as we become experienced, we also develop an individual style. We eventually become 'expert' practitioners.

Schön writes of the very technical acquisition of competencies necessary for a particular profession. He then writes about the *"art of practice"* and how the most successful practitioners progress to this stage not only by working on the job but through feedback and reflection on daily experiences. There is a gradual accrual of learning within practical practice settings.

Eventually we have a store of knowledge, built through our experience of professional practice, and Schön called this *"professional wisdom."* Now this may sound a little soft as a term, but it is all about how we develop in our professional role and that learning is about more than just 'ticking off competencies.' Being successful is about how we relate and interact with others, share our knowledge in supporting clients and carers, and make judgements in everyday clinical situations.

Kathleen Williamson in her *RCSLT Model of Professional Practice in Speech and Language Therapy* (2002) focused on the crucial importance of judgement and decision making. We can acquire isolated competencies, but success in our professional role hinges on how we think and make decisions in everyday action. *"Developing expertise with a given client group relates not just to the development of knowledge and practical skills, but to the making of increasingly fine-tuned, appropriate, accurate and speedy judgements and decisions"* (RCSLT 2002).

There is a recognisable point when we become 'established' and confident in our role and are *"thinking like"* an SLT or assistant practitioner. In simple terms, 'we know our job.' As professionals we are keen to continue learning and build on our level of skills. This is when we have that professional 'know how' and competence in dealing with everyday situations in *"problem infested"* clinical practice (Tripp 1993).

A Set of *"Swamp Skills"*

One of the things an expert practitioner is good at is *"thriving in the dismal swamp."* Schön visualised the arena of professional practice as resembling a dark, muddy swamp. We can get stuck in the middle of it. The swamp represents practice with all the problems, complications, and unique dilemmas we face in caseworking. As early career practitioners we need support to guide us through this swamp. Without supervision we might sink further into this swamp. As we progress we learn to navigate more effectively through the swamp and spend more time overlooking the swampy lowlands, perching on a rocky ridge high above. The expert is different and can dip in and out of the swamp and navigate through it with little difficulty. Some experts will even thrive in the swamp and prefer to be immersed in the most complex aspects of practice.

For a lawyer a specific professional skill could be the ability to retain large amounts of reference information, compose an argument, and be persuasive and organised. For a counsellor this might be the ability to make relationships, set people at ease, listen without tiring, and be empathic.

In speech and language therapy the specific skills which make a practitioner successful vary between specialisms, but there is common ground. For a specialist clinician swamp skills such as critical analysis, interpersonal communication, diplomacy, conflict resolution, empathy, and patience are important whatever the job role. The swamp skills for an assistant practitioner might include the ability to form relationships, track progress, cope with different delegation styles of therapist, and create energy and enthusiasm around therapy plans. All need to communicate effectively, form relationships speedily, put people at ease in communication, notice concerns or dissatisfaction, organise self with admin duties, and so on.

I like how Schön described an expert practitioner as a *"walking set of theories"* which are based on practical experience and learning over time. He maintained that when a practitioner with this type of expertise leaves a team there is a significant gap which is often only recognised after the person has left. This is difficult to set out in a learning and development framework, but colleagues will recognise this level of experience with respect.

What do we need in a professional 'Swamp Kit'? It's very much about continuing professional development and ongoing support. Schön was a parent of reflective practice and strongly advocated the need to learn in the workplace with support and feedback from more experienced practitioners. He compared this to the way we learn to play a musical instrument in a conservatoire or music school, with practice and feedback so gradual improvement takes place. The expression 'shared practicum' is used as a place where we can feel safe and secure and stretch to develop our practice.

Schön also divides 'know how' into technical-rational aspects and the more practical art of practice. In modern terms the art of practice is about 'thinking around cases and reflecting on events' as well as implementing more technically routine processes and pathways. This includes professional 'know how' about casework and making judgements in difficult scenarios.

It's about being able to reflect on events and then learn from experience. Reflective practice is seen as the key to surviving in the dismal swamp. Schön's metaphor of the dismal swamp and experienced practitioners thriving in their clinical and management caseworking has stood the test of time.

There are newer theories of professional development and reflective practice, but they tend to fit well with this swamp imagery.

Reflection

It's interesting to sit for a minute and consider what you might put in your own 'Swamp Kit.' What has enabled you to thrive and have some good days at work, even when facing problem-infested professional practice? I hope that reflective clinical supervision is packed in that kit, alongside a wider supportive network, interest in caseworking, days off, and some essentials like coffee and chocolate (or their equivalents).

Professional practice can be "*very individual, complex, messy with indeterminate situations, demanding an individual and innovative approach*" (Powell 1990). Clinical supervision is at its most effective when the wider dynamics of a situation are considered in a guided conversation. Various models of reflection can be used in supervision to guide the conversation, analysing the client's needs and response, the wider family/carer dynamics, resources available, expectations, and the therapist's 'interaction with the situation.' In effect it is situational supervision.

Whether in early career, developing specialist, team, or clinical lead the tool of reflective practice is relevant to learning. For an assistant practitioner there should be support from the early days of employment in developing competencies through work-based learning and reflective practice. Reflective practice in clinical supervision is a positive practical approach to work-based learning.

This statement sums this up succinctly:

We know that Reflection can enable practitioners to;

- *analyse complex and challenging situations*
- *consider the way we make decisions*
- *make connections between previous cases and current practice*
- *make it more likely that we will put what we have learned into practice*
- *improve our problem-solving skills*
- *identify future learning needs*

(CPD statement, Health and Social Care Professional Advisory Group 2017)

Reflective practice has long been recognised as an important aspect of good practice and is seen as integral to how professionals integrate learning and experience into their development and into improved practice throughout their careers (Argyris & Schön 1978, Kolb 1984, Gibbs 1998, Rolfe et al. 2001).

Other chapters will explore reflective practice, introducing several models which can be used in clinical supervision.

 REFLECTIVE LEARNING

Log your daily dilemmas (in your head or record) for a few days. You won't record all of them!

What are the 'swamp skills' needed in your job role?

(e.g. interpersonal communication, diplomacy, conflict resolution, empathy, patience, creating enthusiasm.) What are your strongest swamp skills and have you any gaps?

Are you a reflective practitioner? Do you enjoy work-based learning? Is it valued enough?

CAMEO – FREEZE FRAMING

Amanda was a senior assistant practitioner supporting a team working in a Stroke Re-hab team. She was struggling in dealing with daily dilemmas and making decisions confidently. Instead of reducing in frequency, the number of 'reach outs' for ad hoc support around a decision about what to move on to when a client achieved success on goal work in a session was increasing. Amanda disclosed to her supervisor, Asifa, that she found it harder to make these decisions now that she knew more; there was more to consider. She was struggling, more and more, and worried she might get it wrong.

Asifa worked as a specialist therapist in the same team and knew the caseload. She listened carefully to Amanda's outpouring about her lack of confidence. This wasn't easy as she wanted to step into 'delegation and direction' mode but knew that wasn't appropriate in a supervision session.

Instead, she encouraged Amanda to talk about the cases she had worked with recently. Asifa wanted Amanda to pause at the points where she had struggled with making a decision. Asifa was able to point out that it was due to her skills as a practitioner that the clients made good progress when working with Amanda. When these pause points were freeze framed and re-visited in reflective conversation then Amanda was able to clearly see how she had actually known the next step and even usually had the appropriate activities and exercises in her bag. She knew her job role and had been successfully working with clients for over five years and her recent promotional post had been well deserved. Asifa validated that Amanda knew her job and to pause in the moment if she struggled with a decision in a session. She might perhaps move to slowly pick up her bag and take out the other resources and introduce another activity – it would be fine.

Then unexpectedly Amanda began to cry quietly. She said that she loved her job and the team she worked in. However she wasn't herself and knew it; there was an issue at home which was causing a lot of stress and involved decision making around a health matter. She was awake at night and unable to make a decision about her own health treatment. The insomnia meant she was tired and snappier with her family. Asifa continued listening and then suggested Amanda booked an appointment to see her doctor to discuss. She also said that she would look into whether there was any counselling support available via their employer.

When they met the following month Amanda was accessing counselling support. She was also feeling more confident in her decision making and enjoying her job again.

5 | An Individual Style and Approach

"The only way to achieve the impossible is to believe it is possible."
Alice, *Alice through the Looking Glass*

Key Themes

- Developing an individual style
- Differing perspectives on events
- Adapting your style
- Tailoring feedback

Supervision Styles

Hewson identified several different *"Supervision Styles"* in *Reflective Practice in Supervision* (2016), and it is helpful to know about these styles and have awareness of when you are using them.

Hewson Supervision Styles

Collaborative – jointly working together
Facilitative – guiding along the way
Prescriptive – directing the way forward
Confrontative – challenging decisions
Descriptive – summarising
Demonstrative – showing practically

DOI: 10.4324/9781003226772-6

Developing an Individual Style

We develop our individual style as supervisors in the same way as we develop our style as clinicians or leaders. It is important to keep reflecting on our personal style and the impact we have on others.

As with management or leadership style it is important to know your preferred style and be aware of when to adjust it. It's possible to be a consultative leader who values involving their team in decision making whenever possible; however, there are occasions when that really isn't necessary and practitioners do not want to be involved in the minutiae of decision making about something like an infection prevention rota. There are also times when style needs to change to be immediately decisive. "OK, yes we need that equipment, just order it now." It's adjusting personal style according to circumstances.

There are times when we need to think carefully and check out our decision making, and there are times when we can engage autopilot or work intuitively. There is a point when we become confident and competent and in 'flow' at work.

When working with early career practitioners it is important for a supervisor to give space and know that the supervisee is not going to think in the same way and is unlikely to have the same style as them. It is important for any practitioner to develop their own approach to interacting with clients and carers. It usually seems to fall into place quite naturally and we only notice this when there is a problem, perhaps a practitioner is struggling with their role, or the early career practitioner has a very different evolving style to other members of the team.

When we first take on a supervisory role this might be with minimal training for the role. There may have been informal, ad hoc supervision of others but not a formal supervisory relationship. Training in the basic theory and models ought to be in place, but it isn't always accessible.

The assumption is that a fledgling supervisor will not be supervising an experienced colleague, and so the following suggestions relate to supporting newly qualified or very early career colleagues.

If a supervisee needs lots of guidance and support around individual cases they are probably at an early career stage. The supervisor can be more directive and give advice. Conversations will be focused on the history of the case, possible directions, and a plan. Although this is tighter and more directive support it can be easiest for those new to supervision. Over time this will become more reflective conversation, with the supervisor asking carefully crafted questions to help the supervisee work out the solutions for themselves.

If a supervisee is feeling overwhelmed and is struggling with workload, then the supervisor's style needs to be an attentive and active listener. There is no need to rush in with lots of advice about how to do things differently as the chances are the supervisee is not going to have the brain space to listen. The chances are the supervisee will have forgotten by the time they reach the other end of the corridor (even if you have carefully noted down the action points). More to follow in Chapter 12 on the restorative function of supervision.

The normative function of supervision is about processes, systems, and doing things in a corporate way. The style of the supervisor can be that of a supportive colleague, and there will inevitably be demonstration and advice. There will be times when a supervisor supports around errors, mistakes, and dissatisfaction. The style is somewhere between advice giving and supportive listening.

If the supervisee is prepared for the session to be recorded this can help a supervisor critique and adapt their style. It is difficult for any of us to do this, but it does give valuable insight into how we can develop and improve. I still find 'gaps' difficult, even after many years of supervisory conversations, so for several months I set myself a personal development objective of giving less advice and listening more. Recording and watching myself was a powerful learning tool.

It is important to be aware of the power of assumption about people. We know that we make decisions about people within split seconds. Research suggests we are often 'way off' in these first impressions of people. As a supervisor we need to keep questioning any assumptions we notice we are making.

It's also essential to remember that although we are tuned in to our supervisee and invested in their success, when we listen to them, we are only hearing one perspective on events. We are hearing our supervisee's story; others involved may have a very different perspective. As supervisors we need to actively wonder about alternative perspectives.

An example:
A relatively inexperienced clinician was working with minimal support in a child assessment centre. I realised as I listened to a story of events which had upset this colleague that we had vastly differing values around what had happened. This was one of those times when I was aware that there must be other perspectives and could perceive the other person's viewpoint right from the beginning of the description.

The clinician was feeling overworked and part way through a busy week needed to undertake a videoconference with some parents. For some reason less than 24 hours' notice was given to the family for this meeting. The parents were unable to make the appointment, which provoked considerable irritation in the clinician, and this was brought to supervision. The focus was on the importance of her time, the lack of commitment of the family to their child's needs, and that she was unlikely to offer them another alternative appointment for some considerable time.

My colleague was expecting a supportive response with some validation. I listened with growing concern about lack of insight and compassion about family life, let alone family life with a severely disabled child where there were probably several healthcare appointments a week on the calendar. I was also unsure why this lack of ability to attend an appointment, given at short notice, had caused such significant irritation.

Through conversation it became clear that the clinician felt vulnerable and inexperienced and there seemed to be some level of avoidance. There were wider difficulties with balancing workload. Stepping back and going back through events, while using a reflective model incorporating questions designed to facilitate consideration of the practitioner role and involvement in a situation, helped to change perspective.

Tailoring Feedback

Giving feedback is an acquired skill. Feedback given clumsily can emotionally bruise someone and also provoke resistance and be a barrier to change. In an ongoing relationship of any type it is important to remember to give positive comments and compliments. The 5:2 or 4:1 ratio of giving positive comments in comparison to negative comments is widely known.

The best outcome is where a supervisee can evaluate their own skills and gaps through a guided conversation. This isn't always possible. So what style of feedback is most likely to empower someone to change and not result in seething resentment?

Feedback which:

- Is conversational
- Is inquisitive rather than forceful. Ask questions 'wondering out loud' what might have happened. *Let's work out together what happened. Wondering is an under rated tool in the supervisory toolkit*
- Is specific not general, e.g. *"when this happened, I noticed that … how did that feel … what was going through your thoughts?"*

   "Any ideas about what you might do differently next time?"

- Is descriptive, e.g. *"the part with the role play game went really well (and I know this because this happened)"*
   "There was less language when questions were asked. Did you notice?"
   "I was trying to work out what might have been happening, what was your impression?"
- Yes, those comments can be powerful compared to questions

   "It would be interesting to try X." "While I was watching I started wondering how this would work"

- Focuses on building strengths instead of highlighting weaknesses
- Does not dwell continually on negative aspects. Looks for glimmers and highlights these too
- Encourages evaluation of role, identifying gaps. This gives ownership to development and improvement. It is an unusual person who never feels fragile when hearing about their weaknesses. *"When you did this there was a definite change in level of engagement. Should we do more of that? Could it be a way in?"*
- Is appreciative
   "This worked well, that could be built into the new plan"
   "The way you waited and let others give their opinions made it a really successful meeting"
   "Could we build something along those lines into every meeting?"
- Isn't too vague – *"that was dreadful, wasn't it?"* without any comment about the specifics
- Is balanced and genuine. Supervisees know about the *positive sandwich tactic* and see right through it
- Is concise. There is a tendency to feel guilty and keep justifying the feedback, just making the experience excruciatingly difficult

 **REFLECTIVE LEARNING**

First Impressions:

Do an online search on optical illusions (also called ambiguous images or reversible figures). You will find images you have seen before, the *rabbit head* which can also be a *duck's head*, the *older/younger woman*; the *Rubin vase/faces*. This is always a good reminder that 'all is not as it seems.'

Catch your first impressions next time you meet someone for the first time. We know there are complicated psychological processes going on when we meet someone new for the first time – personal constructs coming into action, comparison with previous experiences, and unconscious biases. We also know that research consistently shows these first impressions are usually 'way off.' Next time you meet someone at work (colleague or client) notice your response and catch it, challenge it, and override it.

Professional Style:

Think about different supervisors you've known. Whose style did you admire? Why?

What's your individual style as a practitioner? If someone was describing your team then how would you be described? How are you different to colleagues?

If you are a supervisor and feel confident enough then ask your supervisees about your style. It's possible to broach this a little more indirectly when you review supervision by describing the approach you've taken and whether this approach (your style) has worked well or needs adjusting.

Are you happy with your style? Wish it was different? If you would like your style to be different, then what do you need to do to change it?

Feedback:

Find a character you like in a movie or from history and imagine giving feedback in their style. I'll give feedback in the style of Hercule Poirot for example.

What feedback has worked for you in the past? What was different/special about this feedback?

CAMEO – CHANGE OF SUPERVISOR

Fleur was devastated as the early career practitioner whom she supervised had requested a change of supervisor. Not only this, but the supervisee had not discussed this with Fleur and gone formally to Beth the team leader. Now the team leader and Fleur were discussing this in a scenario which was acutely uncomfortable for both of them. The team leader had valiantly brought in a cup of coffee and some biscuits; but it really didn't lighten the situation.

Fleur asked again what had happened and Beth gave the basics. Fleur was both angry and upset. She had, in her own perceptions, gone 'the extra mile' and given her supervisee lots of resources, and been available for ad hoc supervisions as well as the formal sessions. This had never happened to her before, and she felt very emotionally bruised.

Beth guided the conversation to the content and style of the last few supervisions. Fleur did admit that she had ended the last supervision early after taking a phone call and waved her supervisee off to try out the new plan which she had suggested. She had mouthed this at the supervisee while engaged in the phone call. Yes, this directive advice was something neither were supposed to do – as specified in the ground rules for supervision, but surely on just one occasion?

Beth followed up and asked curiously about the 'new plan.' Fleur related how the supervisee had been using X approach and she knew that Y approach was more successful with that type of client and had strongly suggested a change in approach.

Beth suspected that the supervisee had outgrown Fleur's very directive approach, but realised that what had 'tipped this over the edge' was the way Fleur had told the supervisee that her approach was not the right one and advised her to change it. Fleur asked about the supervisee's approach and if there had been problems or limited progress. Was she struggling with the case? Was that the reason for the suggested change? "*Well actually, no,*" Fleur admitted, she just thought that her way worked better … and then the idiomatic penny dropped. She put her head in her hands and admitted that she would have hated this style of supervision when she was an early career therapist. It wasn't difficult for Beth to ask Fleur what style she preferred. This was a tough learning experience for Fleur, but she could now see the perspective of her supervisee.

Beth was able to suggest that Fleur supervise another member of the team and that she consciously change her style and ensure there were regular reviews of the supervision around how it was going. She compassionately suggested that the supervisee had probably been ready for a change soon anyway. Fleur knew she had not given her full attention to the supervisee or she might have noticed some of the dissatisfaction. She also knew she had supervised in a style she would have disliked herself; she had, she reflected, probably been giving directive management supervision and not reflective clinical supervision.

I cannot resist ending this cameo and this section with an Alice quote:

> *"She (Alice) generally gave herself very good advice, though she very seldom followed it."*
> Alice's Adventures in Wonderland

Norming Practice through Supervision

"What do you mean by that? Explain yourself!" – Caterpillar

"The best way to explain it is to do it." – Dodo
Alice's Adventures in Wonderland

Key Themes

- Norming standards and quality
- Accountability
- Clinical or management supervision
- Mediation
- Clarity of role
- Oversight of work

Standards and Quality – Norming

Sometimes the normative function of supervision is called administrative or managerial as in Kadushin's (1992) model of supervision. In essence this is about standards and quality. CQC state that: *"Importantly, clinical supervision has been linked to good clinical governance, by helping to support quality improvement, managing risks, and by increasing accountability."*

In terms of clinical supervision, normative function is closest to management supervision. It is about professional matters such as quality, standards, clinical governance, risk, evidence, and equity in care or service provision.

This chapter is about Proctor's normative function or, with its more accessible label, *standards and quality supervision*.

DOI: 10.4324/9781003226772-7

In any service there is a need for consistency in approach. There are issues ahead if one therapist suggests twice weekly therapy for a child with a language disorder and another suggests training plus monthly support. Within any service there tends to be a consensus about 'the offer' and approach advocated within the team. This is called "*norming of practice*."

Several years ago I was a clinical lead in a newly formed organisation which brought together three Healthcare Trusts in a re-organisation of providers. One of the priorities was to agree pathway standards. Then, the clinical leaders met with each practitioner and reviewed caseloads in the context of agreed pathway standards. Whether this was a good or bad thing to do is irrelevant, but it highlights the critical need in large organisations to 'norm practice.' This function of supervision can become tricky if there is an element of evaluative oversight and 'nudging' practitioners towards changing practice to be more closely aligned to colleagues.

The norming function relates to promoting and maintaining high standards of work. It is also inevitably linked with ensuring that the policies of the organisation and professional and quality standards are adhered to. It is the quality assurance function within clinical supervision. Safeguarding supervision fits neatly under the umbrella of norming.

Accountability

Accountability is an important concept in both clinical practice and clinical management. Since the devastating lapses in care standards and criminal actions of practitioners, such as nurse Beverley Allitt, there has been a strict focus on clinical governance and benchmarks/standards in care to provide assurances of safe service provision. HCPC advocates "*autonomous professionals*," but as such we are accountable for maintaining standards.

There can be a need to review practice in the context of an organisation's policies, protocols, and procedures. Any dilemmas about ethical or practice standards can be brought to supervision sessions. At times when practitioners are covering an absent colleague's work then support around prioritising needs and maintaining quality in provision might be a theme for supervision. Administrative load and personal skills such as managing workload, effective outcomes, and record keeping link to accountability.

This function of supervision focuses more on the organisational background of individual practice. It also relates to national frameworks linked to professional, political, and legal matters.

CQC, RCSLT, HCPC, and NHS organisations have an expectation that clinical supervision will serve as a tool to safeguard practice and implement consistent care pathways. The need for specialist clinical leadership, evidence-based reference points/resources, and recording CPD is emphasised. There is good practice at the practitioner level around pathways, standards, and quality assurance. This may be measured by quality initiatives and clinical audit, but there are few studies in this area.

There is a helpful definition in the RCSLT Guidance:

Normative: relating to the promotion and maintenance of good standards of work, ethical practice, accountability and adherence to policies of administration, including:

- *clarification of roles and responsibilities*
- *workload management*
- *review and assessment of work*
- *addressing organisation and practice issues*

Clinical or Management Supervision

There is more potential overlap between this function of clinical supervision and management supervision. There is a fine line between clinical considerations and service management. For example, a service decision not to offer input to children with behavioural difficulties in eating and drinking, or the fact that many services in the NHS stipulate those children whose cognitive age is on a par with language levels should not receive a service. When services face waiting list demands plus recruitment and retention difficulties there are more conversations about what can't be offered. The impact of these decisions might be taken to clinical supervision by a practitioner, but this is about whole service and organisational restrictions. Addressing organisational issues tends to fall under the umbrella of management supervision.

There is an evolving aspect of clinical dilemma which fits into the function of normative supervision. As an NHS Clinical Lead, I led on developing care pathways in my clinical specialist area. Within any specified care pathway, we need to be thoughtful when considering deviating from the pathway for a specific case. This is a time to engage in reflective thinking about the needs of the client and the reasons for a different direction. When we are moving away from an agreed norm then decision making rationale can be considered in supervision.

Care pathways in a service draw practitioners together and give a shared focus for considering cases and planning care. They are a strong way of alerting practitioners to the research and embedding evidence-based practice. However, there are those occasions when a deviation is needed for an individual client and the need to reflect and justify clinical thinking is positive.

In a team or service, it is necessary to have some norming of practice. Service provision needs a shared ethos and equity in delivery. There are complex issues underlying this normative function of supervision.

There is a 'beware of' warning here too. The normative function has the potential to be hijacked in times of pressure on service and potentially utilised to influence case management. Caseload review and guidance to norm practice at times of service restriction is not the same as clinical supervision. Caseload review and nudging in a different direction may be needed at times of crisis but is not clinical supervision.

So let's look at the normative function with a positive lens. With an emphasis on research-based practice, applying theory to difficult cases in a collaborative conversation, this function is essential.

I reflect that I occasionally might do something similar in my supervision sessions when working with an independent colleague who does not have access to management support. There might be an issue which arises which links with the normative function of supervision. Occasionally I feel I need to say something which is more directive linked to standards and governance; I tend to say that I am aware that I have 'changed hats' and am now speaking more like a manager than a clinical supervisor.

Turner and Hill (2011) looked at implementing a system of supervision for nurses based on Proctor's framework. They utilised the ward manager to clinically supervise the whole team and used a tiered rather than a cascaded structure for supervision. They realised, with hindsight, that this had been positive in *"ensuring the whole team was involved and that no staff were supervised by the least experienced staff."* All grades had the same level of experienced support. For now it seems best to say that supervision can be offered by a line manager, but there needs to be clear differentiation between roles. Some experts in this field of supervision strongly advocate choice of clinical supervisor. The key to success seems to be mutual trust and respect.

Let's pause for a while to shine a spotlight on the scenario of a potentially miserable practitioner who knows they are failing in competence and confidence and under a level of scrutiny.

If this person was being supervised by the same clinician who was dealing with any performance assurance matters as part of an organisational policy, that could be problematic.

> It would be compassionate for the practitioner in this situation to access a clinical supervisor outside of the line. There could be arrangements for sharing information about progress and the involvement of the line manager, with the agreement of the clinical supervisor and supervisee.
>
> However, at times when a practitioner might be acutely anxious about performance and the need to improve skills it might potentially adversely affect wellbeing to have their line manager involved in their clinical supervision.
>
> The self-fulfilling prophecy might not be researched but there are generations who would attest to its existence!

Normative function is *"the quality assurance dimension within supervision"* (Kettle 2015). It is closest to management supervision with more potential overlaps. The dilemma for the clinical supervisor is that on occasion in a conversation linked to standards, quality, and governance there is a need to step outside of the usual supervisory style and ask specific questions to check the situation further and give specific guidance.

Clarity of Role

A practitioner may take a case to clinical supervision where there is positive collaborative working, perhaps joint working between SLT and dietician is evolving, and exploring how this works practically for individuals is very appropriate for clinical supervision.

Clarity of role can often be set out specifically by an employing organisation. Often a practitioner will bring to supervision stress caused by another professional's interpretation of their role. Sometimes other professionals make assumptions about what the speech and language practitioner 'should be doing,' e.g. providing regular therapy. Sometimes a colleague with influence and power attached to their role like a paediatrician, ENT consultant, or educational psychologist has very definite ideas about what the practitioner 'should be' offering. If this is communicated to families an immediate clash in expectations and potential lack of trust in the speech and language practitioner is possible. This is not at the top of the list of topics in clinical supervision, but it scores highly for being a common theme which causes frustration and stress for practitioners. Having access to evidence-based practice/pathways and assertive communication skills helps here, but there always seem to be colleagues who know what the practitioner should be doing differently.

Personal Reflection

Several years ago I was fortunate to be involved in an innovative service initiative to modernise practice in a special school. All the clinicians were feeling overwhelmed and close to burn out. Caseloads were static, and although there was excellent liaison there was little actual joint working.

After a period of evaluating evidence and discussing possibilities, the SLT, OT, physiotherapist, and school nurse devised a new model of collaborative working.

With the agreement of management in the school the teachers were trained in this new model, which involved them 'requesting' input from the therapy team. The team considered the request and decided who would respond. SLT and OT might make a joint visit if the request overlapped, e.g. positioning in relation to eating and drinking needs. The request forms were simple to complete, and the response time was quick.

The SLTs involved would discuss overlapping roles and working differently in their clinical supervision.

Oversight of Work

Oversight of work is not usually part of clinical supervision in speech and language therapy. It happens more in clinical psychology or teaching where there is more joint observation of practice integrated into supervisory systems. However many speech and language practitioners will choose to take cases for discussion where they are seeking evaluation of their decision making in a complex case. Effective practitioners will self-evaluate their work continually and will seek out the opinion of the supervisor and 'take on board' and use supportive feedback constructively.

REFLECTIVE LEARNING

Think about standards across speech and language therapy:

Do you know them? These are outlined on the HCPC website. Have a look and refresh your memory about the professional standards which we literally sign up to in undergoing that process of re-registration every two years.

Consider how practice (clinical approach) is 'normed' across a service:

How does this happen? Is it by care pathways? Case review?

What are your own standards of practice?

What are the red lines you won't cross? What are the situations where you have felt you needed to speak up and protest about something a colleague has suggested? We all have values and standards underpinning our approach to practice, and we're not always consciously aware of these.

Have a think about your values and maybe make a list:

Examples might be excellence, integrity, equal access, respectful relationships, ethical decision making, being supportive and responsive, plus many more.

Take your values out with you for a week at work:

Notice if there are any times when you feel uncomfortable about a clash between your personal values and the values of the service (if you are employed in a team).

Think about Alice:

So far these seem rather heavy reflections for this serious topic ... so ... let's change the tempo. You will have noticed the Alice quotations at the beginning of the chapters.

If you know the book or movie then consider what the values and learning points in the stories might be. I've added some thoughts on this below:

- Without self-challenge we don't grow
- Sometimes taking risks propels us forward
- Valuing the differences of others
- Finding new perspectives and directions.
- Avoiding getting stuck in the past
- Standing up for ourselves
- Discovering who you are (professional identity)

"When the Caterpillar asks Alice, 'Who are you?', she struggles to find a simple answer. This is not just because she has changed sizes several times since falling down the rabbit hole, but because Alice is unsure at this point in time just who she is."

Alice's Adventures in Wonderland

CAMEO – NORMING A PATHWAY

This was an unusual short-term group supervision which highlights the normative/standards function of supervision. The supervisor, Allison, was asked to set up and facilitate a group of six practitioners, which was in effect a team of practitioners who were working together on establishing a new care pathway for young people with a language disorder. The new care pathway was innovative in combining a strong component of training with individual plans linked to the content of the training. Previously the team had worked individually with different secondary schools (11–16 year olds). The team had enjoyed their work but the waiting times were long (at one point approaching 3 years) and there was an increasing pressure to work differently.

The first session explored a tendency, experienced by several, to want to keep things the same way. Allison, the supervisor, asked questions to ascertain the history and gradually began to explore barriers (or perceived barriers) to the new approach. There was honest conversation about anxieties around the training role, and one practitioner had a strong value clash as she felt this was in effect reducing (cutting back) the service.

Over the next three months the group met five times. Allison facilitated the session so that each supervisee could talk about and consider an individual young person in a school context and their likely progress through the pathway. The process of the group was felt by each supervisee to draw their practice closer together and also gave opportunity to fine tune the care pathway. Practice was normed and brought together.

Effective Reflective Conversations

"Would you tell me, please, which way I ought to go from here?"

"That depends a good deal on where you want to get to," said the Cat.

"I don't much care where—" said Alice.

"Then it doesn't matter which way you go," said the Cat.

"—so long as I get SOMEWHERE," Alice added as an explanation.

"Oh, you're sure to do that," said the Cat, "if you only walk long enough."
Alice's Adventures in Wonderland

Key Themes

- The positives of supervision
- Into the dismal swamp
- The default lens
- Introducing reflective models
- Lewin and Kolb's Learning Cycle
- Gibbs' Reflective Cycle
- Driscoll and Rolfe's What, What, What Model
- Boud's Reflection Model
- Johns' Model for Structured Reflection
- Brookfield's Model of Reflection
- Tripp's Critical Incidence Technique
- Page and Wosket's Cyclical Model

DOI: 10.4324/9781003226772-8

Reflective practice and clinical supervision combine together to enable practitioners to reflect on situations in their practice and analyse what happened and whether anything could be done differently as a result of new insights. This is learning and improving practice through reflective conversation.

The Positives of Supervision

In the 'helping' professions there is a danger of moving towards burnout. Signs of burnout include feelings of 'staleness' about our job, rigidity, and defensiveness. Clinical supervision can break the cycle of feeling drained. *"A good supervisory relationship is the best way we know to stay open to ourselves and our clients"* (Ghaye et al., 2000).

When we engage in a positive and constructive supervisory relationship then there are considerable benefits:

- Self confidence in how to move forward and take next steps
- Broader thinking around clinical situations
- Reduced stress generally
- Acknowledging limits – knowing our scope of practice and personal endurance
- Reduction in emotional exhaustion
- Improved relationships with clients, colleagues, and managers

---

Powell (1989) sees supervision as positive tool for learning and change:

- Practitioners have the ability to bring about change with the assistance of a guide (supervisor)
- Practitioners don't always know what is best for them and may be "blinded by their resistance to and denial of the issues"
- Change is constant and inevitable
- In supervision the guide concentrates on what is changeable
- It is not necessary to know about the cause of a problem, even a significant problem, in order to resolve it
- There are many 'correct' ways to view situations and view the world

---

Into the Dismal Swamp – and out the Other Side!

Several models of reflective practice are explored in this chapter. Before we embark on this, let's look again at Schön's ideas about how professional practice develops. Schön uses the metaphor of the *"dismal swamp"* and talks of the need for reflective thinking when we are faced with an unusual situation, also called *"an indeterminate zone of practice."* This is the uncharted lowlands in the marshy swamp, but with reflective thinking we can be confident and navigate through the swamp, integrating our knowledge with a specific client's needs.

In Schön's model he defines his two main types of reflection (sometimes this is called reflexivity, but it veers towards jargon so I will simply use 'reflection'). There is the *"Reflection on Action"* where we rewind and analyse events, re-framing our view of what happened, freeze framing before planning how we might make changes in the future – make a sequel! Then there is *"Reflection in Action,"* sometimes called **reflection in the moment**. This is when, in the middle of a situation, we knowingly make a change in our approach. Schön talks of how our practitioner's 'sixth sense' is activated and we realise something needs to change immediately. There might be a moment of pause and slow motion while we adjust our actions.

There is also a third type of reflection less widely known which is *"Knowing in Action."* This is the intuitive knowledge a practitioner has gained through experience and learning that enables them to do their job or task without thinking. It is their professional 'know-how.' *"The knowing is in the action. It is shown by the skilful execution of the performance – we are notably not able to make it verbally explicit"* (Schön 1983).

The expert practitioner not only enters the swamp but thrives in it. One characteristic of an expert practitioner in any profession is that they are able to see 'the big picture,' not just details like individual trees, but the whole forest and sometimes even sense the smoke coming over a ridge in the distance.

In reflective practice we can re-visit the 'situation,' go into slow motion thinking, and consider events. The scene is re-visited, the story re-told, and through this process new insights can emerge. Hawkins (1982) suggested that in the 'swamplands,' which are the territory of supervision, a guided conversation would consider the client, environment, organisational systems, and the practitioner.

If there is something that feels 'not quite right' about a situation, it can make us pause and it triggers more focused thinking about the event. We all make many decisions every hour on 'clinical professional autopilot,' and it is the puzzling events which trigger this thinking process.

When we are able to sit and talk with a supervisor about a situation, through the use of reflective frameworks we are guided into seeing the event again and the picture changes. This has been compared to moving from 2D greyscale into full 3D technicolour. The conversation can give us a multi-dimensional perspective.

In my own model of reflective thinking (Figure 7.1 adapted from Howes 2005), I drew on film imagery. We consider a situation, something which is a 'daily dilemma,' where decision making is not straight forward. We rewind and view again as if the situation was a movie streaming. The conversation covers the people involved against a background environment (the film set). We hit pause and then view the action again, this time in slow motion. We can rewind, freeze frame, and zoom in closer to consider the situation.

The supervisor not only guides us through describing what happened, but helps us to look through a soft focus lens to re-visit emotional reactions to events and then through a sharp focused lens looking logically at those events and any barriers we might not have previously noticed. This leads to reflective processing and sensemaking about the action event.

So what does it mean? Is there a changed perspective? Would we do anything differently? We can re-frame and edit the plan for the future. After this editing process we can even move into anticipatory reflection and preview events and consider how this might play out next time.

We have a conversation using film imagery to consider a puzzling event and rewind, viewing the event in slow motion, pausing and freeze framing if necessary, or zooming in to consider a small detail in sharp focus which we might have overlooked. Through this process of reflective processing we might gain a different perspective and some ideas about how to move forward.

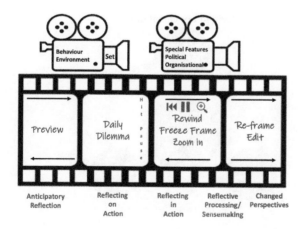

Figure 7.1 My own model of reflective thinking

Introducing Reflective Models

All the models of reflective practice have a common core of guided conversation about caseworking where supervisees examine experience, work with it, and often gain new perspectives (Figure 7.2). There are several different models, but this is the essence of all approaches. Ghaye (2010) feels that "*new knowledge and improved action is only possible by learning through reflective conversations which we have with each other as we explore each other's confusions, anxieties, apprehensions, achievements and relevant lived experience.*"

The same pattern tends to be followed. We look back on our experience of the situation, through a sharp focused lens, considering what we have learned and would we do the same again or change for future action (Figure 7.3). The situations which we bring to discuss are usually based on clinical caseworking – our clients, their carers, relationships, and any 'emotional clutter,' which can make it hard to see clearly.

A skilled supervisor can guide the 'story of practice' and how it is viewed. Supervisees can also develop skills in presenting events, in re-telling a story of practice. There is an appreciation of different perspectives of those involved as we are encouraged to look through the eyes of others.

The supervisor influences how we process our experiences, after visiting the edit suite and slow-motion viewing. In facilitating processing, the supervisor adds lenses and filters (questions and summaries) to give different views and insights. With a wider lens we notice more about the background context; with a long lens we might project into possible futures. We can imagine how things might improve and be better. "*Reflection is much more than simply thinking about what you do, it is about being self-critical without being destructive and overly critical*" (Ghaye 1998 & 2010). The reflective

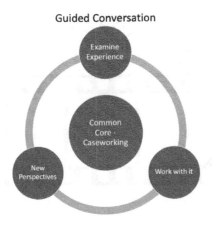

Figure 7.2 A guided conversation

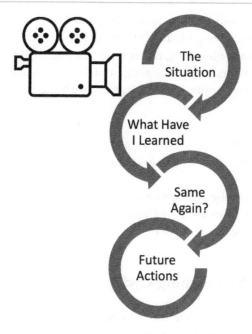

Figure 7.3 Reflecting through a lens

conversation is pivotal in unpicking events and putting them back together; when colour, texture and dimension are added we may notice patterns. We begin to recognise our own action tendencies.

The Default Lens

I divert down a side pathway now for a short time. In his work on managing energy rather than time, *The Energy Project*, Tony Schwartz (2016) talks about a *"default lens."*

Each of us calls this default lens reality, because most of us believe we see things the way they are. However, in truth we see reality through a fixed lens that selectively filters our view of the world. There needs to be some filters to aid processing and help us to focus on key features and avoid totally sporadic attention control. However as mentioned later in Chapter 11 regarding the 'gorilla in our midst' experiment, we know that our impression of events is not going to be the same as someone who might even be standing next to us looking in the same direction.

"Our identity is the sum of the stories we tell about ourselves." We tend to use a default lens which is fixed and filters how we view the world. Schwarz

maintains that we should *"learn to see through a broader range of lenses."* There are new ways of seeing situations through a reflective lens. This should allow us to stand back observing, rather than reacting to events. This links with reflecting in the moment. The suggestion is to ask ourselves two simple questions when we notice 'being triggered' with the reactivity response growing.

What are the facts here?

What is the story I'm telling myself about this situation?

Pausing (and no one else will notice a momentary pause) and considering these questions allows us to *"stand outside ourselves and observe our experience,"* reducing triggering reactivity.

Lewin and Kolb's Learning Cycle

Now, moving on to share some reflective models. The most well-known is Lewin and Kolb (1984). Although it is usually referred to as Kolb's Learning Cycle it was first devised by Kurt Lewin who developed his ideas from control engineering (Figure 7.4 shows an adapted version of the cycle).

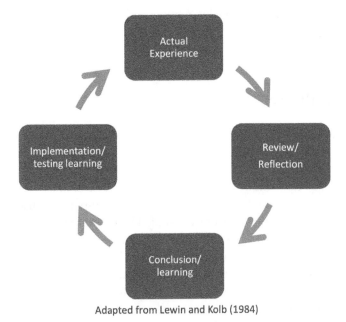

Adapted from Lewin and Kolb (1984)

Figure 7.4 Learning cycle

Kolb's Learning Cycle

Phase 1: concrete experience: having the experience

Phase 2: reflective observation: working with the event, looking back, and reflecting on what happened

Phase 3: abstract conceptualisation: reflective processing, 'making sense' of events with new perspectives

Phase 4: experimentation: planning and testing out what has been learned through the reflective processing

Other models have superseded it, but if anyone says 'learning cycle' they usually mean Kolb. The process begins with the 'concrete' description before reviewing and reflecting on experience. There is sensemaking, considering how to handle things differently in the future. One difference which hasn't been picked up as much by later writers is that the final phase of experimentation involves planning ahead and testing out ideas based on what has been learned.

Gibbs' Reflective Cycle

It is not sufficient simply to have an experience in order to learn. Without reflecting upon this experience it may quickly be forgotten, or its learning potential lost.

(Gibbs 1998)

Gibbs' Reflective Cycle is about telling your story by following stages: description, feelings, evaluation, analysis, conclusions, and action plan (an adapted version is shown in Figure 7.5). The idea of this model is to systematise reflections and isolate feelings. *"It is from the feelings and thoughts emerging from this reflection that generalisations or concepts can be generated and it is generalisations that allow new situations to be tackled effectively"* (Gibbs 1998).

Working through the different stages usually helps to slow down thought processes so that we don't jump to conclusions and take time to reflect.

This six-step model supports a conversation about a situation experienced by the practitioner.

Steps 1–3 connect back to what happened

Steps 4–6 focus on learning and considering how actions might be adapted in future situations

Telling your story

Adapted from Gibb's Reflective Cycle (1998)

Figure 7.5 Telling a story

Gibb's Reflective Cycle: Steps 1–3

Step 1 – description: the conversation begins with a short description of what happened during the event. This is the supervisee setting the scene for the supervisor.

- What happened and when?
- Who was involved?
- What did they do?
- How did events unfold? How did it end up?

Step 2 – feelings: then recalling what thoughts were going through the practitioner's mind and what they were feeling during the events:

- How did you feel during this event?
- What were you thinking while this was happening?
- How did you feel during, and also after, this happened?
- Have you any ideas about what other people might have been feeling?

- Can you remember any key thoughts as you walked away from this situation?
- Did you think about this experience afterwards?

There is an opportunity at this point to identify strengths and any need for professional development to strengthen skills.

Step 3 – evaluation: this step is innovative and perhaps one of the reasons this model is still widely used. The practitioner considers what was good/positive as well as what was bad/difficult about the experience. This is about weighing up the positives and the negatives in this situation. What others did or did not do well can be included:

- How did things go? Focus on positives and negatives
- What went well? What didn't?
- Describe any aspect which went especially well
- Was there anything which stands out as not going at all well?
- Was there something which was tried which did not work?
- Do you think your actions/contributions had a positive or negative effect on the situation?
- What word would best describe this situation as you left it, e.g. was it *resolved*? Was there still *frustration* (irritation) in those present?

Gibb's Reflective Cycle: Steps 4–6

Step 4 – analysis: the conversation then bridges to looking ahead. The supervisor guides an analysis of the situation with reflective processing to 'make sense' of what happened. I find it helpful to use the term 'sensemaking' at this point in a conversation. I learned this expression from my analytical, engineering husband and it is incredibly useful in supervision. The conversation focuses on this sensemaking and any insights which have emerged during the conversation. They often do, it isn't unusual that with space and time and a guided conversation we notice something we missed during the event. It may even be something as simple as a pause and change in body language or intonation by someone, or a comment which disrupted the direction of discourse.

In sensemaking the conversation might consider theory, research, wider context, previous experiences, and advice from others:

- Why do we think things went well or badly in this situation?
- Have we any theories/evidence to make sense of events?
- Could I have responded differently?

- Is there anything which might possibly have helped or improved things?

Take into account points made in the previous steps and identify any factors which helped, e.g. consider your role in the experience and how you contributed to the success of this experience. If things did not go to plan, why do you think this was, e.g. lack of preparation or external factors beyond your control? It can be useful to consider other people who were involved in the experience. Did they have similar views or reactions to you? If not, why do you think that was the case?

Step 5 – conclusion: wondering if there is anything else which could have been done which might have made a difference. Gibbs proposed two conclusions: a general overview and a specific conclusion based very much on this particular situation. Often these are merged together, but considering both broad and specific conclusions can support action planning:

- What have I learned? Both generally and specifically?
- What could I now do better?
- Should I have done anything differently?
- What skills would I need to deal with this/cope with this sort of situation better in future?

Step 6 – action plan: then on to action planning ... if this happened again then what would the practitioner do differently? Thinking about:

- How can I apply my new perspective to improve things in the future?
- What new knowledge and skills have come out of this experience?
- How can I adapt my actions and do things differently in future?
- Is there any training (work based or a course) in this area of practice?

Some practitioners find Gibbs too prescriptive. However, in the early stages of learning to reflect on experience it is a good model for considering the experience and its impact and identifying any learning needs for the future. It is possible for a supervisor to have sight of the cycle and use it as a shared reference point in a session, but not stick rigidly to it if a different conversational direction emerges.

This model is also often suggested for reflective writing on experience. It is worth remembering this option after a difficult scenario; working through the cycle as self-reflection, jotting down thoughts and ideas, in a type of self-de-briefing can 'settle the mind' and reduce any stress attached to events (Chapter 18).

Driscoll and Rolfe's What, What, What Model

John Driscoll's book *Practicing Reflective Practice* (2007) is a good place to go for anyone looking for an academic source of information about reflective practice and supervision. He occasionally mentions speech and language therapy and often refers to AHPs, so is thinking more widely about healthcare and not just a nursing perspective.

On the surface it appears simple, but it is a strong sequential model for exploring events and perceptions of what happened.

Driscoll What, What, What Model

What? Describing the experience

So what? Reflecting in conversation on the experience, including what has been learnt

Now what? How learning will be used in future practice

It is put forward as a simple way of helping to *"form a basic plan when learning from experience."* It starts with asking *"What?"* and returning to the situation. The conversation then moves on to *"So What?"* and an attempt to understand the wider situation. The focus then moves to *"Now What?"* and how a practitioner might modify future actions and do something differently. It is another model useful for self-reflective writing.

A supervisor's individual style of conversation can be used to explore each step of the process. Others have worked on extending this model, and Rolfe's model (2001) presents the three questions as a cycle adding specific prompt questions (Figure 7.6 shows an adapted version).

Rolfe and colleagues (2001) devised a series of questions to extend the three What questions. These questions give a plain English, accessible way to *"refine reflective thinking and isolate the key elements of the situation or occurrence so that they can be understood in more detail."* The questions have been adapted a little for speech and language therapy as they were originally written from the perspective of a practice educator.

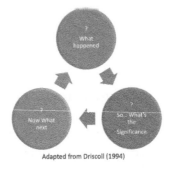

Adapted from Driscoll (1994)

Figure 7.6 What, What, What cycle

Adaption of Rolfe's Questions

What?

Is the difficulty/reason for feeling stuck/unsure what's happening?
Is the reason communication is breaking down?
Was my role in this situation?
Were my motivations?
Was I trying to achieve?
Actions did I take?
Was the response of others?
Were the consequences for those involved?
Feelings did it evoke? For myself? Others involved?
Was good/bad about the experience?

So what?

Does this tell me about relationships?
Does this tell me about my client's care?
Does this tell me about the therapy approach I am using?
Does this say about my attitudes/my client's attitudes?
Was going through my mind as this happened?
Did I base my actions on?
Could/should I have done to make it better?
Are any new perspectives on the situation?
Broader issues arise from the situation?

> **Now what?**
>
> Do I need to do in order to make things better/resolve the situation?
> Do I need to do to feel better/get on better?
> Wider issues need considering here?
> Might this situation turn out?
> Might the consequences be?

Boud's Reflection Model

Boud's Reflection Model (Figure 7.7 adapted from Boud's model) was devised by David Boud, Rosemary Keogh, and David Walker (1985) and focuses on learning through reflecting on experience.

They devised a reflective model which loops round more than once, while considering what happened in a situation. The supervisor returns the practitioner to the experience in a guided conversation. Emotional reactions are considered, but this model emphasises utilising positive feelings as well as scrutinising obstructive feelings which might be barriers to moving forward. The supervisor guides re-evaluating the experience through reflective questioning. In this model there is always a link out to the behaviour, feelings, and thoughts which the practitioner experienced. The conversation eventually leaves the loop and moves into 'outcomes' and considering new perspectives about the experience, changes in response/behaviour, and an action plan; a readiness to commit and try out a new approach.

The difference with this model is it emphasises the opportunity to go round the loop several times, consider solutions, and then go back into reflective thinking. It is more dynamic with structured looping and linking leading to learning.

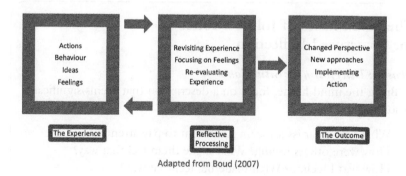

Adapted from Boud (2007)

Figure 7.7 Reflection Model

Johns' Model for Structured Reflection (MSR)

Johns' model appears in the Helen and Douglas House supervision materials (2014), the NHS Scotland Study Units on supervision, and the RCSLT Reflective Writing pack.

When describing Johns' Model for Structured Reflection (1996), the Helen House Supervision kit singles out a significant difference in this model. In a busy working environment, Johns' MSR begins by *"inviting the practitioner to bring the mind home."* This describes the process of stepping away from the busyness, burden, and pressures of our work to really bring ourselves into clinical supervision so that we are present in the space not only physically but also psychologically and emotionally.

I admit to having missed this. I always tended to feel a little overwhelmed by Johns' model and its long list of questions. MSR has been revised and updated many times. I would make a guess at this currently being the 13th edition, but that could easily be superseded. It is an excellent model for those who are new to reflective clinical supervision and need a tool which gives specific and comprehensive direction. The reality is that a more experienced supervisor will probably know the model, have access to it, use some of the questions, and share it with supervisees as a learning tool because this model really zooms in on reflective questioning.

I have noticed that Johns is now writing on *Mindful Leadership in Healthcare* (2015) so the need to create a safe space and begin by *"bringing the mind home"* fits with mindfulness and 'being in the moment.'

Johns' Model for Structured Reflection is a guide to help navigate conversation. It can be used for personal reflection and within clinical supervision by individuals and groups. MSR is widely available and a summary is given here.

The model uses *"reflective cues"* which are divided into five phases.

The Five Phases of Johns' Model for Structured Reflection

Phase 1: Describing the Situation
 Bring the mind home, focus on a description that seems significant in some way.

- What particular issues seem significant to pay attention to?
- How were others feeling? What made them feel that way?
- How was I feeling? What made me feel that way?

Phase 2: Reflection

- What was I trying to achieve and did I respond effectively?
- Why did I approach this the way I did?
- What were the consequences of my actions for me, the client, others?
- How did I feel during this experience?
- How did others feel during this experience?
- How do I know how others felt during this experience?

Phase 3: Factors Which Influenced the Situation as It Happened

- What factors influenced the way I was feeling, thinking, and responding?
- What internal factors influenced my decision making during the experience?
- What sources of knowledge were available?
- What sources could I have consulted?
- What sources and information would have impacted my choice?

Phase 4: What Could I Have Done Better? Considering Areas for Improvement for Similar Situations

- To what extent did I act for the best and in tune with my values?
- How does this situation connect with previous experience?
- How might I respond more effectively given this situation again?
- What other options did I have?
- Have I considered all options?
- Have I selected the best option?
- What would be the consequences of alternative actions for the patient, others, and me?
- What factors might constrain me acting in new ways?

Phase 5: Learning and Planning around Areas for Improvement as Identified in the Previous Phase

- How do I NOW feel about this experience?
- What will change because of this experience?
- How do I feel about my experience now?
- What does this situation have to do with past situations?
- What would have been a better way to approach this situation?
- What are the consequences of alternatives choices I've made for patients? For others and for me?

- How approachable and available am I to better help my patients and colleagues?
- How has this experience changed my knowledge? In one of the following ways:
  - Empirical – scientific
  - Ethical – moral knowledge
  - Personal – self-awareness
  - Aesthetic – the art of what we do, our own experiences
- Am I better able to support myself and others as a consequence?
- Am I more able to realise excellence in practice?

There is a lot here, and this explains my conflicted approach to Johns' model. It is clearly sequenced, updated over time to include new ideas and thinking about practice development, and it links more closely to learning and development than many models. Does it help me create a positive supervisory experience? Well no, the structure takes over the session and there is potential overload in the number of questions plus some jargon too. However it cannot be ignored and is a valuable reference point. There is nothing else like Johns. Know about it, refer to it, use it, but with common sense and awareness of the needs of your supervisee and potential 'overload' of information processing.

I believe there are practitioners out there who can make MSR work in an accessible, supportive style. I suspect it might work well as a framework for co-supervision, where there might be a tendency not to push forward with challenging questions. If both practitioners use MSR or an adaptation of it to structure their shared time, then it would result in a wide ranging co-supervisory conversation which covers all angles.

Brookfield's Model of Reflection

Developed by Stephen Brookfield (1995) this model comes from the teaching profession. Reflection was originally about events in the classroom and school day. There is more on Brookfield's model in Chapter18 on reflective writing as it is one of the models in the RCSLT reflective writing pack. In the learning pack it is suggested that this model *"can work very well if you're reflecting on a new or different intervention – especially if it's your first experience applying it in practice."*

The model has four lenses which can be used by practitioners for looking at events and giving their views about a situation.

Brookfield's 4 Lenses

The Autobiographical Lens – experience from your own perspective
   The Client Lens – experience through the eyes of the client
   The Colleagues Lens – seeking other viewpoints, this is about feedback and support from those around you – both SLTs and other professionals
   The Theoretical Lens – considering relevant research or other sources of information

This approach gives another systematic tool for looking differently at a complex situation. Viewing through the different lenses can lead to creative thinking and noticing patterns in events. Brookfield suggests using tentative questioning as each lens is applied in an informal 'investigative approach' to viewing events. It's all about keeping a curious mind. Brookfield notes that *"critically reflective teachers make excellent teachers that are able to convey their own voice to others in an authentic way."* Reflective driven power, in action!

Tripp's Critical Incidence Technique (CIT)

Tripp's Critical Incidence Technique (CIT) (1993) is a rather different model which takes a story-based approach. Practitioners share stories about different types of incidents. There are five story titles for these incidents. The practitioner tells a story about their practice, which is then scrutinised through a sharp focused lens.

Tripp's Critical Incidence Technique Story Types

Making a difference
Went well
Broke down
Typical
Demanding

More detail is found in Chapter 17 where CIT is applied to group supervision.

Fleur Griffiths (2002) adapted CIT and called it *"Telling Practice Stories"* using slightly different story choices:

Fleur Griffith's Adaptation of Tripp's Stories

Sunny

Success

Turning point

Blunder

Routine

Something new

This framework also works well as a structure for group supervision (Chapter 17). The inclusion of 'sunny' ensures there are stories about achievements and good days.

Page and Wosket's Cyclical Model

NHS Scotland's Clinical Supervision Resource (2017) presents several models as helpful when practically implementing clinical supervision. Unit 2 showcases the model by Wosket and Page (2001) (Figure 7.8 shows an adapted version). It stands out as a little different, and the key features are summarised below. This Cyclical Model is explored in some detail in the NHS Scotland Resource.

This model falls between being a framework for organising a supervision session and a reflective model.

The Five Stages of Page and Wosket's Cyclical Model

Contract: this is the starting point covering ground rules and expectations before the supervisor focuses on the supervisee's presentation of the information.

Focus: here the supervisor brings in comments and questions connected with any goals in development, e.g. confident decision making.

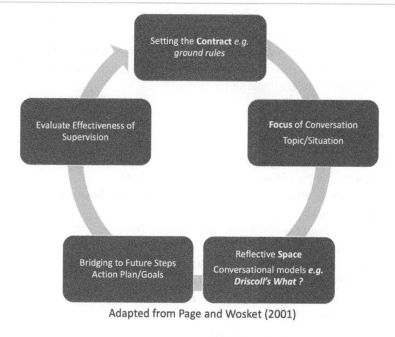

Adapted from Page and Wosket (2001)

Figure 7.8 Cyclical model

Questions that may be used to establish the focus:

What would you like to bring to this session?
What do you hope to get out of our time?
Where do you want to get to by the end of this session?
What would be a good outcome for you?
What would you like the outcome to be/look like?
Do you know what you want?
Do you know what you don't want?

Space: stepping into a safe space for reflective consideration of the case/situation.

There is emphasis on challenge at this stage. Challenge is seen as *"a significant benefit of facilitated reflection and an important aspect for enhancing awareness and development"* (NHS Education for Scotland 2017).

Carefully chosen challenging questions strengthen reflective thinking. *"In reality the purpose is not so much to 'challenge' as to offer and encourage consideration of an alternative perspective."* Through reflective questioning the practitioner becomes aware of assumptions (possibly unconscious ones) and what might be influencing the situation.

The questions and statements are actually very good for challenging and could be used in any reflective conversation. They suggest warmth and guide reflection into more challenging territory.

Challenging Questions

You talked about ... I'm wondering why you thought that?

There are a couple of things here ... are they linked?

You seem to be saying ... but I don't think your body language is saying the same thing.

Is there anything you could have done differently?

What difference would that have made to you?

Remove assumptions: if this wasn't happening? If things were different?

Can I tell you what I think you're saying?

I'd like to talk about something you said earlier.

What is it that makes you think that?

Is there anything else you could do?

If you did that what might be the impact on others involved?

What other ways could you approach this?

What might you have wanted to do instead?

Bridge: is about being a reflective practitioner and using work-based learning to develop and identify any changes we need to make. It enables us to:

- Identify what we need to know (knowledge)

- Establish what we need to do (skills)

- Evaluate our practice (competence)

Responding to a gentle challenge to our practice with reflective processing increases insight into our level of competence.

Questions that could be used to facilitate action planning are:

We talked about a number of things you could do, which would you choose?

Ideally who would you get support from?

What would support look like?

What have you done in similar cases that could be relevant here?

> *Are there any other options you could consider?*
> *What might the repercussions be if ...?*
> *In the future what could you do to ensure that ...?*
> *How has your perception changed from when we first started?*
> *What are you going to do now? Anything else?*
> *What support do you need?*
> *Who could you go to for help/support?*
> *How are you going to get that support?*
> *Are there any potential barriers to you achieving this?*

Review: feedback and evaluation of previous actions, today's session, or the overall success of clinical supervision.

This is clearly a very wide-ranging model. I suspect supervisors either love or hate it!

In effect Page and Wosket give a model which integrates a reflective model into a structured framework for organising clinical supervision sessions. This model would not be my preferred, 'go to' model of reflection. It is complex and I have other preferred models. For someone new to reflective practice it gives a comprehensive framework for the development of skills. If you are interested in using this model then locate more in-depth information in the Scottish resource.

There are other models of reflective practice, but common to all is in-depth consideration of a situation/an event in a structured way. Some models work well for self-reflective writing, but when used by a clinical supervisor in a guided conversation the effect can be enhanced. We are in a safe space, slowing down our thinking, re-viewing events, and gaining different perspectives. A reflective conversation gives structure to learning from experience.

 REFLECTIVE LEARNING

The Positives of Supervision

Think about your own experiences of supervision.
    What is needed to make a positive supervisory relationship for you?
    Remember a great supervision session.

85

Now one which was difficult, dreadful, devastating (we've all known these and you may now be able to recognise what contributed to the negative experience).

Toolkit Techniques

Into the swamplands: what would you put in your 'Swamplands Kit' for dealing with a day of difficulties and dilemmas? This might be a strategy for de-escalating a situation or something more light hearted like hot chocolate or an imaginary invisibility cloak.

A Day at the Movies

Choose a day in the weeks ahead and put it on your calendar. On this day you will be focusing on slow motion thinking; you will be purposefully slowing down your thinking speed ... going into slow motion. You are probably going to be more likely to be able to 'think in the moment,' which is really difficult but improves with practice.

Getting to Know Gibbs

Look at Gibbs and the stages involved in considering scenarios. When you are talking through an event in supervision do you consider all these aspects? Do you reflect on your feelings and reactions? Do you consider the feelings of others who were there? Do you think analytically and try to make sense of it all? Or go with your emotions and gut feeling?

Think about your action tendencies: we all have these habitual responses and a reflective model can help us realise there are different ways of interpreting events and responding in the future.

OK; So What?
Remember Driscoll ... it is a very short and memorable model.

What? Describing the experience
So What? Reflecting in conversation on the experience
Now What? New perspectives for future situations

Look through Rolfe's questions and choose two or three to put in your own words. Use these, as occasion arises, during the next week.

Choose Either Brookfield's, Johns', or Page and Woskett's Model

Brookfield: look at the lenses and decide if these are for you. You might prefer to create and choose your own lenses.
   For me, this might be:

A visual memory lens (what do I remember of tone of voice, body language?)

A worry lens (was there anything which I was dwelling on after the situation?)

A helicopter (or balloon) lens (what do I notice if I look back on events as if I'm seeing them from a helicopter/balloon and hovering over the scene?)

Johns: look again through the phases and the linked questions. Choose two questions for each phase and put these in your own words, in your own style.
   Suggest to a colleague that you schedule a peer supervision session and use John's MSR. Remember to include in your CPD log afterwards.
   Page and Woskett: if you think this model might be the main tool in your supervision kit then look at the Clinical Supervision Resource compiled by NHS Scotland and work through Unit 2. Website: https://learn.nes.nhs.scot.

A Story for a Sunny Day

Think of a sunny story: a feel good story from your own experience. Just remembering a good day enhances motivation!

CAMEO – BRINGING STRUCTURE INTO A 'STUCK' SUPERVISION

Stuart was supervising a specialist practitioner working in an Adult Learning Disability service. Giulia the therapist was struggling with the transition to specialist, following an internal promotional opportunity. She had been surprised to get the job, and 'only applied for the experience.'

The supervisory contract was to meet every month for 90 minutes. Stuart was aware that over the last three months Giulia was looking more tired and her conversation becoming more rambling and going off at a tangent. He had noticed that she seemed to have become convinced that a colleague who had been competitive with her at interview was behaving differently now. She had initiated a training approach at a number of group homes, and it wasn't going well. The training was scheduled mid-week after the homes' weekly staff meeting, and everyone looked tired and disinterested. These two subjects were brought to supervision each time, but there was no 'settling' or resolution of the issues.

Stuart was beginning to wonder how to change the supervision to avoid the same scenario at a session scheduled the following week. He took this to his own supervision and reflected on the tools and frameworks he had used. He had a fairly informal, conversational style, and this usually worked well, but he wondered if this was contributing to the long, directionless monologues of the last two sessions.

After reflecting on the next step in his 'supervision for supervisors' he realised that he had been using the same style and approach with all his supervisees. For Giulia's next session he did some preparatory work. He sent out an email before the session with a short questionnaire asking what Giulia was planning to bring to the supervision meeting. Giulia had returned the questionnaire saying she would be bringing the same issues as before. Stuart had re-visited reflective models to find inspiration for structuring the next session differently.

After the usual introductory 'catch up' conversation Stuart suggested using a reflective framework to consider Giulia's two issues. He had selected Rolfe's adaptation of Driscoll's What … Now What? Model.

Stuart suggested starting with the training situation and guided the conversation in a structured way, while Giulia considered the questions and issues. She had already paused the training for several weeks. From the conversation a plan emerged for her to contact the group home leaders and suggest a different approach to the training, involving each staff member reading some information, undertaking a small project around a client's communication needs, and then sharing this with the others; and this could be via Zoom or on a designated training day. Giulia was clear there should be no more after-work training sessions.

Stuart used the same framework, slightly adapting the wording to cover communication with a colleague rather than a client. Giulia had already worked through the framework once and was able to consider the feelings and behaviours of her colleague with a different perspective.

The following questions were particularly valuable for Giulia in considering perspectives and being a little more positive about moving forward.

- What could/should I have done to make it better?
- What do I need to do in order to make things better/stop being stuck/resolve the situation/feel better/get on better?

Her colleague's behaviour had certainly not been supportive but talking about different viewpoints helped her to consider trying a different style with this colleague.

Stuart felt exhausted after the meeting, yet confident that the supervision was no longer 'stuck.' He thought the key had been slowing down thinking and reflecting on different perspectives which had given Giulia some compassion for her colleague. He suspected the situation around the training might have resolved more easily if Giulia had not been so stressed in her new role.

Focused Listening, Tools and Techniques

"I can't know everything." – Cheshire Cat

"Only a few find the way, some don't recognize it when they do – some ... don't ever want to." – Cheshire Cat

Alice's Adventures in Wonderland

Key Themes

- Active listening – go with the FLOW (Focus Listen Observe Wait)
- Decisions and dilemmas – 2000 decisions an hour!
- Questions can make a difference

The skills of active listening, noticing, and carefully crafting questions are key tools for effective clinical supervisors. They come from counselling and have been adopted into supervision. They are combined with other techniques in an evolving 'supervisor's toolkit' of techniques such as metaphor and solution-focused and appreciative questioning.

Focused Listening – Go with the FLOW (Focus Listen Observe Wait)

Sometimes it really is the simple things which make a difference. As a new NHS manager and clinical leader I had so many ideas about developing the service. I cringe when I look back at some of my actions. Occasionally there is a significant learning point which 'jolts our thinking' and totally changes how we approach situations in the future. I learnt to listen. I had been one of those people who wasn't listening but was 'waiting to speak.'

DOI: 10.4324/9781003226772-9

I'd used nondirective therapy and delivered Hanen Parent Programs for many years before becoming a manager. I believed in these tools clinically, and they gave me my values as a therapist. I didn't always utilise them when supporting colleagues. Instead I was keen to offer advice and give suggestions about case management. I know that I sometimes listened to colleagues who were feeling overwhelmed by their casework at a shallow, superficial level, before giving advice and adding to their already burgeoning list of things to do. When I read Sonya Wallbank's (2013) research about supporting those who were at risk of burnout primarily by listening it made uncomfortable reading. It also gave me practical tools for supporting others differently (specific strategies in Chapter 12).

The basic message is that if someone is stressed and not thinking clearly we don't jump in and dispense advice. Instead, we listen. We bring in active listening techniques and keep listening. Eventually it will be time to bring in reflective questioning or coach towards new directions, but listening is key to reducing stress about work.

For those who are new to active listening, it is a skill originating in counselling. It includes techniques like *summarising* and *wondering aloud* if we have understood. The suggestion to 'go with the FLOW,' and to focus, listen, observe, and wait before speaking, is a helpful reminder for those developing this skill.

Active listening requires a focus on listening and noticing wider non-verbal communication and giving signals that we are attending carefully. After a while we judge it appropriate to make a comment. We show we are working hard to understand the situation. The key is giving total focus and then checking with summaries such as:

"it seems to me that this is happening"

"I'm working out that you feel ..."

"So after this happened then you felt ..."

"I can see that you've tried a few things and at the moment it seems nothing is helping"

"I am wondering ..."

The comments are often tentative as we are checking out that we are 'tuned in.' In counselling a focused listener might move on to ask specific, probing questions. In supervision, I find this is rarely needed. The 'wondering out loud' strategy leads to further discussion and I listen again. When a supervisee is ready I often move into reflective questioning about the situation. The reflective 'and then,' 'and then' (Driscoll 2006) is often my next tool after listening.

Decisions and Dilemmas – 2000 Decisions an Hour!

All practitioners make many decisions every hour. It is thought that we make up to 2000 an hour. When researching for this book I mistyped as 200 an hour and thought that sounded a lot! Two thousand is another matter. Of course in psychological terms some of these decisions are barely conscious and others are routine decisions about moving to get out of bed, how much coffee to add to a cup, and so on. If you close your eyes and think of a typical clinical session then you get an idea of the number of decisions made. I give up after a few seconds, as there were just too many to quantify. Closely monitoring the reactions and responses of others can be relentless and exhausting. Some time and space to think can be incredibly restorative during a professional day.

Eva Krockow (2018) points out that *"personality aspects also influence our decision-making."* She gives an example of choosing a flavour of ice cream. It's a good example as it isn't an everyday occurrence and needs some focus but doesn't have a high stress load attached.

> *Those who have a tendency toward perfectionism also have the urge to weigh all options precisely, which may seem realistic but is simply impossible — even if it would, of course, be nice to try all 50 types of ice cream before the final decision.*

I think this explains how some professionals can become stuck in a quagmire of decision making, unable to complete tasks. I also believe it isn't always perfectionism which causes this as factors like tiredness, empathy in seeing both sides of a situation, lack of confidence, and fear of criticism can impact on the speed and effectiveness of decision making.

Structured Questions Can Make a Difference

There is an approach devised by Nancy Kline, *Time to Think* (2002) and *More Time to Think* (2015), which creates time and space to think and takes a more structured approach to listening attentively. It can be used very effectively at the coaching level of supervisory support.

Several years ago I was working in an NHS Trust where several clinicians in my team were offered places on an in-house leadership programme. All who attended spoke positively of the experience. They returned to share a key feature of the programme – Nancy Kline's listening approach. I knew Kline's work and liked the way it had been brought into a leadership programme. The basic foundation is a promise not to interrupt.

This is described as *"the promise that changes everything: I won't interrupt you."*

Kline maintains that in learning situations the *"mind works best in the presence of a question."* The approach has ten effective ways of helping people to think innovatively, including using incisive questions. She feels strongly that a key factor in the quality of someone's thinking is affected by *"how they are treated by the people around them, to the importance of appreciation."*

Kline's Ten Ways to Support Innovative Thinking

1. *Attention* – listening with focus
2. *Asking incisive questions* – to challenge limiting assumptions
3. *Equality* – treating each other as thinking partners
4. *Appreciation* – a ratio of five positive comments to each critical one
5. *Ease* – space to think without rushing or urgency
6. *Encouraging* – supporting others in clarifying their thinking
7. *Feelings* – allowing emotions to be there in the conversation
8. *Information* – painting a detailed, accurate picture of situations
9. *Place* – choosing spaces to meet which give the message this time is important
10. *Diversity* – recognising and valuing differences and cultural inquisitiveness

---

Through a combination of space for listening, questions, and positivity the Thinking Environment is created. The promise not to interrupt is highlighted as the most important, but most difficult to keep promise. This is because *"when we interrupt each other, we interrupt our thinking, and that interrupts the quality of everything we do."*

Certainly when I write this my mind wanders to parents I've worked with who truly struggle with Hanen strategies like OWLing, where we Observe, Wait, and Listen and follow the child's focus of attention before we contribute to the interaction. It's hard work. Even more acutely the work of Keena Cummins, developing her VERVE video interaction-based approach, has this same important feature. When a child is involved in an activity and an adult begins to question, or even comment, we are changing the focus of the child's thinking. Parents attending VERVE therapy are supported in stopping doing this and in effect giving a child space to think.

The Thinking Environment challenges our assumptions. For those new to this type of approach, think about first impressions when you meet someone. We form first impressions in split seconds based on previous experience and whether the person reminds us of someone we know. There is that little poster in clip art about the 'ass' in assumption. Assumptions can be dangerous! Yet the reality is our thoughts, emotions, decision making, and actions are affected by assumptions. Kline turns this into a positive, brings assumptions out into the open, and believes that *"The good ideas and feelings come from true liberating assumptions. The bad ones come from untrue limiting assumptions."* The Thinking Environment helps break through the barrier of 'bad assumptions.'

Assumptions Scenario

A helpful example is based on a conversation around wanting to change something and setting a personal goal:

> *"What might you be assuming that is stopping you from achieving your goal?"*
> *"Of these assumptions, which do you think is limiting you the most?"*

In this framework there are three types of assumption.

- Clear facts, e.g. I am not in charge of the Care Pathway
- A possible fact, e.g. Jenny thinks I'm hopeless at time management
- A bedrock assumption about the self or life, e.g. I'm useless, I can't change this job, everything is against me on this rotation

A bedrock assumption is limiting. Incisive questions were devised by Kline to topple these assumptions. We listen and support as a supervisor by being curious about bedrock assumption and exploring these via questioning. For example:

> *"That is possible, it might be true. But what are you assuming here that makes that stop you?"*

When we have a goal and a barrier to dismantle (a bedrock assumption) then the hard work begins for the supervisor in formulating incisive questions. The structure of an incisive question could be:

> *If you knew + freeing assumption + goal*

A freeing assumption is simply the positive opposite of the negative assumption. So you might ask:

"Have a think. What could you be assuming which is preventing you from achieving this goal?"

"Let's look at the barriers to making progress with this. What assumptions are you making which are getting in the way of this objective?"

Assumptions can be wide ranging:

"No one else is interested in doing this and the clinical lead will think I'm arrogant."

"That's possible. But there's an assumption in here. What are you assuming that makes you stop trying? You're assuming you haven't enough skills to carry it off and the Clinical Lead won't like it."

"Let's leave the clinical lead for a moment. What would the positive opposite of feeling hopeless be in this situation be for you?"

"Hmm. Being 'able' and confident in trying out this approach."

"If you knew you were confident and able to do this then what would you do next to achieve this goal?"

The supervisor is guiding away from bad to good assumptions. The process follows the sequence of:

- Working out what assumptions are limiting a supervisee's thinking
- Pinpointing what is most limiting
- Thinking and deciding if there is any truth in this assumption
- Considering what might be the positive opposite of this assumption and a positive, 'liberating' assumption
- Finally working together on a carefully crafted incisive question … 'If I knew I was capable of doing this complex assessment, what would I think/feel/do now?'

Kline suggests it is important to keep going over the question several times until there is a solid, unchanging answer. This is giving space to explore thinking around a barrier, a difficult situation, and find a different way of looking at things. The supervisor might jot down the question and give it to the supervisee to take away and keep exploring after the session.

How would a supervisor create this Thinking Environment in a session? This is basically a tool which starts with focused listening, giving space and structure for supervisees to think about issues and problems before gaining more positive perspectives.

Let's imagine the topic is time management and re-structuring a working week. If the goal was re-working time then the supervisor would facilitate identifying as many assumptions as possible. Then move on to consider what is the most limiting assumption and if there is any truth in it. This is the key barrier. Once this is out in the open then it's about identifying a positive, opposite viewpoint and dismantling the assumption which is in the way of moving forward with the supervisor building an incisive question.

Kline focuses on the use of this incisive question. The supervisor is continually listening for limiting assumptions and working on devising a question which will lead to insights about how to disable the barrier.

So, the main limiting assumption here is that the supervisee feels a victim of time pressure. They are a victim of circumstance and can only endure this dreadful position. All job satisfaction has gone as the stress of never getting work completed is carried home every evening. The liberating alternative assumption is that there is some choice about how the supervisee spends their time at work. The incisive question follows: *"If you knew that you did have choice, how would you structure your time differently?"*

Kline's work has been used in coaching and supervision in a wide range of organisations across the world. It starts with focused listening and works through a process to practical, positive solutions. It's tricky for the supervisor at first but the attentive listening, tracking what's being said for limiting assumptions, and then gently working to explore and dismantle limiting beliefs works very well indeed.

The key 'take aways' are:

- Listen without interrupting
- Focus on the content of what's being said
- Notice limiting beliefs and assumptions
- Remember that we dislike being told exactly what to do (except in an emergency situation) and our minds work more effectively when considering a question
- Formulating questions isn't always easy, but incisive questions are powerful questions which come out of careful listening and encourage supervisees to challenge their assumptions about themselves

REFLECTIVE LEARNING

Write some brief notes about Nancy Kline's Thinking Environment approach:

Just key words in a diary or an e-note to remind you about thinking space and incisive questions. Use as a memory jogger for a week.

Keep noticing whether you are listening or 'waiting to talk':

Are there any patterns: any times, places, or people where this happens more?

Where are you the best listener you can be?!

Interrupting in one-to-one conversations:

Track your style. Do you interrupt a lot, hardly at all ... what's your pattern in interrupting? Do you want to change anything? Set a personal objective to listen and wait ... to truly go with the FLOW ... focus, listen, observe, wait.

Assumptions:

When you feel frustrated or irritated about something, e.g. a colleague not doing something they promised to do or a client not complying with a treatment programme ... pause ... and consider whether you are making any ASSUMPTIONS about the other person and the situation. Does this 'assuming' affect your choice of actions in the situation? *It might be easier to reflect on a situation which has happened than 'work this out' in the actual moment.* See how it goes.

Think about incisive questions:

If the opportunity arises have a go at compiling a carefully crafted incisive question.

> *"If you knew you were capable of undertaking this complex case with strong support from others, what would you decide to do? How would that change things?"*

> *"If you knew you had confidence plus the skills to do that presentation how would that feel? Would that change your decision about offering to present at the team meeting?"*

CAMEO – FEAR OF PRESENTING

Safna had been working in her team for a year. She was well supported and enjoying therapy and her new job. Some colleagues were more career focused and already looking for band 6 posts in other services, but she was happy to build her skills and develop at her own pace. She had positive feedback from the centres she supported and had helped carers introduce a new approach to conversation skills groups.

Word had spread, and now her manager had suggested she might share this experience and give a presentation at a team meeting. This resulted in something approaching total terror. She also had conflicted feelings, as she knew the group was an achievement and would be interesting to others but presentations were something she avoided.

Through conversation her supervisor clarified that when Safna had given presentations before (at university) they had gone well and she had received positive feedback. The anxiety around this request to present at a team meeting was growing stronger and she was realising it was a barrier. The supervisor listened ... and listened again. Then when Safna paused and seemed to have offloaded most of 'her angst and anxiety' the supervisor used the terminology of barriers and different kinds of barrier, how they looked, and helped Safna create a visual picture of this situation and the barrier she was facing. It was huge and there was no obvious way round it.

The supervisor then began to craft a question to facilitate Safna in thinking about the situation differently. She began by mentioning all the positives which she had picked up from the conversation – and there were many – the innovative approach, the use of evidence-based practice, the collaborative working with a centre, the ability to plan and complete this mini-project, and the fact that her manager and colleagues were interested in hearing more about it. Her supervisor also suggested that Safna imagine a scene where she had given this presentation, it had gone OK, and the sorts of comments and questions which her colleagues might make afterwards.

If you knew this was going to go OK then how could you begin preparing for it? How would that look? What would you need to do? And then? This was a variation on an incisive question and had the effect (unplanned and unexpected by the supervisor) of helping Safna move from inertia to actively considering how the presentation 'might look.'

The supervisor had intended to explore other options, e.g. sending out a sheet to colleagues outlining the project, reflecting on her experience with references to the evidence. This would potentially have been a way of stepping around the barrier and a valid approach, but it wasn't needed. Once Safna had begun to consider and plan the presentation her confidence level increased considerably and she left to email her manager and put in a date for her presentation.

Building on the Positives, Searching for Glimmers

How she longed to get out of that dark hall and wander about among those beds of bright flowers and those cool fountains, but she could not even get her head through the doorway; "and even if my head would go through" thought poor Alice, "it would be of very little use without my shoulders. Oh, how I wish I could shut up like a telescope! I think I could, if only I knew how to begin."

Alice, *Alice's Adventures in Wonderland*

Key Themes

- Solution-focused supervision
- Ten Minute Talk
- An appreciative approach
- Strengths-based supervision
- Positive psychology tools
- Solution-focused questions

Solution-Focused Supervision

Solution-focused approaches can change the direction of supervision. In simplest terms it is about looking for what's worked well, the positives, and working out together how to build on these. We imagine how the future might look if we take certain actions. Solution-focused questions are thought provoking and different. Scaling is utilised alongside the questions.

In solution-focused supervision the supervisor and supervisee give close attention to casework and the supervisee's interests and goals. The supervisor

DOI: 10.4324/9781003226772-10

does not need to know about the clinical area; it is about an evolving relationship with focused conversation about chosen topics with the supervisor bringing in tools from solution-focused therapy.

Tools from Solution-Focused Therapy

The key tools are purposeful questions and scales:

- Exploring strengths and personal resources
- Imagining and finding ways of getting closer to a supervisee's imagined future
- Being purposefully curious and asking questions to clarify positions. The supervisor is not an expert and asks questions from a 'not-knowing' position
- Always seeking out glimmers, noticing small positives, little bits of movement
- Giving thoughtful compliments
- Adapting the pace
- Scaling and self-rating for evaluating progress

The supervision always begins by talking about the supervisee's existing strengths, abilities, achievements, or learning. The supervisor guides towards recognising what is working well in casework. The supervisor helps the supervisee work out their unique strengths and identity as a clinician.

The session agenda is linked to job role with a focus on clients or casework. There is visioning about hopes for the future and how to move closer to this future state.

In this approach the supervisor can guide the conversation in different directions and find new pathways. Having a supervisor with experience in the same clinical area is not necessary as the focus is on the supervisee's skills and their learning and development.

Personal Reflection

One of my own most gifted supervisors knew nothing about my clinical area, in fact little about speech and language therapy. Yet he did know about clinical care, the complexities of relationships at work, and the emotional frustrations of caseworking. By asking thoughtful questions he found out more about my role and understanding of my profession. The questions, curiosity, and insights were thought provoking. When

I described a problem-infested multi-agency situation to a supervisor who was asking curious questions I was prompted to reflect on how I tended to approach things, including communicating with others, in the same way. This position of curious 'not knowing,' but with a focused interest in finding out more, was powerful in triggering insights into my actions and the beginnings of solutions around my addressing the attitude of other professions towards speech and language therapy.

At that point I didn't always feel valued by some of the educational colleagues I worked alongside. Change in my problematic situation didn't happen immediately, but the supervision helped me to notice glimmers (small positives) and ways of building stronger relationships with some colleagues, while challenging others as necessary.

It is important to guide the supervision and keep the conversation flowing with careful questions. The curiosity results in new perspectives and solutions. The supervisor does not see themselves as wiser than the supervisee.

One difference to a reflective approach is that it is not necessary to hear a detailed history or story about a case. In a solution-focused approach, the supervisor is exploring skills, abilities, and ideas, and identifying strengths and facilitating these further in caseworking. The term 'looking for glimmers' is useful: identifying small positives which might give part of the answer about how to move forward.

Scaling is a key tool.

If 10 means this supervision was very useful and 0 means it was not useful in any way, where would you place today's session?

What went especially well, or what was the most useful aspect of our conversation today, which made you choose that number?

Is there anything which should be different next time, to move up the scale one or two points?

If this was the best clinical supervision ever, what would that look like?

Using a scale leads to a detailed conversation where a supervisor listens and finds out more about how the supervisee hopes things will become different, stay the same, or improve. As with all frameworks it is important to re-word questions in your own style.

A supervisee might bring something like the following request to supervision:

"Could we do some more work on the way I close cases and communicate around this with clients/families?" The supervisor will use questions adapted from ones like those below to guide the conversation and search for solutions.

In Supervision

- What are your best hopes for supervision generally?
- What are you hoping for from supervision today?
- What will success look like? How will you know it is working positively?
- How will you let me know if I need to change anything?
- What is needed for this session to rate as successful?

In Casework

- How has your approach changed in the last X months?
- What has been your most successful moment?
- What has been your greatest challenge?
- When something isn't working, what helps you to make changes in your approach? How have you made successful changes in the past?
- What do you think this client has found most useful about your support/therapy?
- What would you need to notice to stop you feeling anxious and worrying about this?

Solution-focused clinical supervision is about searching for glimmers; it's conversational treasure hunting. The supervisor will be listening, looking for glimmering positives which may be hidden in a treasure trove. The approach is about identifying positives and using these more of the time.

Another Personal Reflection

I reflect on a significant change in my own casework after I attended training in solution-focused approaches. We were looking at how to build a positive alliance, devising goals for clients, and mapping a way towards a solution.

My transformational change was around considering a client's **strengths** in language and communication as well as their **gaps and needs**. My care plans began to incorporate ways of building on positive skills to strengthen communication as well as impairment-based goals. It was helpful to talk with parents about what their child was achieving.

Speech and language therapy is a problem-focused profession, and as clinicians we are always evaluating skills and determining the next step. Sometimes though we can take a solution-focused approach to intervention and build on positive skills so they become stronger and strengthen communication overall.

Ten Minutes Together

Kidge Burns (2008) gives enthusiastic insight into using a solution-focused approach in supporting SLTs working with adults in a hospital setting. Burns implemented an innovative approach to peer and student supervision called the *"Ten Minute Talk,"* which was based on a solution-focused co-coaching formula.

The team had found the aspiration of an hour-long supervision with students on placement was unrealistic and they needed to adapt this to cope with workload. The ten minute co-coaching was piloted and proved very effective with students.

This Ten Minute Talk around *"Best hopes?"* or *"What's better?"* was extended to co- supervision. The team set up a rota and a crib sheet of questions for confidence in the early stages.

The Ten Minute Talk is *"different from a quick corridor conversation"* with planned, ringfenced time to discuss issues in a solution-focused way. Interestingly, those involved usually felt ten minutes was long enough. The positives were in having some planned time to talk, *"we can trust in the process that talking about only one small change can have a ripple effect in terms of outcome and that a simple (but not simplistic) conversation can make a difference to peoples' lives."* Each team member was asked to evaluate the impact of the approach using the *Clinical Supervision Evaluation Questionnaire (CSEQ)* (Horton et al 2008). The results showed that there was 100% 'strongly agree' or 'agree' on all 14 items.

A solution-focused approach, rather than a problem-focused one, helped busy practitioners identify what's 'working well' at work. It seems *"evidence points towards a tendency for us to recall successful experiences far less frequently than unsuccessful ones; this has important implications, for example, when evaluating intervention given to clients and carers"* (Graves 2007). The focus on *"best hopes," "what's better?"* proved positive and time effective.

Appreciative Leadership Approach

David Cooperrider and Diane Whitney (2008) developed this approach for transformative change and leadership. It is also used as a coaching framework. With roots in positive psychology, the basic idea is that we leave problem solving aside and focus on more positive aspects. These positives are the key to moving forward – plan to do more of 'what's working.' It is relevant for individuals or service development projects. It is empowering to leave negative problems behind and design a solution which builds on existing success. What works well is magnified and extended (the 4D model is outlined in detail in Chapter 14).

> ## The 4Ds
>
> *Discovery* – seeking positives, e.g. when is the service most effective?
> *Dreaming* – building on the positives and abandoning the negatives
> *Designing* – the future and how this could look
> *Destiny* – planning to get to the newly designed future state

In supervision the expression 'look at everything with an appreciative eye' is key. If you are keen to work from a positive perspective, then appreciative supervision/coaching is a simpler, more adaptable framework than the structured scaling and questioning of solution-focused supervision.

Strengths-Based Supervision

Strengths-based supervision is a technique with practical potential which is still in the early days of development. My interest in positive psychology, aka positive therapy, has been consistent since I attended a training course aimed at preventing relapse in adult clients who continually re-accessed health services. At the time I was working with a small number of voice clients. I am one of those unusual clinicians who has been able to work across several clinical areas over time. I was an RCSLT specialist clinical advisor in children's complex needs for 22 years until I left the NHS to develop an independent practice. However I always enjoyed working in voice and fluency and had opportunities to work with those clients to a specialist level. Such was the wonder and privilege of a career in speech and language therapy before adult and children's services split into different organisations. My voice work led me to this training day on positive psychology. I never looked back, took away and utilised many of the ideas, and tracked further developments in the field. I probably applied the techniques much more in my management/leadership roles than clinically.

The idea was that we could prevent relapse in some client groups by focusing on wider happiness levels rather than specific deficits. Positive therapy techniques were the route to this point. The clinician recognises but leaves the health problem to one side and looks instead at how we process events and live a little more happily. In simple terms I suppose this was about seeking happy endings after an episode of care. The idea is that we all have a set level of happiness, but with focused application of techniques, some adjustments are possible which boost happiness levels and outlook on life.

The work from the Positive Psychology hub at Penn State, led by Martin Seligman, gave me additional insights and ideas after the training course. So what is positive therapy/psychology? It is not positive thinking. It is a research-based approach with the aim of changing the focus from preoccupation with *"repairing the worst things in life to also building the best qualities in life"* (Seligman & Csikszentmihalyi 2000). The spotlight shines on peoples' strengths and what's going well in their life at work and home. Key tools include identifying signature (character) strengths, flow in work, gratitude, forgiveness, and mindfulness.

Ryan Niemiec (2017) looked at integrating signature strengths into supervision. The theory is that if we know our individual character strengths and life and work allow us opportunities to use and develop these strengths then we will become more positive and content. Based on emerging research, the identification and use of character strengths may be useful in increasing a feeling of general life satisfaction and competence (Fialkov & Haddad 2012; Proctor 2010). Exploring and using signature strengths has also been linked to a decrease in depression (Gander, Proyer, Ruch, & Wyss 2013; Seligman, Steen, Park, & Peterson 2005).

The character strengths framework has been researched in over 30 different countries to validate the existence of 24 character strengths cross-culturally (Biswas-Diener 2010).

The Values in Action (VIA) character strengths survey identifies strengths; locate a survey via the Penn State Positive Psychology Centre website.

A signature strengths framework gives a basis for supervisors to use a strengths-based approach (Niemiec 2013). The first step is for a supervisor to complete the VIA character strengths survey and know their own signature strengths. I'd encourage anyone interested in this approach to supervision to complete the signature strength survey. Reading the printout is valuable and reinforces any supervisor's self-esteem. I admit to making my family compete the VIA questionnaire after returning from the training course. It is essential to know the framework, the different strengths, and the terminology.

The VIA character strengths survey is organised into six areas; these are strengths in:

Wisdom (e.g. creativity, curiosity, judgement, love of learning, and perspective)
Courage (e.g. bravery, perseverance, honesty, and zest)
Humanity (e.g. love, kindness, social intelligence)
Justice (e.g. teamwork, fairness, leadership)
Temperance (e.g. forgiveness, humility, prudence, self-regulation)
Transcendence (e.g. appreciation of beauty and excellence, gratitude, hope, optimism, humour, spirituality)

After completion of a survey, a document outlining top signature strengths is produced. When someone is doing something which draws on their signature strengths then this will *"energize and empower."* Exploring with a supervisor how these strengths could be higher profile in life at home and work is a starting point. Indeed, *"capitalizing on signature strengths may be one useful strategy for mitigating the effects of stress and self-doubt experienced by beginning supervisees"* (Fialkov & Haddad 2012).

One study indicated that students who participated in an intervention focusing on strengths identification and application showed reductions in anxiety and depression (Brunwasser & Gillham 2009 and a similar study by Proctor 2010). Supervisees who took part in activities specially designed around their strengths demonstrated increased levels of life satisfaction not seen in a control group.

The identification of these signature strengths in supervision can be a tonic for self-esteem. Unlike most types of supervision there is often some homework for the supervisee.

> **Supervisees are encouraged to consider their top strengths and explore how these could be extended at work:**
>
> - How might you bring these strengths to your learning and development?
> - Let's consider how you could draw on these strengths in your caseworking
> - How do you hope your clients see you as a person? What strengths do you think they might see?
> - Think of ways you could build on your strengths
>
> Sometimes supervisees are asked to write reflectively about their strengths and then keep referring back to these notes during the course of supervision.

The most important 'take away' technique for supervisors is strengths spotting. Not every supervisee is going to have time or inclination to complete a survey. Strengths spotting is about the supervisor knowing the strengths model and highlighting the supervisee's strengths.

For example,

> *It seems to me that you were using one of your strengths there – you had clear perspective and were compassionate and kind in your response. This meant the relationship was not so disrupted that the service lost a contract with that school.*

It also gives a specific way of giving compliments to a supervisee. Strengths spotting can be used to help a supervisee recognise successes which their current mindset might block them from seeing.

> **A supervisor can 'strengths spot' in the following ways:**
>
> *"As I listen to you remembering this experience, it seems to me that you were bringing in bravery, giving perspective, and then kindness in your approach with this client."*
>
> When a supervisee gives themselves harsh judgemental feedback, the supervisor can bring in character strengths to help re-view events.
>
> When strengths spotting, it is incredibly important to label the strength and connect it with a particular action.

"OK. Let's just rewind and look at that again. I'm wondering, it seems to me that when this happened you were ..."

"When I listen I'm noticing and thinking of these strengths? I'm not sure you are realizing that you brought in those strengths and it made a difference?"

"This does seem a tricky situation. It's difficult to work out which way to go forward. Let's pause and think about your character strengths ... What strengths could you bring in to adjust your approach to this situation?"

Once again this is a basic template to be re-worded in your own individual style.

Using a framework for strengths-based support can also act as a *"buffer against burnout"* (Dreison et al., 2018). It boosts self-identity and confidence levels. I was recently doing some training on managing anxiety with clients and listened to one of the presenters saying that "everyone is frightened of other people." It struck a chord. It didn't seem as exact to me as the presentation suggested, but I could see that many people are worried about people's reactions and apprehensive about interactions. Feeling confident about skills and abilities via a 'rockingly good' supervision session which specifically references our signature strengths can only boost self-confidence. The identification and utilisation of character strengths are associated with feelings of competency and connection to clients (Fialkov & Haddad).

A strengths-based approach is helpful when coaching and considering the future. Identifying signature strengths gives a different focus to the more usual personality index such as the Myers-Briggs style questionnaire. Bringing in a signature strengths profile as a starting point for reflective conversation about a current job role and aspirations for the future can be a very positive conversation.

Even if someone prefers not to complete a survey there are simple visual summaries of the signature strengths (via an online search), and one of these simple diagrams could be shared as a focus of conversation in a session.

It is also perfectly possible to just explore someone's personal strengths without reference to the VIA framework. Talking together, identifying strengths, and perhaps recording the conversation on a mind map is tapping into strengths principles. If, as a supervisor, you know about signature strengths, then you can bring these into the conversation.

Interestingly, strengths which are practical and involve social interaction rate a little higher in creating happiness. Similarly, those with an aspect of caring or supporting others give more contentment when compared with more insular character strengths.

Other Tools Originating in Positive Psychology

Considering what is positive in working life, those people or things you are grateful for, is a positive therapy tool. Identifying someone you are grateful to at work and writing them a letter/email enhances positivity. If you write, outlining why you are grateful, e.g. appreciation of joint working on a project, and actually send it to them, then research shows they will get a boost of positivity from reading it and you will also feel better for writing it. It seems a true win-win situation.

I certainly incorporated more well-deserved compliments and gratitude into my supervisions and emails after learning about this simple yet very effective technique. I began to write 'thank you' notes to my direct reports at the end of each year and on a couple of occasions prepared a presentation which showcased each team member's key strengths and just shared this on an automatic loop on PowerPoint for the whole team. I felt very positive after considering each team member's strengths and contributions and it seemed appreciated. That part of the theory, that writing expressing gratitude gives the writer as well as the recipient a boost, was certainly true for me.

The concept of being in 'flow' at work can be explored in supervision. It fits with job satisfaction and is important in terms of 'having a good day at work.' Flow is those times when you realise that you know what you are doing, and feel confident, competent, and that today you are good at this. This is what you enjoy at work and hope to do more of in future. For me, being in flow is facilitating training. Knowing about flow as a concept helped me to realise what I wanted to do more of at work. Flow is different for everyone and what I've just described will be someone's worst nightmare. Bringing the concept of flow into a supervision and exploring what this is with a supervisee can influence future career choices.

Some Solution-Focused Supervision Questions

- What works well?
- What could you do more of ... in future?
- What would be your "preferred future/options"?
- How would you like it to be?

- How could it be better?
- How do you imagine the situation where it has improved?
- When does this problem not occur?
- Are there any times (of the day/week) when this doesn't occur?
- Tell me about a better day. What was it that was different?
- If you could change one thing what would it be?
- Let's look at your resilience. How you've managed, in the face of this difficulty, to keep going. What have you achieved with your resilience?
- What are your best hopes for A (client/colleague)?
- What would "good enough" look like?
- Imagine that …
- Imagine a scenario with this 'new you.' Imagine any new skills/behaviours and a different self-image. How does that look?
- OK. Let's stop doing what doesn't work. Let's look for anything which has worked well so far
- What's a better situation? What's a different outcome?
- What is better now?
- Think of that scale of 1 to 10. If 1 is 'unbearable' and 10 is 'comfortable,' where are you now on that scale?
- Can we think of the way to move just one point up that scale? What would need to happen?
- Have you noticed any small changes? Let's look back and think about any positives which have happened that might have been missed
- Sometimes these are called glimmers – a glimmer of hope, a glimmer of something improving
- Is there anything you can do tomorrow/next week/next month to make it more likely to happen?
- If you woke up tomorrow and the situation had changed totally, there was no longer anything to make you feel anxious or worried, then what would be different? Let's walk through this new situation and work out what's changed (adaptation of the miracle question)

REFLECTIVE LEARNING

Solution-Focused Questions

If you are new to using solution-focused questions then:

- Look through the list of questions
- Choose two or three which look relevant to your role. It's a shift in thinking but worthwhile taking the time to acquire the skill of compiling a solution-focused question. You are wondering out loud often and looking for small signs of positive progress or development
- Use these questions or variations on them during your day at work. This might be in a supervision session, with a client, or in a meeting

If you have experience using solution-focused questions in clinical work then:

- If you are a supervisor then bring scaling questions into conversations

For example, on a scale of 1 to 10, if 1 was 'worst possible session' and 10 was 'fantastic' where would this session be?

- Focus on 'What's working well?' Re-read the information on Kidge Burns' approach and consider locating the article online (it is short, interesting reading)

- Try out this Ten Minute Talk. If you work in a supportive team then it may be others might join you in using this approach

A Sparkling Moment

- Think of a time during the last year where you felt you sparkled at work
- Perhaps you felt you were using your skills, making a difference, making good connections, or perhaps you simply felt fulfilled in the work you were doing at that moment

Signature or Character Strengths

- What do you intuitively feel are your signature strengths? This does not need to be within the VIA framework – just identify strengths

- Ask a colleague you trust to share with you what they think your character strengths are. Return the favour. It is a good thing to do during a dull or miserable week as you will inevitably both feel better
- The online Positive Psychology Centre at Penn State has links to various surveys for discovering your signature strengths. Complete and identify your individual profile of strengths
- Knowing your strengths means you can use your strengths more

Flow

- We are in flow when we are doing an activity where we feel confident and don't need to overly think about our actions. We know what we are doing and everything flows along
- When are you in this flow state? Identify those times

CAMEO – APPRECIATIVE INQUIRY PROVIDES A SOLUTION

Isabelle was feeling totally overwhelmed at work. She worked part time but often appeared in the office on her day off to just 'catch up with paperwork.' She never seemed to catch up with paperwork, and her manager was becoming concerned when she asked for time owing for the additional hours in the office, which had never been agreed. Her manager worked in another town and was unaware of the additional hours. When the manager asked questions about the time accrued Isabelle became very angry in the office. Her clinical supervisor worked in the same building and walked into a scene of angst and extreme upset. She checked her diary and then suggested an immediate ad hoc supervision.

After the outpouring of anger about her line manager, Isabelle began talking with extreme resentment about her role supporting care home settings. This covered communication and swallowing needs in several settings across a wide geographical area. From listening the supervisor worked out that the service was provided totally by Isabelle with no involvement of care home staff. Taking a chance the supervisor moved into a solution-focused/appreciative inquiry style. She asked what Isabelle liked most about her work, then explored how much of the time she could focus on what she enjoyed and how the rest of her time was spent. She asked about the care home staff and how interested they were and what their knowledge and skills were. Were there positive examples (glimmers) of staff contributing to the therapy activities? It seemed there were people who would be keen to be more involved in therapy provision.

In a fairly rapid turnaround the reflective discussion resulted in a realisation that there was an untapped resource of carers who could be interested in supporting the therapist's work. Isabelle rang to arrange a meeting with one of the larger care homes to discuss possible approaches.

Then she emailed her manager and explained the new plan, while apologising for accruing the time without alerting her manager to this, and a compromise plan was agreed.

The Developmental Function, Reflective Routes to Learning

"And what is the use of a book," thought Alice, *"without pictures or conversation?"*

"Curiouser and curiouser!"

Alice's Adventures in Wonderland

> ## Key Themes
>
> * Valuing work-based learning
> * Anticipatory and in-action reflection
> * Practice development

Work-Based Learning – Learning from Experience

The learning approach of reflective supervision can be applied to any activity or occupation. The essence is pressing the pause button and considering events while in a safe space with a supervisor who guides a conversation in a direction which allows for reflection and picking out learning points. Supervision can be seen *"as a lens, a way of looking at any situation and oneself; a way of being in the world; a way of seeing with new eyes"* (Shohet and Shohet 2020).

Proctor identified the developmental function of supervision, and this links closely with reflective practice as a tool for learning. We become reflective practitioners who are always looking at experience as an opportunity for developing skills. Learning is an active process; it is integrated in daily professional activities. It is not set apart like learning on a training course, it is rooted in the situations and relationships of working life. Whatever our role, whether

DOI: 10.4324/9781003226772-11

clinical manager, highly specialist, early career, specialist clinician, or senior assistant, there is the opportunity to learn from experience every day.

Work-based learning (WBL) is not always valued the same as formal training which is frustrating. The research on short course learning for adults is sparce. We know there are ways we can structure courses to make learning last and continue after the course has completed. These include:

- Reflective logs/journals
- Case studies
- Identifying individualised 'take aways' and using these

For successful adult learning there is a need to practically implement and personalise new skills after the course. The 'go to' technique for establishing long-term learning seems to be reflective practice.

Schön talked about the lovely *"sheltered practicum"* or learning place where we learnt from those who were more experienced, our performance critiqued with supportive guidance and feedback until we were competent practitioners. Those who learnt in this way were rounded in their learning. It was not only about the knowledge required to do the job, it was also the subtle 'swamp' skills needed to be successful in a profession. If a practitioner was unable to engage in communication, share ideas, and influence others to commit to an intervention plan, we would worry. If the therapist was unable to diffuse conflict and form constructive relationships with colleagues and was totally disorganised in record keeping and statutory paperwork then eventually it would become a professional competency issue. Those who work in speech and language therapy, whatever our caseload, whether independent, NHS, or employed in education, know what a successful practitioner 'looks like.' We know the speech and language practitioner swamp skills.

In the modern workplace there is no sheltered practicum. However, there are support mechanisms, and clinical supervision is advocated for all practitioners by RCSLT, ASLTIP, HCPC, and CQC. The recommendation is a session every four to six weeks, which is enough to feel supported and safe in practice. If supervision is frequently cancelled then the support may drift and become less effective.

For assistant practitioners the RCSLT Framework for Training and Development is competency-based and rooted in reflective practice. There should be a competencies coach who listens and sets direction for developing skills.

The challenge is to implement clinical supervision which is strongly linked to continual professional development. It is by engaging in reflective conversations about events and situations that new insights emerge.

Reflection – Anticipatory and in Action

Reflection is not only about pausing and re-viewing events, but also engaging in anticipatory reflection. This tool reduced my stress levels considerably when I learnt about it. I had always been aware of potentially difficult sessions or meetings approaching in my diary. However, it was only after learning about reflective practice that I began to focus on a difficult review meeting and plan to pre-empt difficulties. Reflecting ahead using a mind map gave me confidence plus a much more organised and persuasive approach in meetings.

In time I began to acquire skills of reflection-in-action. Specifically, when in a difficult meeting, I began to track the conversation and note down salient points and embellish my prepared notes/mind map. I began to be able to listen and reference what others had said when it was my turn to contribute. I was far more focused and attentive, and the stress of most meetings evaporated.

Personal Reflection-in-Action

We were discussing reflection-in-action at home this week, while I was working on this book. I realised that my greatest reflection-in-action is when cooking and specifically when baking. For some reason the bread I had set to rise was wet and sticky and didn't seem to be rising as much as usual. I was convinced the measurements had been the same, so it was a mystery why today the result was less successful. I adapted and added more flour. I turned it out and kneaded the mixture a little more. Some progress. It is my habit to make small bread rolls with this recipe. I began to cut the mixture into rolls and paused and decided to follow the shape of the dough and form it into a loaf shape instead. I added some Italian herbs to the top and coated with olive oil to stop the bread hardening when cooking – this is a soft focaccia-type recipe. My actions were different, unplanned, and it was an example of reflection in the moment. Thankfully it worked well, and I shall do the same again in future. I now have two options whenever I make this recipe.

This does of course resemble a practical, direct therapy session. We have our plan and an idea of the direction but will adapt and change the plan during the session. It is one of the first skills we learn on placement.

Practice Development

We talk about CPD and know what it means. The concept of practice development is less well known in speech and language therapy, but it is appearing more and that is a good thing. Practice development is simply 'our practice' and how we approach our role, how we carry out duties, the impact we have on clients, and how we communicate and interact as a professional. It is a dynamic, action-filled concept. It is not flat 2D learning but 3D multi-faceted learning from complex situations. Work-based learning through reflective clinical supervision is a powerful way to develop and extend our 'practice.'

As reflective practitioners we know that this learning process never ends. As long as we are working in the profession we are learning from experience. Clinical supervision is a way of ensuring that life-long learning is strong and continues.

 REFLECTIVE LEARNING

Work-Based Learning (WBL)

WBL is the Cinderella of CPD. Short courses have more prestige, yet 'proper WBL' is a strong way of developing and extending our skills. Think back over your own learning (recent or in the past). What's worked well for you? In terms of practice development how have you become the practitioner you are today? What have been the strongest, longest lasting strands of learning? How does WBL feature here?

Are You a Real Reflective Practitioner?

Think for a moment about how you bring reflection into your working week.

Learning Logs – Preparing for a Supervision Meeting

How do you log your learning? Is it using the RCSLT diary? Do you have a reflective journal? It is valuable to keep jotting down possible issues to take to your next supervision; then as the date gets closer glance at the list and choose what to take to the meeting. It can be re-assuring to see that some issues have resolved since you jotted them down. Others remain prominent and make the topic short list. This is a good way of making sure you don't always take something which comes up just before the meeting. It is surprising how many of us take something to supervision which arose that week. Choose carefully and by jotting down possible issues you will have a more considered choice.

CAMEO – WORK-BASED LEARNING

Sonja was working with two recently appointed assistant practitioners. The difficulty was that when the last assistants had joined their small team there hadn't been a long waiting list. There was enthusiasm but no time to train new colleagues. The previous approach had been to allocate half a day a week to a rota of training seminars offered by various team members. There had to be an alternative to this. She emailed out for ideas. She got one response with a suggestion for an external course which the assistants could attend. It was a good idea and she jotted it down; but it wasn't going to be the answer to providing necessary training and development to fulfil roles and give assurances of safe practice.

Sonja got inspiration from a colleague in another region. His service was using work-based learning within a structured framework and it was going well. Their assistant practitioners had received initial induction around the RCSLT Competency-based framework for assistants and were now developing these competencies during their working week. They did need a weekly meeting where they discussed their experiences and learning was carefully tracked.

Sonja had her solution: a revised internal training programme delivered via work-based learning. She prepared Competency Profiles for the arrival of the assistants (with suggestions for accessible online study material). Then she scheduled weekly 'professional training and development' meetings with herself as competencies coach.

It went fairly smoothly, and over the next few months additional learning opportunities such as short courses and attendance at a regional assistants' Clinical Excellence Network augmented this programme.

It actually proved easier to contact therapists in the team as the need arose to ask them to share some information about an aspect of therapy and offer shadowing rather than asking to prepare and deliver a half-day seminar.

She found that she did need to deliver a half-day seminar in reflective writing, but she based this around the RCSLT Reflective Writing e-learning pack. It would have been helpful to have something ready made to further reduce the admin involved, e.g. Competency Profiles, information about work-based learning; but she hadn't located anything like that. She had been approached to give a presentation on this new approach at a regional study day, and she would be presenting alongside the two assistant practitioners who would be talking about their experience of developing in role.

Crafting Conversation

"Now, here, you see, it takes all the running you can do, to keep in the same place. If you want to get somewhere else, you must run at least twice as fast as that!" – Queen of Hearts

"Well, in our country, you'd generally get to somewhere else—if you ran very fast for a long time, as we've been doing." – Alice

Alice's Adventures in Wonderland

Key Themes

- Crafting conversations
- Structuring sessions
- Making things CLEAR
- Slowing down thinking
- Roles
- Open questions
- Challenging
- Shifting sands of story telling
- Personal constructs

Crafting Conversations

A skilled supervisory conversation is the key component in successful supervision, but what makes a skilled supervisory conversation? It starts with a framework which could be as simple as having a plan/agreeing an agenda before beginning the meeting. Or it could be an in-depth framework from Chapter 7 such as the 7 Eyes of Supervision, the Triangle, Rolfe, or Johns.

DOI: 10.4324/9781003226772-12

Over time a supervisor will probably move from using a framework to guide their sessions to their own individual approach. Within a framework the supervisor will bring in specific tools/techniques to strengthen the conversation, e.g. focused listening, metaphor, visual referents. Models of reflection, like Brookfield's lenses, add depth and texture to a conversation.

There are other approaches which augment the conversation. These would include tools like appreciative inquiry, strengths-based conversation, Kline's Thinking Environment, adult-child interaction (Berne 2010), and solution-focused approaches.

Personal Reflection

When setting up my own independent supervision practice it took several days to think of a title which fitted with my individual style and approach to supervision. It gave me an opportunity to stand back and consider my supervision style and my values as a supervisor. There were acronyms written on scraps of paper, moments of inspiration which quickly faded. Then it clicked into place – my approach is conversational; I know the reflective models and bring them in, but nowadays I don't adhere to a specific model. I also adapt the questions to make them as 'informal' in wording as possible. There needs to be a wide ranging, yet comfortable conversation. I also pull on positive therapy; as mentioned earlier, focusing on 'strengths' was a 'turning point' in both my clinical and managerial approach. The acronym ARC surfaced as a possible label for my approach. There needs to be an appreciative, reflective conversation, and the metaphor of an arc or rainbow across the horizon worked well.

Structuring the Session

There needs to be a structure to a supervision meeting. The following format is simple but works well for both individual and group supervision. In a group the agenda setting is a little more complicated as supervisees may be vying for time.

Structure for a Supervision Meeting

Greetings – and a quick catch up
Agreeing an agenda for today

Re-visiting topics from the last meeting (if wanted by the supervisee)
Prioritising the topics (in case time runs out)
Considering the topics (client or situational)
Using an agreed approach, e.g. reflective model or solution focused
Summarising any learning points (could have done that differently; next time I will do this instead, etc.)
Highlighting strengths and skills demonstrated by the supervisee
Noting any continuing action points/professional development needs
Reviewing how the session has gone
Making arrangements for the next meeting

There needs to be a structured agenda, plus a tool which drives reflective conversation. Whether this is informal or structured questioning (e.g. Rolfe) or bringing in metaphor, the supervisor needs to choose and use tools which work for supervisees.

Making Things CLEAR

Hawkins and Shohet summarise what underpins a successful, positive supervisory relationship. That *"supervision can be an important part of taking care of oneself, staying open to new learning, and an indispensable part of the individual's ongoing self-development, self-awareness and commitment to learning"* (Hawkins and Shohet 2012).

Robin and Jean Shohet come from a social care background, but train healthcare practitioners. I warm to their reflective style of writing. They actively reflect on their activities and engage in some very honest critical self-reflection.

One of their frameworks, CLEAR, pulls together both the structure of the session and the tools/techniques for reflective analysis. CLEAR was developed in the 1980s but has evolved over time. They describe CLEAR as *"a handy way of thinking of a session, almost 'how to' structure a supervision meeting."*

In CLEAR there is a focus on the practicalities of the actual conversation. The elements of CLEAR are compared to an ordinary, everyday conversation. The Shohets say the conversational structure of CLEAR is the same as when we meet someone, perhaps in the street, and talk with them. When this meeting happens, there is always an element of unspoken negotiation before we begin the conversation. Human communication is complex with much below the surface. There is unspoken negotiation about who will lead, how long we keep talking, and when the conversation ends. Non-verbal signals are given and read on both sides – this is complex situational pragmatics in action!

We don't usually analyse our everyday conversations this way, but there is a lot going on. There is a structure and an agenda. There are non-verbal greetings. One person speaks first. We tend to expect this will be a short conversation but this isn't always the case, there might be unexpected sharing of surprising news about a mutual acquaintance for example, but usually there is unspoken agreement that this will be a short interaction. The agenda is introduced, we listen to each other, we share recent news, while all the time tracking the conversation and non-verbal signals which show us when to draw the conversation to a close. Phew!

This ordinary conversation gives a **CLEAR** Framework:

Contracting (agreeing the agenda for the session)
Listening (active listening)
Exploring (careful questioning; working through a reflective model)
Action (so, what happens next ... what have I learnt, what's the plan?)
Review (how did it go? What are the arrangements for the next session?)

That's it – all CLEAR!

A CLEAR Way to Structure a Session

CLEAR provides a structure to work through a session. Shohet calls this framework "*the journey of the session.*" The loose structure guides the conversation.

The brief contracting at the beginning of each session sets the agenda. Agenda setting seems to be something which we speech therapists are quite attached to. For example, "Have you got a list?," "OK, what's on your list today?" In technical terms this is the supervisor asking "What are you bringing to supervision today?" There is, of course, a subtle reminder that the supervisee ought to have given some thought to what material to bring to supervision. We look at the items on the list (aka agenda) before deciding together on priorities and time allocation.

Slow Motion Thinking Makes Things CLEARer

Shohet tells us supervision is essentially a good conversation between two or more people. Importantly and easily missed is Shohet's view that one of the cornerstones of supervision is to slow down the conversation. I like this technique, this critical importance of slowing down. This not only slows down the conversation but reduces the speed of thoughts too. A layer of calm is added to the conversation when *"instead of a race, we slow down the pace"* (Hanen).

In my model of reflective conversation I use the film imagery of going into slow motion and freeze framing when we are analysing and reflectively unpicking events. When slowing down thinking and reconsidering a situation it is likely that we will see something differently, notice something that we hadn't considered when we were 'in the moment.'

With the agenda comes considering outcomes for a session. The supervisor asking "What are you hoping to get out of today's supervision?" The supervisor might also ask if there is any emotional load attached to this topic. If it is something which caused considerable stress at the time, the supervisee might still be dwelling on what happened which could influence the choice of questioning style.

An aside here is that experienced supervisors tend to know intuitively (a good example of Schön's knowing-in-action) if a supervisee is looking to just check over their thinking or if they are totally submerged in a situation, unclear about clinical direction, and need more of a directive/advisory style to allow them to get their head above water again. We bring to supervision those situations where things didn't go quite as well as expected, to mull over events, and work out what might need to be different next time. It's having a safe space to share something which didn't go to plan or felt a little uncomfortable at the time.

And so, there is a CLEAR plan for supervisory conversations. *Contracting* the agenda, then the supervisor *listening* and making sense of the situation, before guiding the supervisee into *exploring* events further, with a reflective, analytical lens. This is where different questions are asked to trigger reflective thinking. Then there is a discussion about learning and identification of *action* points and noting these down. Finally, there is a *review* of the session and what's gone well, or needs to change. I hope that's **CLEAR**!

Personal Reflection

I worked with a supervisor who tended to bring her own agenda into sessions and was hyper challenging if I wasn't on the same wavelength. After one session I felt quite dysregulated and perturbed for an hour or so. I did have a gap and if I'd been straight into another session or meeting I might have focused less on the supervision. As a supervisee I felt something was wrong with the dynamic.

I was also member of a reflective supervision group and had the opportunity of discussing the same topic in that group. There were still challenges, but also understanding of the rationale for the approach I was taking. I realised that I had taken the same subject material to individual supervision and expected an exploration of the situation and potentially some challenging questions, but before we had reached that point my supervisor had stepped in and given strong opinions and advice.

Looking back, I had been taken by surprise and become reactive and defensive. If the challenge had happened after some analytical exploration of the topic, then I think (hope) I would not have felt so dysregulated and rather confused.

In the CLEAR Framework my supervisor had missed out the exploration stage and jumped straight into what felt like a superior teacher role.

It is also interesting what might have been happening on this occasion in terms of the games we play in supervision. I suspect I became guarded and contributed less. I knew that I was never going to be on a wavelength with my supervisor about the approach she favoured with such passionate enthusiasm. I wasn't going to spend time discussing it as there was clearly a clash of values on this subject. For much of the time we did share clinical values, but on one particular case we clearly had widely different positions. Both were acceptable and professional positions, just very different viewpoints.

Developing a Facilitative Style – Using Open Questions

We looked at some formal structures for reflective questioning (Chapter 7) and solution-focused supervision (Chapter 9). Often questions used to clarify are not part of a specific framework.

Questions are an important technique in the supervisory toolkit. Using open questions is a way into exploring complex situations, relationships, and emotional responses. We use closed questions when using a supportive, advisory style. Closed questions are certainly a quick way of finding out the key facts of a situation. Open questions give a more facilitative style. They also provide a rapid route into the reflective thinking.

If you are at an early stage of developing your skills as a supervisor, then spending time looking at a framework with questions such as the Triangle or Rolfe's model and re-wording these in a style with which you feel comfortable will not be time wasted. You will be creating a useful resource for your supervisory toolkit.

Challenging

Giving feedback is tricky. We know we need it and challenge helps us develop as practitioners. Most of us also know that we feel more comfortable and less stressed when there is no challenge.

The ideal situation is for a supervisee to feel comfortable and trust their supervisor and welcome challenge. Trust gives a safety net. Some supervisees seek out a supervisor whom they know will give a low level of challenge, which may be comfortable but is a concern in terms of reflective learning. This is one of the issues around peer or co-supervision where there needs to be a strong commitment to ensuring the relationship doesn't become 'too comfy.'

Hewitt suggests that when reviewing supervision there is consideration of the level of challenge. Grinder and Bandler (1989) wrote about the magic or alchemy in supportive relationships. Their phrase "*Match for rapport; mismatch for change*" is astute. Basically this is about there being a level of 'challenge to thinking' in a supervisory relationship. The supervisor might have strong rapport with a supervisee, but it means there is likely to be less challenge.

It's possible to use the diagram (Figure 11.1) and mark X where a single session, or the whole supervisory relationship, is in terms of challenge. It's best to bring challenge out into the open and talk about it.

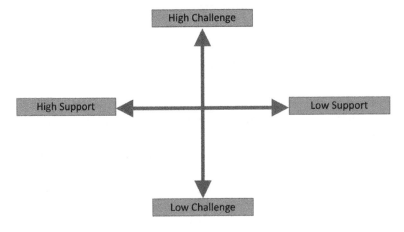

Figure 11.1

Shohet says supervisors need to support supervisees by guiding them into the *"learning space between the comfort zone and the panic zone."* The place where we can calmly consider events without defensive reactivity. Gilbert and Evans (2000) point out that one of the main jobs of a supervisor is *"to reduce the supervisee's fear and anxiety."*

Personal Reflection

I reflect about a coaching relationship which I set up while transitioning between jobs after a difficult re-structure. I was fine but missing my old job (which I'd loved) and was busy evaluating a new team and forming relationships with lots of new people.

I met with this coach for several weeks. I gained insight into my personality type and response to stress and events.

I was startled to be challenged about 'authenticity' and from the conversation, which was guided skilfully by the coach, I realised there was something in this. I had, over time, become used to hiding my thoughts and going along with things. I'd previously been quite vocal in giving my opinion, but tumultuous change meant I was being more passive and accepting of decisions.

A skilful challenge around my 'authenticity' made me realise that I had stopped challenging others!

Roles in Supervision

What roles do we take as supervisor?

Who Am I?

A teacher?
    Am I asking questions to check level of clinical thinking?
An expert?
    Am I dispensing advice?
A parent?
    Am I saying 'it's OK' rather than challenging aspects of practice?
A challenger?
    Am I challenging directions and decisions to encourage critical reflection?
A friend
    Am I taking the role of a friend and sharing concerns?

Supervisors need to have the flexibility to adapt their style and support supervisees differently, moving out of their 'preferred' style and comfort zone when necessary.

It might just involve a slight adjustment of style.

Shifting Sands of Memory and Story Telling

When we bring a topic to supervision and talk through the actions and events, retelling 'the story,' there is inevitably going to be some bias. We've already thought about it and potentially justified our actions. We know that when two people are in the same room and something happens they will probably give different descriptions, emphasising different aspects of what happened with different interpretations. Daniel Simons and Christopher Chabris in their paper *"Gorillas in Our Midst: Sustained Inattentional Blindness for Dynamic Events"* (1999) give a thorough overview of studies in this area.

Gorilla in Our Midst

One of my favourite pieces of psychological research is the gorilla in the room experiment. The strong results were replicated in a second experiment where the gorilla appeared for longer.

In a video, a gorilla walks from right to left into a live basketball-passing event, stops in the middle of the players, turns to face the camera, thumps its chest, and walks off.

This gorilla appeared for 9 seconds in a video of 62 seconds. Only 50% of viewers remembered the gorilla. Most were focusing their attention on a set task, counting how many times players passed the ball.

Chabris and Simons concluded *"these findings suggest that we perceive and remember only those objects and details that receive focused attention."*

It is easy to find a video on YouTube, but now you will notice the gorilla as you know it appears!

Sometimes there is a situation where a colleague recounts a distressing event. We immediately focus on the colleague's stress. We put cooling balm into the conversation. I imagine myself and others saying, "That's terrible, how awful for you." Yet, what do I really know? My colleague might have triggered the scenario or contributed to its deterioration. Support for the distress is appropriate but strongly agreeing, reinforcing their perception of events, without even asking any questions is not going to help reflective processing. There may be time for an ad hoc supervision or suggesting key points are noted to take to supervision.

We need to be able to stand back and reflect on a difficult situation and wonder if perhaps we had a small part (or even on some occasions a significant part) in how a situation evolved. Why did the visit not go to plan? We can be attached to our story and memories about what happened and potentially have 'a little bit of a blind spot.' Reflective practitioners accept we have triggers and blind spots. We need to remember the gorilla in the room.

Shohet suggests the approach of Byron Katie (2007) in challenging the assumptions we make when we are telling 'our story.' It gives a way of challenging assumptions when a supervisee is telling a story of practice. We remind ourselves to think 'how exact is this?' and 'how can we really know how close this is to true?' Or more formally 'What evidence do we have to form this opinion?'

Someone may strongly believe something is the case, but is there actually any evidence that the other person holds that position? In supervision take a step back; if we didn't think this way about the other person, if we abandoned this thought, then how would it look? Katie is very clear that she is not asking the supervisee to drop the thought at this point; what she suggests is simply asking is 'Is it true? What's the evidence?'

An Example of Utilising Byron's Approach

Take an example of a supervisee saying that an adult client with a voice disorder does not value therapy sessions. It's possible for the supervisor to pause and then suggest ways that the client does seem to actually value something, e.g. the client is still turning up for therapy.

There might be issues about engagement with therapy but there is a glimmer of positivity, and it may be the current approach is not a 'best fit' for this client.

What's tricky is that we can all be judges and make judgements and will certainly keep doing this. If we are aware of this, we can diffuse this tendency to make assumptions by asking ourselves questions like 'Do I think this is true?' or 'How much of this is true?' and 'OK, so what does that mean?'

Personal Constructs

Next is something which needs to be treated with a little caution as it comes out of the psychotherapy field, which isn't my area of expertise. However, in my own supervision when my supervisor has asked me the question "Who does that person remind you of?" it has sometimes been quite useful and enabled me to think 'ah yes' and see why my decision making in this situation is more challenging than usual. Perhaps I'm more cautious or warm towards someone's style. It can work both ways.

With improved self-monitoring and earlier recognition of my action tendencies I started to recognise that I needed to pause and consider my emotional responses to events and people. So, when a relationship with a family member or a client isn't working quite 'to plan' then answering questions like 'who do they remind you of?' can be valuable. What irritates, disappoints, or confuses you about the person? How do you want them to change? Also, turn this totally on its head and consider 'What is it about them that you like?'

I considered including Fransella's personal construct psychology approach (PCP) (2005) and decided against it as it requires training and is less used in therapy, though it remains significant in adult dysfluency. If you know this PCP then use it in supervision. A gifted supervisor used this as a tool as we got to know each other and built mutual trust. At the time I was a specialist but comparatively new to the role. I'd moved to a different region and role and was struggling with a dynamic with a colleague who seemed cold in their communication with me. I could find no reason for this and it was something I dwelled on (probably more than was necessary). My supervisor, who was also my immediate manager, spent time with me reviewing and reflecting on weekly events and brought in the personal construct approach to add depth to our sessions.

What a revelation; I discovered my concepts were quite tight and narrow in some areas. I have since worked on widening these and hope I've had success. I still have no idea why my colleague was cold in her communication; perhaps it was just a clash of styles. She left a year or so later and moved to another profession entirely, so had perhaps been struggling with wider issues; I'll never know and made a decision to try not to make assumptions!

I also considered including an overview of transactional analysis (Berne 2010) here. Most therapists will be acquainted with this model from their initial training: the terminology of Nurturing Parent, Controlling (or Critical) Parent, and Adaptive Child. Berne suggests that many of our problems come from interactions (transactions) which have been unsuccessful. Practitioners in transactional analysis recognise which ego states people are 'transacting from' and work out how to intervene to improve communication by supporting changes in style. It can be useful for a supervisor to reflect that what is being described resembles a Controlling Parent resulting in Adaptive Child behaviours.

Berne's model is actually very complex. If interested go to Berne, *The Games People Play* (2016) as a starting point. This gives a basic introduction to the different ego states people adopt with ways of understanding challenging conversations and helping others explore their interactions and responses to others.

There are other more easily accessible tools such as Signature Strengths, Appreciative Inquiry, or Birkeland's Stories of Practice which give insight and different perceptions of a situation without the specialist training required for PCP or transactional analysis.

The supervisor will make sure there is a structure to the session with an agreed agenda and bring in tools like reflective models and crafted questions. Working through a structured approach brings extra dimensions and insights to a reflective conversation. Remember CLEAR can be used to structure a session and was developed to flow in the same way as an ordinary conversation.

 REFLECTIVE LEARNING

Slow Down Supervisory Conversations

- Practice slowing down your thinking and contributions when in a supervisory conversation
- It might be that focusing on breathing and taking slow and steady breaths will help you achieve this. It isn't easy, but it's worth pursuing this skill
- When you slow the movement of your hands, face, and head slightly this may feel slow motion to you but no one else is likely to notice anything. Yet it will make a difference
- Pause, breathe, or count in your head before asking a question

Roles

- What are the roles you tend to take in supervision? Reflect on your habitual roles and whether you might need to vary your style sometimes
- Roles include the Questioning Teacher, the Monitoring Teacher, the Protective Parent, the Compassionate Friend, the Challenging Supervisor, and the Supportive Supervisor

Challenge/Support

- Which are you?
  - A High Support/Low Challenge Supervisor
  - A Low Support/High Challenge Supervisor

- Can you adapt your style to be more challenging or more supportive as necessary? Is this easy or difficult for you? Monitor your responsive style and notice your action tendencies. Do you need to develop greater flexibility and stretch in your style?

CAMEO – SUPPORT OR CHALLENGE?

Adele and Dani worked together in an independent specialist school for children with autistic spectrum disorder. Adele had worked there for eight years and was a highly specialist therapist. Dani had worked there for two years and knew she wanted to specialise in this area. From the time when Dani began working at the school there had been a high level of support from Adele.

Adele felt it was time for Dani to begin to take more responsibility and lead on areas of development. Yet when this was broached Dani was reluctant and said she felt unable to do this without support. As each half term passed there was no change and Dani continued to expect a high level of support. In the supervision Adele broached this and then Dani re-iterated her reluctance and Adele found herself back in supportive mode saying that was OK.

Adele finally managed to take some protected time for her own CPD. She was going to spend time offsite at home and work through some developments in evidence-based practice. Yet her thoughts were preoccupied by her feeling of inadequacy and being unable to motivate Dani to move out of her comfort zone and take on some leadership and co-ordination duties. This situation could not continue for much longer.

Some time and space away from school allowed Adele to consider possible solutions. She didn't get much CPD done but she did emerge with a realistic plan. Adele got permission from her line manager for funding for an external supervisor/coach for Dani for a six-month period. Adele felt that at this time the dual roles of line manager and clinical supervisor were incompatible. If she continued with management supervision and focused on developing Dani's Personal Development Plan, she could guide objectives which were linked to

Dani developing into a senior therapist. The external supervisor/coach would be asked to give clinical supervision with coaching around specific skill development.

Dani was happy with this plan. She saw the external supervision and coaching as an opportunity and felt the school was investing in her. Adele was able to structure management one to ones differently so these were service and goal orientated. Dani took on the oversight of a Parent Support Group and support for Key Stage 3 and 4. Adele realised that she had partly created this scenario by being High Support and Low Challenge. She had found it hard to increase the level of challenge. The dual role of manager and clinical supervisor had been difficult. After the initial six months she suggested the arrangement continued as it was quite insular working in a small team and she felt it was positive for Dani to network with colleagues in other settings and the supervision had made this possible.

The Restorative Function, When the Going Gets Tough

"I wish I hadn't cried so much!

I shall be punished for it now, I suppose, by being drowned in my own tears!"

Alice, *Alice's Adventures in Wonderland*

Key Themes

- Mental grime
- Restorative supervision
- Emotional intelligence
- Positivity
- Resilience

The Mental Grime

The restorative function of supervision links closely with wellbeing at work. As Clutterbuck says *"Supervision can gently restore the balance, offering calm space to refocus on being rather than doing"* (2014).

In simple terms this is about how we re-charge our batteries as practitioners through clinical supervision. This restorative function also connects with ideas around resilience and dealing with what comes at us in the working day. I have always used the concept of 'mental grime' or in my Yorkshire vocabulary, 'mental muck,' with regard to supervision. The concept came from the miners' case in the early 20th century for time to be given to wash off the grime acquired during work down the pit within working hours, rather than going home filthy where there might only be a tin bath in front of the fire (and yes my Grandpa was a miner in Darfield). This was about

DOI: 10.4324/9781003226772-13

'Washing off t' muck in't bosses' time.' The concept transfers from actual muck to mental grime. In each day at work we acquire a little mental grime. This accumulation of grime can and should be washed off in work time through clinical supervision.

This grime varies in nature; it might be someone was sharper in tone than usual, challenged a decision, or said we were unable to have our dates for annual leave. Some days it's minimal grime and other days considerable stress; perhaps dissatisfaction from a client has resulted in a formal complaint. We all react differently to events and have different thresholds in resilience. There are practitioners who pick up very little mental grime at work, but the majority of practitioners admit to some emotional load from the job. There is also the impact of the inevitable sadness, anxiety, and concern for the future of our clients and their families.

There is a point where a practitioner moves from general stress to approaching burnout. We know we are at increased risk due to working in a caring profession. We work closely with people and that involves forming multiple relationships and communicating continuously. These two factors of caring and building relationships put practitioners at higher risk of burnout compared to other professions.

This chapter covers more general supportive approaches for wellbeing at work for supervisors to draw upon. Supervisors need to be skilled at noticing signs of burnout and using resilience strategies to support colleagues.

Then there will be specific reference to the approach of Sonya Wallbank (2013) in the restorative function of supervision. Wallbank recognises that a practitioner who is particularly stressed and emotionally exhausted requires active listening and not a new To Do list and a training plan. Her model's three-tiered levels of support moving from active listening, through reflective practice to goal-based coaching give a structured framework for supervisors.

> **In the RCSLT Guidelines the following definition of restorative supervision is given:**
>
> *Restorative: relating to the maintenance of harmonious working relationships, with a focus on morale and job satisfaction, including:*
>
> - *developing a sense of professional self-worth*
> - *sustaining practitioner morale*
> - *dealing with job-related stress.*

When reading literature on clinical supervision I have, several times, come across the belief that it is experienced practitioners who are most likely to need this function of supervision. In Proctor's model, the theory is that the specialist practitioner predominantly needs the 'offload' chat covering workload and attritional relationships. There may be a need to discuss cases and therapy approaches (developmental function), but the suggestion is that at this stage of a career the focus is on restorative conversation.

For me, it is much more individual than this. There are times when, although I was expert in one area, I was learning new skills in another. The need for developmental/learning supervision may recede over time but is relevant if we consider ourselves lifelong learners. Early career practitioners also need to deal with the emotional aspects of caseworking and in working in a team for the first time. The need for differing emphasis on different functions of supervision can vary month on month.

For many, the primary need is for restorative supervision monthly or six-weekly with a trusted clinical supervisor. In between supervisions many have the opportunity for a snatched cup of tea with conversation about something which has happened which is difficult to set aside. Other practitioners are more isolated, but modern technology allows email and videocalls if urgent ad hoc conversations are needed.

So, what does this basic restorative supervision consist of? Let's look at some common factors.

Restorative Supervision

Restorative supervision focuses on the emotional load of work. It incorporates feelings (inevitably) and discussion around other issues such as tiredness, energy levels, and what we often call 'juggling' priorities, for example:

- The stress and anxiety of being behind with administration
- In the pandemic, the change in some services from face to face to remote teleconferencing contacts
- Issues at work around feeling undervalued or unable to prove that we are ready to apply for a promotional post

Sometimes practitioners feel 'OK' at work and then there is a change in management resulting in different clinical emphasis or even what seems a personality clash.

I've never been entirely sure if 'personality clash' is a technical term in any classification, but I've supervised many colleagues over the years who are experiencing anxiety because they don't feel comfortable with a manager or clinical leader. They move from being confident to a sudden lack of self-esteem and doubt about skill levels. I generally suspect the manager or leader really doesn't have a clue of the impact. Sadly, even in a profession which is focused on communication with others, we are not always able to talk with colleagues about difficult subjects like feeling our skillset is not appreciated anymore. Sometimes it is purely a clash of styles and sometimes in management we really do get it wrong.

Assistant Practitioners

Assistant practitioners are especially vulnerable as far as experiencing sudden changes in direction or role in a team. As registered therapists there is general consensus about the skills and directions of our role. Even in very specialised services there is a clear scope of practice. For assistant practitioners there can be sudden changes. This has been reported in many services, e.g. children's community, adult community, and head and neck services.

Assistants find that different therapists have different ideas about their role and delegation approach. Even with a care pathway specifying the role of the assistant in a service there can be widespread difference between therapists in the work and level of delegation, e.g. arm's length support or close specific guidance. I imagine myself in the position of an assistant who is motivated and working to a pathway when there is a change in leadership and a decision to change that role and sadly the assistants are not always involved in those decisions.

Even in a supportive team with identified roles there will, for the assistant, be minor differences in style between therapists which cause some mental grime. Restorative supervision is important for assistant practitioners. This is more clearly identified by NHS Scotland in its framework for learning with focus on restorative supervision for all practitioners. This is different to a case-related discussion with a therapist who has delegated work. This is day-to-day caseworking supervision.

The skills the supervisor uses in a restorative supervision session are simple. The build-up of mutual trust is always critically important in supervision. The 'setting at ease' and providing a safe place to talk, whether online or face to face, is important. Even back in 1985, Boud, Keogh, and Walker were advocating listening and supporting emotional resilience. The list below includes some of their points:

- Listening closely
- Clarifying and checking understanding of the situation
- Incorporating feelings in the conversation
- Making sure the session highlights any positives around work-based learning
- Making it an active process to notice learning and positives and comment on this
- Working towards positive consolidation of skills and any changes made

The conversation needs to find the positives and highlight how the supervisee is extending skills and dealing positively with situations at work. Sometimes I realise, as a supervisor, that I can say the obvious, and to me it stands out as obvious, but a supervisee may not have realised their achievement. Noticing the positives is incredibly important.

Boud et al. also say that the supervisor needs to model empathy and emotional intelligence. There is no prescribed way for doing this modelling, but listening, pausing to summarise, and 'offering insights' can work well. If a supervisor knows about emotional intelligence and the publications of David Goleman (1995, republished 2020) it is easier to label specifics and use his terminology. Some of it is already in the practitioner's toolkit, e.g. empathy, but others can be a surprise. One of the cornerstones of emotional intelligence is self-regulation of our emotions which is something I have always needed to work on myself.

Goleman's Model of Emotional Intelligence

This well-known model has evolved over time. Now there are 4 domains with 12 elements underpinning each domain (Goleman and Boyatzis 2017) (Figure 12.1 is a version adapted for use in practice situations).

It was developed by studying the strengths of outstanding leaders who possessed "a well balanced set of Emotional Intelligence competencies for dealing with tough challenges."

Having a balanced range of competencies spread across these 12 elements gives a firm foundation for roles linked to influencing and supporting others, such as people management and leadership. These competencies are linked to resilience.

Self Reflective	Resilient Responses	Social Insights	Interpersonal Actions
Aware of Emotional Response in Situation	Regulate Reactions	Empathic /Compassionate	Influencing/Guiding
	Flexible in Thinking		Supervising/Coaching
	Outcome Focused	Reading emotional 'current' in situation	Reducing conflict
			Valuing Teamwork
	Positivity		Inspiring Others

Emotionally Reflective Response in Practice Situations

Figure 12.1

Goleman and Boyatzis give the example of Esther, a 'well-liked manager of a small team' who is positive with empathy for others.

She is a problem solver who re-frames setbacks as opportunities and is a source of calm to her team.

Esther is often complimented on her emotional intelligence but feels stuck and knows she isn't progressing in her career.

Esther is strong in empathy, self-control, and social awareness but lacks other critical competencies which could make her a stronger, more effective leader.

She needs to develop in conflict management (including giving difficult feedback), influencing others, teamwork, and inspirational leadership.

Goleman has always been consistent in saying that many misunderstand his model of emotional intelligence and define it 'much too narrowly.' Successful people management and leadership need a balance of competencies. It is important to have a spread of competencies across the model.

If Esther becomes an inspirational leader then she should become successful at identifying areas for innovative change, influencing and motivating others to carry change forward.

She needs to focus on the team moving in a clear direction and set objectives around innovation.

Esther is currently a good manager of a team staying in the same place, but she wants to be a manager who is leading teams forward in an inspirational way.

The Four Domains of Emotional Intelligence

Self-awareness: being conscious of our own feelings and thoughts when we enter a difficult situation.

Self-management: the fight or flight response of the brain allows a rapid response to threats, real or imagined. In modern life this response can be out of proportion to what's needed, with flooding of stress hormones like cortisol. Skills like strategic thinking and planning are reduced. Richard Davidson and Jon Kabat-Zin (2003) have mainstreamed the practice of mindfulness to support self-management resilience. Woods et al. (2021) gives a thorough background to mindfulness-based stress reduction (MBSR) and the practice and teaching skills developed by Kabat-Zin. There is also growing literature on mindful leadership to help maintain emotional balance and effectiveness.

Social awareness: the ability to connect in empathy with others and perceive the wider impact of events is the essence of this domain.

Relationship management is about managing various relationships among people at work. Relationship management includes inspiring others, managing disagreements, supporting teamwork, and guiding people to work together in the same direction.

Skills in each domain can help people face difficult situations with lower levels of emotional reactivity. The importance of emotional reactivity is often overlooked in supervision. I reflect that if I am tired or distracted with a busy diary and want to finish work for the day and then another crisis lands, I need to work hard at not being reactive. Restorative supervision is a process which can cover strengthening emotional intelligence skills at work, e.g. reducing reactivity, standing back and just noticing the responses of others, and building resilience.

If a supervisor knows about restorative supervision and values its importance then positives include:

- Emphasis on strengthening resilience
- Increasing self-reliance
- Developing leadership skills
- Helping practitioners develop awareness of their impact on others
- Inspiring others to be autonomous, emotionally regulated, enjoy teamwork, and move forward in positive directions.

Picking up on Positive Themes

Conversations can focus on themes which are restorative and boost positivity.

The supervisor stays objective and brings in their own experience/ knowledge to help the supervisee examine the situation. This is about helping a supervisee to step back and re-gain a balanced view of themselves and their practice. The supervisor sensitively helps a supervisee let go of emotions and assumptions which are clouding perspective. Often this seems to result in renewed energy and enthusiasm. *"It's all too easy to have feelings of self-doubt, or a 'helicopter' perspective acknowledges both what is happening on the ground and the bigger picture"* (Clutterbuck 2014).

Some themes that can support positivity are:

- Supporting awareness that acceptance is sometimes needed to tread water and leave things as they are for now

- Talking in terms of energy management, rather than time management, can give a positive and different perspective. This can link with coping skills such as how to restore energy when this is flagging (ensuring we take breaks and structure our working day around energy patterns) or focus energy on identified priorities

- Things won't always work out – it's inevitable. Sometimes, not always. If we don't try things out or do things differently then there is 'sameness' and in more dramatic terms 'stagnation.' When we try a new idea/ approach we risk assess (even if this is in our heads) and if it is clinical, consider the evidence/rationale. Sometimes it goes well, sometimes it partly works out, sometimes it fails. Thinking of new initiatives in the same way as an Action Research approach with evaluation then adjustment in a new cycle (iteration) can be helpful both for small, personal projects, such as a new approach to structuring our working week to create more 'headroom' for admin, and larger service initiatives. Self-belief is important, and a supervisor can work at shifting focus from 'beating oneself up' (self-blame) to learning from experience

- The supervisor can help the supervisee consider how things seem different when they are 'at their best' and how to work towards things being at 'this best' more of the time

- Without laughter, work, for me, becomes dull and difficult. Clutterbuck points out that numerous studies have demonstrated that *"laughter has the ability to restore energy."* Intuitive and respectful supervision helps the practitioner to see absurdity in some situations (helping put them into perspective and diminishing their effect) and most important is the ability to laugh at ourselves

- Sense of profession; many practitioners go through phases of wondering why they are doing the job. Clinical supervision can facilitate reconnection with our individual values and aspirations. Increasingly in supervision I talk about individual professional values. Sometimes there can be a clash of values which is difficult to navigate through. Knowing our values (many of us don't think about this, but our values are there and will surface if we step back and reflect) can be a key tool for recharging our professional batteries and refreshing our enthusiasm for the job. It has to be added that sometimes someone is ready for a change in job or even a different profession. That's positive and always better than a feeling of futility and being stuck. Another way of describing this is having a sense of purpose at work. If we have totally lost that then it may be time for a change in direction

- A supervisor can highlight positive changes in clinical skills. They can notice and point out changes in levels of motivation or in personal skills such as time management. Knowing we are getting better is good for motivation. Sometimes it takes a supervisor to notice how we are developing and to pinpoint new directions for learning

- There are also those times when it can be helpful for the supervisor to share an experience where they changed their approach in a similar situation and it helped. Supervision is not counselling, and it is possible to give examples from the supervisor's practice which enhance insight or perspective

- Opportunities for service growth and development; the skills of being a gifted practitioner and running a successful independent business don't always go together. In independent practice supervision time might focus on talking about new developments and directions. Sometimes this is simply refining the core business offer. Sometimes this is looking at maintaining income during a difficult period. At the beginning of the pandemic there was a need for a dramatic move to remote therapy via teleconferencing in independent practice. Suddenly access to clients and schools was removed. After a traumatic realisation about both the impact of COVID on working approaches and income ASLTIP led in a move to support ways of working remotely. RCSLT rapidly collated evidence, mostly at that point from ASHA, presenting it in an accessible way. These dramatic changes happened in a short timescale. Certainly when there are problems and barriers, effective supervision can bring perspective and helps practitioners achieve a balance in considering their personal professional identity, preferences, and the needs of their business

How do we boost positivity when feeling disillusioned professionally? Some of the core tools from positive psychology are useful here.

- Journaling and noticing what went OK/better today
- Considering gratitude – flexible working, having annual leave, colleagues we value, opportunities for training, even as basic as being glad to have a job, etc.
- The version of gratitude which my Yorkshire Mum advocates (and I didn't realise this till I trained in positive psychology) which is the 'You don't have to look far for someone who is worse off than you our Ruth' and then the 'get a grip and get on with it' conversation
- Looking for 'glimmers,' or the small things which are going well or we like about our work
- Writing yourself a letter about what you are hoping will be different in six months' time and then putting it away till that point in time. Usually something has changed
- Writing a note or card to someone, saying thank you or how much you appreciate them, can have positive benefits for you and them
- Talking about individual strengths can raise positivity. Chapter 9 covers signature strengths which is a valuable approach, but simply chatting about perceived strengths can be helpful in increasing self-worth
- And finally adapting your environment to have more indoor plants and greenery or even a water scene on your screensaver. It seems we humans tend to be more positive when looking at scenery with trees with open gaps and views to the distance. If there is a pool of water showing through the trees then that's even better

Goals in Self-Development and Reflective Practice

This is about setting goals which are not clinical skills but professional 'swamp skills' (Schön) which tend to lead to success in a profession. Self-development is also about skills in emotional resilience and time management, and books such as Covey's *7 Habits of Highly Successful People* and Goleman's *Emotional Intelligence at Work*. These are general, easy reads which can help with confidence and self-esteem. In formal performance development reviews/appraisals it can be helpful to have a self-development goal, e.g. a skill linked to presentation skills, leading meetings, giving more time to home, and keeping work in perspective.

143

Personal Reflection

I reflect here on my decision to leave my NHS post and work and live differently. Some months before I left we were unexpectedly introduced to a new human resources IT system with a short run in. With a different approach it could have been very positive. It wasn't. This additional work coincided with my garden being at its best. I remarked to a friend that I hadn't even had time to smell the roses and the sentence stuck with me and helped me realise that I needed a different perspective on my role at work.

Resilience

We all know what resilience is until we try to define it.

(Padesky 2009)

As practitioners we need coping strategies to restore confidence in our competence after a setback or knock down. At these times the supervisor provides listening support and empathy. However sometimes it is practical support in developing and applying strategies for coping at difficult times that is needed. A working knowledge of resilience is essential in the toolkit of the supervisor.

Resilience is bounce-back ability. It is having strategies for picking yourself up, getting a grip, and starting all over again. I once heard the singer Lesley Garrett talking about difficulties in her early career singing in London, and how her mother from Doncaster, South Yorkshire, occasionally sent her a tiny bag of soil at low times and called it 'Yorkshire Grit.' I can certainly relate to this supportive style, though I don't suggest that we supervisors hand out small bags of Yorkshire grit – I mentioned earlier about supervision being about getting rid of mental grime, but there is no need for visual support here.

I have not read research on 'giving oneself a talking to.' I worked with a colleague who used this phrase a lot. If she felt herself sinking down or becoming low in spirits at work, then she would give herself a talking to. I used this expression recently in a supervision session, when saying to a supervisee, "you know listening to what you've said, it sounds as though you gave yourself a talking to," and we both laughed and agreed. It won't work for everyone, but there is something in there. It's a realisation that something has to change and it is possible to think differently and change direction, even if that is not an immediate, screeching hand break turn.

There are many accessible books on this topic, such as *SUMO (Shut up and Move on)* by Paul McGee (2015) and *Flourishing* by Maureen Gaffney (2012). SUMO gives a framework to work through, and there are sometimes training courses available. Gaffney summarises research on resilience, positive psychology, and mindfulness with lots of practical techniques. She describes how she began writing after a re-structure when her hours of work were drastically cut and she had to bounce back and writing the book was her way of doing this.

Gaffney also covers mindfulness as both a tool for stress reduction and clarity/flexibility of thoughts. It is a topic which can provoke strong views. It is also an area which does have an evidence base. I came across mindfulness on a training course for adult fluency but became interested in this as a tool for reducing anxiety and encouraging compassion at times when tiredness or overload of work might make that difficult. I certainly became more accepting of times when I had hoped to be doing something else, but a crisis situation or distressed colleague needed attention and to be prioritised. I'm conscious of a difference in my own approach now where I usually close my eyes briefly and take a deep breath (no one notices) and reluctantly shift into another mode.

Sometimes if someone is clearly struggling then the important thing is to bring it out into the open and ask if they think that they are 'OK to be in work.' Make a suggestion about potentially having a chat with a GP or accessing a counselling support line if one is available. The key for me is to risk assess the ongoing conversation and decide whether to continue. By continuing to listen and give support am I preventing this supervisee accessing help from someone who has far more training and knowledge around mental wellbeing than I have? I am now able to make these suggestions without worrying about reactivity from supervisees. That's never happened, and there is usually a conversation about the reality of a period of low spirits and evaporated motivation at work.

Resilience seems to be a combination of the following. Each heading has some suggestions for strategies to support and guide supervisees:

Confidence Levels

- Knowing strengths
- Feeling valued for contributions at work
- Being receptive to challenge
- Feeling physically well

Network of Support

- A social and supportive network
- Gratitude in role
- Empathy for others

Flexible Thinking/Adaptability

- Resilient thinking – knowing it is possible to bounce back
- Thinking space – a safe place to share thoughts
- Mindfulness – refreshed thinking or re-booting thoughts
- Working smarter not harder – considering solutions/innovative approaches rather than longer hours

Having a Purpose

- A set of personal values and beliefs
- Goal-focused approach – knowing goals and expecting to achieve them
- Looking to the future and reflecting on the past (aka 'positive mental time travel')
- Part of a team with strong purpose and direction

Underpinning this is the knowledge that it is important to focus your energy on what you can actually control. Accept that there are some things we can't influence and stop wasting energy on them. It is sensible for wellbeing at work to avoid getting entangled in mental anguish about a policy decision over which we have little influence.

There is specific research into the efficacy of restorative supervision. Milne and Reiser (2020) prefer the term *supportive supervision* to restorative. Supportive function is the term used as an alternative to Proctor's restorative function by Kadushin. They prefer this term because they feel it gives stronger emphasis to the wide scope of supportive supervision. This includes *"a positive strength-based emphasis, active prevention of stressors; valuable personal development."* I like the term 'supportive' supervision, but there is also something re-assuring about 'restorative' supervision with which I identify: time out, safe space to talk with headspace and headroom. The suggestion is to use whichever you feel fits most closely with your individual style.

Restorative Resilient Model of Supervision

It is time to showcase a specific model of supervision, developed and researched by the clinical psychologist Sonya Wallbank (2010), which stands out as different. It is widely known in midwifery and health visiting as these professions formed the research cohorts, but the approach is very relevant for AHPs.

> *Restorative clinical supervision is a model of supervision designed to support professionals working within roles where they have a significant emotional demand.*

> (Wallbank, 2010)

The model has been piloted (Wallbank, 2010) and substantially tested with a range of community staff (Wallbank and Hatton, 2011).

Wallbank has specialisms in resilience and restorative approaches to wellbeing at work, as well as leading service delivery, change, and improvement programmes. The practical materials resulting from the research enable services to introduce a structured approach to restorative supervision.

A key feature of the restorative resilient model is that focusing supervision and support on the needs of the individual, not just their work, reduces stress and burnout and improves job satisfaction.

There is a booklet which covers the research, how restorative resilience developed, and the practical tools. This is *The Restorative Resilience Model of Supervision: A Reader Exploring Resilience to Workplace Stress in Health and Social Care Professionals* (2016).

There is also a programme for services to 'take off the shelf' and implement with a guide for a training day and setting up this approach in teams. What follows is a basic overview of the model, tools, and techniques adapted for speech and language therapy, but readers are directed to Wallbank's work for in-depth information.

It is clear that

> *attending to the emotional response to the work is more important than merely support. In this function, the primary issue can be seen as being the emotional impact of practice and the potential of this to undermine safe practice, as well as the impact on health and wellbeing of the practitioner.*

> (Hughes and Pengelly 1997)

Wallbank's work has fed into the NHS professional midwifery advocate model. The benefits of this advocacy approach include:

- Having a positive impact on the immediate wellbeing of staff
- Helping staff to feel valued by their employers for investing in them and their wellbeing

- Influencing a significant reduction in stress and burnout
- Improving compassion, enjoyment and job satisfaction
- Improving the retention of staff
- Improving working relationships and team dynamics
- Helping staff to manage work/life balance more effectively

NHS England (2018b)

The goal of restorative clinical supervision is to give *"a safe environment to consider options, reflect constructively and challenge negativity; this in turn could empower the individual to realise what they can do themselves to improve their working life and reduce stress and burnout"* (de Haan and Christiane 2012). It is about providing practitioners with the space and time to reflectively process work-related experiences, giving support as they strengthen resilience and consider relevant coping strategies.

As with all aspects of self-development, including resilience, it is the practitioner who makes the decision to change and focus on developing skills and strategies for the future. Restorative resilience gives an easier way into strengthening skills because it is part of a structured package.

"The prime candidate for burn-out is the nurse who strives for excellence in a toxic environment" (Cullen 1995). If we change the word nurse for speech and language therapist the message is blunt (and backed up by evidence), and it is more likely that a therapist who strives for excellence in practice, but works in a difficult, toxic environment (team or organisation) is most likely to suffer burnout.

Sarah Calkin wrote in *Nursing Times* (2013) that some nurses were *"more stressed than combat troops."* The suggested solution was to give nurses protected space for clinical supervision to discuss and reflect on practice which more than halved levels of stress and burnout, drawing on Wallbank's research.

From experience, it can be incredibly difficult for practitioners who have a strong set of values and a preferred way of working to adapt to a change in direction in a service. However this does happen: perhaps a pressure to work differently in order to meet waiting list pressures, or even a new clinical model introduced as part of a service re-design. There can be a clash between strongly held values and a new way of working, especially if it is difficult to immediately see specific advantages in the new way of working. This fact cannot be 'swept under the carpet,' and clinicians experiencing this level of stress need to be taken into account in any change management plan. The change may still happen, but the underlying stress needs compassionate attention.

Tony Ghaye and Sue Lillyman (2007) integrated their interest in reflective practice in healthcare with clinical supervision. Ghaye (2001) pointed out that in reflective practice we focus on client-centred care, but that for successful teams in healthcare it is essential to consider *"colleague-centred care."* We should re-frame clinical supervision so that wider relationships, and conflicts across teams which can impact negatively on practitioners, as well as affecting service delivery are included in supervisory conversations. There are still many practitioners who see supervision as just about individual cases, and variability in accessing quality training in supervision hasn't helped matters.

Spotlight on Triggers for Stress

Wallbank's restorative resilient model was designed to support practitioners working in complex clinical scenarios. The starting point is actually shining the spotlight on stress and its signs and symptoms. We often say "I'm stressed" without analysing specifically why we are experiencing stress. Or we acknowledge that the stress exists but then focus on what's happened because of it: the build-up of admin, reports which are overdue, cancelled supervision meetings, because there is 'no time.' We might sit in supervision considering the impact without addressing the stress itself. Restorative resilience provides a way of specifically tackling the stress and building resilience to prevent future build-up of stress.

Stress can affect our behaviour in various ways. Typical signs might be:

- Feeling overwhelmed
- Being late (lots of the time)
- Withdrawing – reluctance to be involved at work
- Absence
- Low motivation
- Snappier style of communication
- Struggling to make effective decisions

Stress can eventually lead to burnout with a lack of interest and motivation in our job. Those in caring professions are more at risk of burnout. Wallbank uses the term "compassion fatigue" for a lack of enjoyment and satisfaction with our work. There is a disengagement due to stress. We can consider changing profession, but someone who experiences burnout didn't want to get to this point and is probably still committed to the idea of their profession; they just can't engage and feel involved with it right now.

Personal Reflection

I do remember three occasions, at varying points in my NHS career, when I had this 'compassion fatigue.' At those times I was in work going through the motions, but I was unable to give mental focus, compassion, and energy to colleagues who sought support and advice.

For me the causes of this mental fatigue were varied: recovering from a miscarriage, concern about a family member who was seriously ill, and a re-structure where my post was at risk.

The first was at an early point in my career and the last was close to my leaving the NHS (not due to the re-structure but I know the experience of intense anxiety and uncertainty eventually impacted on my decision to leave). I can step back in time and see an older colleague who had taken up a locum post in our adult learning disability setting, who had endless enthusiasm, but no clinical experience. I had mentored and supported this colleague and enjoyed the experience, yet after my return to work I just could not listen very well. Of course, I didn't recognise this as compassion fatigue at the time.

Restoring the Ability to Think

A key point to remember is that restorative resilient supervision is all about "*restoring a practitioner's ability to think.*" Stress is a biochemical reaction to perceived threats in the environment, and the resulting flood of stress hormones affects our ability to think clearly. The levels of stress hormones and changes after clinical supervision were tracked (blood samples analysed) as part of the research.

When we are stressed the secretion of stress hormones like cortisol affects brain function and thinking. When this flooding of hormones happens it "*prevents the brain laying down new memory, or very significantly reduces access to already existing memories.*" Sustained stress can even damage part of the brain called the hippocampus in the limbic system which is connected to learning and memory functioning.

During times of perceived or real threat the adrenal glands release adrenalin. Then after a few minutes cortisol is also released into the blood-stream. Cortisol stays in the system far longer than adrenalin and continues to impact on the brain, changing its functioning. Thinking is affected by stress hormones.

Another Personal Reflection

When I first read this, I immediately understood events from the past, times when colleagues under intense stress had seemed more forget-ful. There is a vicious cycle here, in that someone who has memory issues linked to stress becomes a focus for additional support around their performance at work, which results in more anxiety and stress and more stress hormone.

I realised that during one of a series of re-structures my own mem-ory had at times been appalling. I'd assumed this was linked to the menopause. I realise now that this was more likely the effect of cortisol on my thinking. In fact, a combination of the effects of stress hormone plus menopause is awful to consider – and there is a research project in here somewhere.

The research on restorative resilience measured the cortisol and glucose levels of supervisees to monitor physiological changes. The results showed restorative supervision calms the brain and slows down thinking.

So, with a calm brain and slower thinking, cortisol levels reduce and the ability to store and retrieve memory effectively is restored. This has to be a good thing for our wellbeing and clinical practice. Restorative supervision reduces stress and protects us from burnout. Our *"compassion satisfaction"* at work stays steady and can even increase.

Supervising Differently – a Structure to Restore Resilience

The first time I read about restorative resilient supervision was transforma-tional. As I read about the different types of support linked to the restora-tive resilience model (Figure 12.2 is adapted from this) all sorts of memories from the past came to mind. Situations where I had 'sagely dispensed advice' and given what I thought were helpful and practical strategies to someone who was struggling with just coping that week. I recognised the signs of

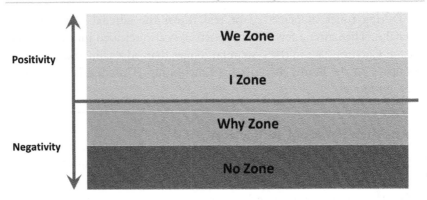

Figure 12.2

stress, the effect on memories, and those times when my supervisees (both in management and clinical supervision) had not had that slow, calm thinking.

Restorative resilient clinical supervision was given to over 2500 healthcare professionals in research showing consistently positive results in reducing stress and preventing burnout. It is resource heavy in the early stages. Wallbank's research team initially provided training and six individual sessions for supervisees. Over time this changed with supervisors trained at an early stage to make the approach cost effective and sustainable.

Initially supervisees were offered around six individual weekly sessions of supervision. It is more usual to have monthly or half termly supervision, so weekly supervision seems a large resource commitment. However when a supervisee is struggling and focused support is needed, the interval between supervisions is often shortened. Also, the reality is that the six sessions will be spread out due to meetings, sickness, annual leave, etc. The difference is planned consecutive sessions with an agenda focused on coping and resilience.

In 2013 a group approach was piloted as a more sustainable approach. The results were positive showing that after the initial one to one sessions, supervision could continue through groups. The groups helped clinicians deal with the emotional demands of their role.

How Is This Approach Different?

In the restorative resilience model there are four Work Performance Zones linking with levels of stress and motivation. In each zone the supervisor uses different skills and techniques to support a supervisee.

These four Work Performance Zones are:

- No
- Why
- I
- We

The supervisor uses different techniques depending on where the supervisee is in terms of zones ("compassion satisfaction"). Techniques are familiar tools drawn from the wider evidence base. Alongside this there is additional specific work on ways of reducing stress and strengthening resilience.

For those approaching burnout then the approach is giving safe space and listening. For those who are motivated and thriving at work there is a coaching approach. There is a continuum of strategies linked to the zones.

Each zone has a different style of supervision. I think of the levels as:

- Listening Level
- Reflective Level
- Coaching Level

These are not Wallbank's terms, but are helpful to me when using this model.

If a supervisee is showing significant stress, stuck in a negative place where they think nothing can be done to improve the situation, and unable to consider any alternatives, it is worth considering using an adapted restorative resilience approach individually.

The impulse is often to try to help the supervisee and suggest possible solutions. An example might be a supervisee who is submerged by administration and cannot perceive of a way of ever catching up with their workload. The supervisee in this negative zone is unable to take on board advice and does not need a longer To Do list. In restorative resilience the supervisor abandons the "Why don't you?" or "Why not try?" or "How about doing this?" approach. The need is for space, time, and most importantly someone to acknowledge the situation and listen.

It may be that supportive advice is given later, and sometimes there is a risk to clients of not providing reports and delayed paperwork which might involve onward referrals. There can be a need to balance compassion for a colleague with the need to practically sort out their casework. However, Wallbank's research is clear about listening being the priority. The use of active listening makes all the difference.

When emotionally and physically drained we are in danger of burnout. The supervisor acknowledges the demands the supervisee is facing. On the surface it seems incredibly simple, but when the supervisor simply listens this has significant impact. Talking about the situation, verbalising the difficulties, is the first step out of 'compassion fatigue.'

The Negative Zones

In Figure 12.2 there are two positive zones above the work performance line and two negative zones below. When in the negative No Zone or Why Zone performance is restricted and veers into negativity. We might not realise when we are in these zones but we are not going to be effective in our job roles. Let's look at the zones in more detail.

> *The No Zone*: when someone spends lots of time in the No Zone they will show signs of stress. People show stress differently. Signs include being withdrawn, avoiding situations, and disengaging. Sometimes people are disruptive or even subversive. Energy levels are low and even general social conversation can be difficult. This is not just a 'bad week,' it is pervasive, impacting on others. If someone does not participate in a team and continually says "no" to reasonable requests that negativity can be infectious. Gaffney (2015) pinpoints how *infectious negativity* can spiral out into a team. At the very least colleagues start to pick up extra duties to compensate for lack of engagement by a colleague.
>
> People in the No Zone are more likely to talk openly and often about disagreements and differences of opinion, their dissatisfaction with others, their manager or possibly just everyone they're working with. There is often more emotion expressed in the office, not just low mood.
>
> In summary it is the intensity of hopelessness in this zone which is different. There is little sign of any positive enjoyment of the job and general negativity about work and colleagues.

Escaping the No Zone

What does a supervisor pull out of their toolkit when working in the No Zone? The supportive techniques used by supervisors in the No Zone are drawn from counselling skills. The term *"emotional containment"* is used to describe this support.

The supervisor begins by supporting the practitioner in dealing with negative emotions about work, processing anxiety and any fear of work situations. This sounds daunting, but usually when people have reached the No Zone they are talking openly and negatively about work, so it is possible to engage in conversation. Those near burnout in the No Zone don't want to be there and want to talk about how they feel.

As supervision sessions progress the focus changes to looking together for what actually triggers emotions and behaviours. What pulls individuals into the No Zone varies. We all have action tendencies, and this can be a helpful way of reflecting on what's happening. I don't like using the term 'behaviour' with colleagues, even positive behaviour, e.g. leadership skills, and prefer talking in terms of action tendencies. With space and focused conversation a practitioner can stand back, wash off accumulated mental grime, and work out what has been happening.

Techniques used by the supervisor:

- Asking open-ended questions
- Asking questions needing a simple affirmative answer
- Listening closely
- Making supportive comments
- Validating the supervisee, e.g. their clinical skillset, support of colleagues

---

For the supervisor it is about listening, acknowledging that 'it isn't easy right now,' and then reflecting together with the supervisee in recognising symptoms of burnout and processing feelings about work.

The Why Zone: this is the other negative zone. It is still a negative place to spend time but is one level up from the hopelessness of the No Zone.

Someone in the Why Zone tends to question everything which is suggested. This isn't productive questioning and has roots in *"nervous or fearful energy."* Wallbank describes that there is *"often just too much on the mind."* Productivity at work (i.e. getting things done effectively) is affected.

Someone in the Why Zone may be carrying around considerable work-related baggage. They are dwelling on something which happened, an event or situation at work which caused distress. Something hasn't gone to plan or these is a culture of conflict in the office. They may have a perceived lack of progression in their career, maybe been unsuccessful at interview. The feelings around lack of success in an internal interview can be very difficult to process. Of course, we are all supposed to accept, move on, and contribute positively. Just recognising this isn't an easy time and verbalising about the experience can help.

We know that venting our feelings as a 'one off' can help. Venting continuously and being stuck is very different (Gaffney 2015). The process of talking through events in a reflective conversation (Wallbank calls this *verbalising*) can be valuable and help a supervisee take the first step in a positive direction. Often, as a manager, I would suggest some external support for someone who has experienced disappointment. Working with a coach to help prepare for the next interview or mentoring around wider career plans can make all the difference and widen horizons.

We all visit the negative zones, but it is when we are stuck there that it becomes a problem. We can visit, but need a trail out. Being in a negative zone most of the time signals we are close to burnout. The No and the Why Zones are the burnout zones. In these zones our thinking is affected, so it is harder to find the route out. In both the No and Why Zones the supervisor is focusing on 'emotional containment' and keeping attitudes around work steady, while finding a path into more positive zones.

As the sessions progress and the supervisor notices glimmers of positivity a more reflective approach is pulled out of the toolkit. Once the supervisee is spending less time in the negative zone then one of the models of reflective practice (Chapter 7) can be used to help the supervisee stay in the positive zones.

If a practitioner is in the No Zone, then it is NOT necessary to go into the Why Zone before moving into positive zones. It's possible to move straight from No to a positive zone.

The Positive Zones

The I Zone: the reflect and connect zone.

Here a practitioner has more energy with a positive outlook, contribution, and performance at work; with focus on what's needed in their job role, and interest in learning and developing their skills or improving general wellbeing at work. There is thinking space for looking ahead and thinking about what "I" could do to develop and progress.

In this reflection connection stage, in-depth consideration of case-working in a guided conversation is the 'go to' approach.

The We Zone: a great place to be. There is high energy, creativity, and interest in thinking of solutions and suggesting innovations for the service and clients. It is a pleasure to work with someone in the We Zone – their positivity and energy are usually infectious.

When a practitioner is in the We Zone then the supervisor can bring in goals and a coaching approach. Supervision becomes future focused, supporting learning with coaching for career progression.

The Reflection Connection

In the positive zones the supervisor can choose a reflective model and guide the conversation. The focus can be on identifying personal and professional strengths, considering feelings and reactions at work, e.g. around requests or tasks. It's possible to consider job role and what might need to change so the practitioner feels comfortable at work again. Are processes in place to support their work, any gaps, or suggestions for improvement?

The supervisor is still listening and noticing patterns in a practitioner's thinking style and expression of feelings. The focus of the conversation might be caseload related or it might spread out to wider issues such as working with others in a team. The supervisor can begin to summarise impressions and feed tentative insights into the conversation. This is one point where I think it can be helpful to talk about and identify strengths outside of the workplace. It is important to highlight some positive contributions and abilities. Most people feel better for a compliment, and when emerging from the negative zones positive comments will help and validating achievements outside of work is relevant. It gradually becomes possible to work together in looking at patterns of thinking, feelings about work, and action tendencies.

Of course, some supervisees are already comfortably in this I Zone stage and content to stay there. This zone is reflective space with guided conversation about events, describing situations in detail. By using one of the models of reflective practice as a basis for conversation then reflective insights and possibilities emerge and the supervisor can reinforce learning points.

An example might be an experienced practitioner who has an action tendency to volunteer at team meetings for more than she can possibly cope with. Often in meetings she feels awkward when no-one else steps forward and so she volunteers again. By recognising this action tendency in a reflective conversation with a supervisor it becomes possible to consider ways of doing things differently at future meetings.

In this zone the tools are similar with active listening, summarising, contributing insights, and asking questions which clarify a situation. There is more structured reflection and focus on the future, e.g. considering how a situation might play out, what those involved might say or do, and how to respond. It is possible to think about other people's perspectives and motivators. This can be a strong antidote to the rigid thinking of the negative zones. The supervisor can start to ask questions to challenge and clarify the supervisee's story about a situation, guiding them into considering other perspectives.

There are another two other important components of the restorative resilient model. At the point when the practitioner begins to feel more positive, then the supervisor brings in stress inoculation and resilience strategies. The objective is to equip practitioners with insight so they notice when they enter the Negative Zones and use individual strategies to ensure that it is only a short visit.

Stress Inoculation

In stress inoculation the supervisor talks openly with the supervisee about stress and individual patterns of stress, what triggers stress, what and how might this be different in future? With insight into individual stressors, then coping with stress in the future should be easier. Protective strategies are identified during the conversation based on the practitioner's responses to situations and events, including anything which works already to reduce the impact of stress.

So in stress inoculation stress triggers are identified with a focus on maximising strengths. Strengths can be linked to work or home. The supervisor brings in general stress strategies including assertiveness and negotiation skills to strengthen resilience for the future.

I don't use supervision sessions as a teaching place and consider stress strategies in the session, suggesting resources and then letting the supervisee try these out before reporting back at the next session.

Assertiveness

Assertiveness is about knowing yourself, your values and capabilities, and what is possible for you that day, week, or month at work. You will put forward your point of view, take the views of others into account, and work towards a positive outcome which doesn't cause you stress.

Assertiveness Skills

- Valuing everyone as an equal and behaving as an equal to others
- Giving your opinion clearly and calmly – strength and dignity
- Use positive body language to support your message
- Being authentic about thoughts, feelings, and hopes and supporting others in doing this too
- Appreciating others and regularly letting them know they are appreciated
- Taking accountability, e.g. for mistakes
- Accepting responsibility, e.g. for role, duties
- Diplomacy
- Apologising when necessary
- Seeing mistakes as learning opportunities
- Delegating to others with care and consideration
- Respecting and listening to the perspective of others and then responding appropriately
- Seeking consensus and solutions wherever possible
- Generally being positive about self and job role
- Self-awareness and self-regulation

Ann Dickson (1983)

Negotiation

Negotiation skills integrate communication, problem solving, solution seeking, and organisation skills to facilitate a mutually agreeable compromise.

Negotiation Skills or Seeking Solutions

- Knowing the current situation
- Preparing for discussion
- Mirroring communication style
- Listening to whole message – intonation/body language/emotion
- Considering various solutions
- Problem solving approach
- Discussing options
- Building rapport
- Choosing options/making decision about preferred option
- Talking about goals and objectives in a clear way
- Outlining benefits
- Having a backup plan
- Listening and working out what someone's unmet need is – why are they asking for this and acting this way.
- Valuing win-win solutions
- Talking about win-win solutions

Have a range of suggested resources around assertiveness and negotiation and signpost supervisees to these. The resources can be referenced in conversation with examples of how they might be applied. Resources include extracts from *SUMO* by McGee (2015); *Flourishing*, Gaffney (2012); *Getting to Yes*, Fisher and Ury (2012); *Don't Sweat the Small Stuff and It's All Small Stuff*, Richard Carlson (1998); *The 7 Habits of Highly Successful People* (Covey 1989, 2020); and my personal favourites *How to Have a Good Day: Think Bigger Feel Better and Transform Your Working Life*, Caroline Webb (2017), and *Emotional Agility*, Susan David (2016).

Also signpost to websites with short, accessible articles for supervisees to dip into. Everyone has a different learning style and sometimes it is a video on YouTube or an app (there are many mindfulness apps) rather than reading which makes learning around resilience stick. Another alternative is attending a training course or online seminar on a topic like positive psychology or time management. It is finding something which fits for an individual supervisee.

A key difference at this stage is that although there is still ample opportunity to reflect on past events, there should be more emphasis on projecting ahead, imagining situations, and talking through likely events. Some practitioners might even feel comfortable role playing a possible scenario. The emphasis is on reflection on future as well as reflection on past events.

Restorative Resilient Group Supervision

Following initial research an adapted group programme was proved successful in reducing stress, maintaining job 'compassion satisfaction,' and reducing burnout. (Wallbank 2013). Groups enabled less experienced supervisees
to learn from listening to others. The format allowed practitioners to discuss
complex situations and consider different perspectives and ideas in a safe
space created and shared by the group. The practitioners reported that it
was helpful to consider potential options, e.g. scripts of what might be said
or done with the support of others in the group and no anxiety about saying or doing anything wrong. This does sound an ideal learning space with
similarities to Schön's *"sheltered practicum"* for extending professional skills.

**Supervisors were encouraged to share any key themes in supervi-
sion. Regular topics included:**

- Specific strategies for conflict situations (a consistent theme)
- Situations where a decision by an organisation had a perceived
  adverse impact on practitioners' ability to do their job to the best
  of their ability
- Differences between personal values and team direction
- Dealing with difficult situations and anxiety about future
  involvement
- Anticipating difficulties and practicing potential solutions

---

Overall, it helped practitioners to know others were feeling the same way.
Structural changes in some organisations had led to isolation and practitioners not spending as much time working together with limited opportunity
for sharing experiences. Attending the group helped practitioners realise
that they were not alone with their workload difficulties.

In summary there is a need for the restorative function of supervision
for all practitioners: a supervisor who listens and provides a safe space
to recuperate from the emotional demands of the job.

This section has highlighted the restorative resilient model of supervision because it stands out as an evidence-based approach providing
practical tools and strategies for supervision with training materials
available for services.

Restorative supervision has benefits for the individual, their colleagues, the service, and any wider organisation.

Practitioners benefit from "feeling stronger and having greater thinking capacity"

More able to "interact more positively in the workplace, which benefits both the rest of the team and the families or patients they are working with."

(Charlotte Louise Giltinane, Nursing Standard, 2013: 21)

 # REFLECTIVE LEARNING

Emotional Intelligence (EI)

How can you tell where your EI needs improvement – especially if you feel that it's strong in some areas? Goleman suggests that simply reviewing the 12 competencies in your mind can give you a sense of where you might need some development.

Picking up on Positives

Practice noticing positive skills and contributions of others and highlighting these. Look over the list again. It will give you ideas for a wide range of positives.

Restorative Resilient Approach

- Re-read the information about restorative resilient supervision. It won't be time wasted. Are you surprised that the research suggests supervisors bring in active listening with supervisees who seem very stressed and approaching burnout rather than giving them solutions to help them sort out the situation?
- Positive or negative zone: don't worry about the specific names of the zones and instead just think in terms of positive zone (above the line) and negative zone (below the line). Notice times when you enter the negative zones. Is it easy or difficult for you to find the way out?

- Burnout: you may be someone who never approaches burnout. I have been there but didn't recognise this when it was happening Make sure you know the signs and symptoms of stress-related burnout so you notice it in colleagues
- Stress inoculation: what are your own ways of reducing stress if you notice it creeping in?
- Have you a range of assertiveness and negotiation skills to boost your protection against stress? What are your strongest assertiveness skills? Look at the list – is there anything surprising? Evaluate your own skillset. Any gaps?

CAMEO – RESTORATIVE SUPERVISION BEFORE DEVELOPMENTAL SUPERVISION

Anna was a new supervisee working in a large NHS Trust. She had moved to a different team focusing on Adult Re-hab with a Multi-Disciplinary Team approach. This wasn't going well. Anna had thrived in her last role and welcomed the move as a positive development. She was, however, missing colleagues, who had become friends over time, and felt less enthusiastic about this new role. Her new manager had suggested she accessed additional supervision to support her in this transitional period. Anna had been reluctant and felt this was a sign of failing in her performance but agreed to a more frequent schedule of supervision with a supervisor who was outside of the team.

The first two meetings were cathartic. They were scheduled close together as the reality was that there was not enough time to complete everything Anna brought to the first meeting. The supervisor listened and booked in a second meeting the following week. This was unusual but felt to be necessary. Due to calendar complications the second meeting was arranged as an online teleconference.

In the first meeting there had been a cathartic 'offload' of regrets, anxieties about failure in the new role, and a very miserable picture. As per restorative resilient supervision the first action of the supervisor was to listen and summarise to check out her understanding of what Anna was talking about. The first session had ended with simple validation by the supervisor that this change was difficult and for Anna to know she had been exceptional in her previous role and those skills were still there.

Towards the end of the second meeting the Supervisor felt able to do more than listen. It was possible to begin to ask questions and use a reflective model to begin a structured exploration of what Anna was experiencing. The supervisor facilitated Anna in choosing two or three particularly stressful situations in the new role and exploring reactions, feelings, and any common patterns. There were also the beginnings of a search for glimmers (small positives). This continued into the third session (the following week) where relationships, strengths, and gaps were considered.

The supervisor made the decision to schedule weekly sessions, and there was time, availability, and support for this.

Anna began to network in the wider team more. She built relationships on shared joint working with the assistant clinical psychologist and OT. Her relationship with an especially dogmatic senior colleague improved over time, but the difference in values and beliefs about how to approach therapy meant Anna felt she was always 'working hard' to maintain the relationship. Eventually Anna left to work in a similar post in a neighbouring department. Interestingly she stayed in this specialist area and maintained contact with her supervisor.

Potholes and Pitfalls in Practicing Supervision

"If there's no meaning in it, that saves a world of trouble, you know, as we needn't try to find any."

King of Hearts, *Alice's Adventures in Wonderland*

Key Themes

- Dilemmas and difficulties
- Differing philosophies in supervision
- Sabotage
- Supervision games
- Stuck in a supervisory relationship

Dilemmas and Difficulties

Supervision can prove difficult for either supervisor or supervisee. It may have gone stale or got stuck but for whatever reason there are difficulties emerging and the relationship does not feel constructive. The games we can play in supervision, perhaps to protect ourselves when we feel vulnerable, are explored. It's important to have awareness of these games and recognise when we are drawn into building barriers. When I first learnt about these games it was uncomfortable reading as I looked back and recognised I'd brought some into play, without even realising it.

There might be practical difficulties such as the logistics of meeting. It seems simple but if one person works Monday to Wednesday and the other works from Wednesday to Friday there are limited times to meet. It might have been a fantastic supervisory arrangement, but it is going to suffer due to limited options.

DOI: 10.4324/9781003226772-14

Another difficulty can arise, most usually in peer supervision, if the relationship is between 'therapy friends' who know each other and have a similar level of experience and knowledge. These relationships are important and can be a positive supervisory arrangement. However it might just be too comfortable with little challenge or opportunity to learn. If there is a shared time type arrangement between two colleagues, then give the meeting a clear structure and put those supervisory hats on. Supervision needs to be supportive, but not always within our comfort zone. I'm going to go as far as saying that when we have supervision with a comfortable peer that it is not actually supervision. It's part of our support network and important for wellbeing at work, but it doesn't count as clinical supervision.

Differing Values

Another 'biggie' to consider is our values as practitioners. I don't mean the value statements of organisations with their emphasis on integrity and compassion. These values should be part of our professional identity whatever our clinical field. No, this is about values underpinning practice. I began to realise I was supervising a colleague who had a very different set of values. I've supervised those in different clinical areas, e.g. support around resilience, time, and energy management. This was more fundamental and could easily be a barrier to successful supervision without very careful thought. I have a strongly interactionist approach, and my supervisee was the absolute other end of the continuum. When something like this emerges it needs discussing openly. As a supervisor I could listen, ask questions, and support a supervisee with differing clinical values, but this was only possible with appreciation of each other's viewpoints; without respect such relationships need to end.

Sabotage in Supervision

Sometimes we throw up barriers in supervision and know we are doing this. Most of the time though we probably don't realise that we look as if we are engaged in a supervisory conversation but are really crouching behind a barrier. It's often quite an unconscious thing to sabotage supervision. It happens. I've done it myself and not realised till months later how I expertly evaded being challenged about a situation when I could have reflected in a guided conversation and developed as a practitioner.

So, what are these games we can play in supervision? How do we sabotage supervision? Strangely the list doesn't seem to have changed much over time. While researching I found the same list re-hashed and re-worded but the same essential content. Here is a summary and a warning to be prepared for some uncomfortable reading. You will recognise the tactics. It's inevitable. We've all used them, even unknowingly. Once aware though, it's possible to change our response and stand back from sabotage.

This is where trust and respect in the supervisory relationship are so important. Shohet (2007) uses the word *"camouflage"* for when we feel vulnerable and might camouflage to try to save face.

The debate about whether a manager should also be a supervisor links here. As a manager we might listen and be tempted to step outside the clinical supervisor's role to address something. However it is more likely that a supervisee, who is clinically supervised by their manager, might be more inclined to hold back if they need their manager to think highly of them. By holding back learning through reflecting practice is sabotaged.

It's helpful and interesting to know that we are often acting to preserve our self-esteem. Glasser (1982) pinpointed that we are acting instinctively to protect ourselves from a threat. The work around polyvagal theory by Deb Dana and Stephen Porges, *Anchored: How to Befriend Your Nervous System Using Polyvagal Theory* (2021), has brought this into a modernised framework. It can be helpful to be aware of this framework and how we react at different levels and ways to regain equilibrium.

In originally identifying the games we play in supervision Glasser advocated that we use thoughtful, reflective learning to recognise and step out of game playing and work towards a constructive supervisory relationship.

It also takes two to keep a supervisory relationship productive. A supervisor might realise a relationship is struggling, but not wish to have a difficult conversation addressing this, which would need effort, time, and energy.

Let's look at the different games both supervisees and supervisors can bring into play in supervision.

Supervisor Games

"I'm special and very busy": if your supervisor is too busy to meet then you need another supervisor. The supervisor is giving the impression of being important with a demanding role, but this is no excuse for being rarely available and poorly prepared for supervision. Supervisees then stand back and make fewer requests as they have got the clear message that their supervisor is overwhelmed by work. It may be a relief to have

such an undemanding supervisor with few meetings in the diary, but it can't continue.

"It's dreadful round here": the supervisor gives a clear message that they understand and feel the same way. There might be long discussions about how difficult it is working in this place. Villeneuve (1994) describes this as the supervisor *"abdicating power"* in the relationship. There is no solution-focused discussion and a joint 'moan fest.'

"It's working, why change it": the supervisor gives a clear message that there is no need for change, this is how things are done here. So, the supervisor keeps control. The supervisee either gives up thinking creatively or looks for a new job.

"Let's do this my way": here the supervisor is keen for everyone to do everything their way. If the supervisor and supervisee have different styles then there is a clash in approach, or the supervisee just feels stifled and parented. The supervisee is going to resent this and want to 'break free'. This happens most in situations where a therapist joins a different team or is rotating into another section of a service. I have listened to early career therapists working in a setting such as a special school or child development centre where the senior clinician has a supportive, supervisory role, but always wants things done their way, in their style. There will be friction, even if it is below the surface.

"That's interesting, but ...": Villeneuve says the supervisor wants to *"appear open-minded (recognizing the supervisee's good ideas), while leaving the actual decision to some anonymous authority."*

Supervisee Games

Avoiding or deferring our supervision meeting (again!): we are too busy, so at the time when we most need supervision we cancel, with an ostensibly very good reason. We avoid and feel a little righteous that we are so busily overcommitted that we just don't have time to meet this month.

Being overly complimentary: most of us need compliments. I certainly do and they are good things. Usually compliment giving by a supervisee is genuine, but occasionally it is possible to be overcomplimentary with the hope that this will divert the supervisor from asking the difficult questions.

Painting with camouflage: Sometimes it's a lack of confidence, vulnerability, or being out of our depth. Maybe a supervisee worries about judgement or feels uncomfortable discussing a difficult situation. That's when the story told might be painted with camouflage. We are vague or focus on a detail, not talking about the whole picture.

"I'm snowed under" and there is no way out: in this scenario it is always dreadful. The supervisee may often turn up late to reinforce how dreadfully busy they are. "I'm snowed under, you know what it's like ..." Nothing has worked and nothing will work. Sometimes being 'snowed under' with reports and routine admin almost seems somehow needed by some of us. We throw this 'snow' into a supervisory conversation. The stress levels and emotional despair can be high. I know myself I now have the option of re-structuring my workload and taking breaks as I need to. I'm lucky and it didn't use to be this way. However constructive solution-focused conversations in supervision can reduce that feeling of overload, even in very difficult situations, e.g. where we are covering our own and a colleague's work. Time management and assertiveness strategies can be brought in.

Some therapists always feel overwhelmed and unable to pull out of the quagmire. If this is the pattern at every supervision and workload is comparable to colleagues, then some challenge is needed. I know colleagues who have been 'snowed under' for years, and for a professional career to be stuck in this quagmire is dreadfully sad. Of course, if there really is too much load on a team then there needs to be wider whole team strategies.

Don't you think? You know what it's like?: "I can't see the point, my time would be better spent with clients" is something many might sympathise with, but administration is a 'must do' and part of employment and professional standards. It is possible as a supervisor to be drawn into an ad hoc conversation about the demands of the 'paper load' and wonder where the time went.

"Please rescue me": when someone is asking for help, because they feel they are in a mess with their workload, the purpose of supervision has changed. Chapter 12 covers restorative supervision. Sometimes there are serial cries for rescue and support given and nothing ever improves. After many years of responding, I reflect that rescuing, e.g. removing a duty, is rarely an effective solution. The same issues re-emerge as the root cause is still there or occasionally the cry for rescue is a smokescreen.

Clouding supervision with personal issues: sometimes a personal issue or issues arise and supervisors listen with compassion. If a supervisee is totally absorbed with something outside of work at every meeting then the supervisor needs to broach accessing support outside our scope of practice (GP, counselling, or NHS Occupational Health).

On occasion a supervisee may be so absorbed by a personal emotional or health issue that they are unable to function in their job role but also unable to realise this and gentle broaching is needed.

I know more than you about this: "well I know what you are saying but when I went on this course this is what I was told," "that isn't what they did in my last team." The relationship is not productive as joint discussion about new approaches should usually spark clinical interest and an in-depth conversation.

I have a list: often a list is useful. Supervisees need to prepare and plan for supervision. However, the list can be so long and time so limited that there is little time to reflect. The agenda needs jointly agreeing between supervisor and supervisee.

A different diversion is when a supervisee asks lots of questions which fill the time that way. It can be flattering at first to be asked to give advice, but can become a pattern. As Villeneuve points out *"the little list"* encourages the supervisor to demonstrate knowledge, and the supervisee need only listen to the wise answers.

I know, I did this, but should done…: the supervisee is aware they are struggling and keeps one step ahead by pointing out their errors (queryable decisions) before the supervisor guides conversation in that direction. This gives the impression and re-assures the supervisor that the supervisee knows what to do, it just went wrong on this occasion.

If you don't know about it, then we can't talk about it: over time a skilled supervisor learns to listen and draw out information in a supportive conversation. If many details are left out or the supervisee never has problems to share it is noticed.

Group Games and a Cautionary Note

Chapter 17 covers group dynamics. Sometimes one individual can influence the positivity and success of a group. Once when three supervision groups were set up in my team, each group led by a nurse colleague, one group failed after three meetings. The attendees dreaded attending as the supervisor took a very authoritarian and superior approach to supervision. She was 'the expert' and not knowing speech therapists made a mistake by telling everyone how serious this was and not a place for coffee or biscuits. The group folded. My group had a supervisor with a different style and thrived, and there are several anecdotes in this book based on my learning in that group setting. We had a leader with an enquiring, interested manner who asked the right questions and made sure that everyone contributed over time. Coffee was expected and added to a relaxed and sheltered setting.

I do recall though that an early career therapist found the group challenging as the other members all had more experience and the leader worked to reduce her vulnerability. Facilitation is about vigilance. A learning point for me in groups has been the necessity of making sure that everyone is involved or has the option of involvement. There needs to be some point to giving time and turning up.

An Example from Shohet

Shohet (2020) devotes a chapter to experience of a group which went dreadfully wrong. Some of the group members recount how their resentments had built up and were expressed. One supervisee was subversive for reasons she later realised were spurious. The group was a combined training course with integrated supervision sessions. Some of this situation developed, they felt on reflection, due to their stress levels. Shohet missing a training session due to adverse weather shouldn't have caused such extreme negativity.

The group rapidly became a toxic place where negativity spiralled, and Shohet as group facilitator was a target for perceived grievances. Shohet describes how he 'named this for what it was' and described to the group the effect it was having on him. I've never been in this type of situation, and it makes for uncomfortable reading.

I once observed a colleague leading an Action Learning group as part of a leadership course. It had involved significant planning with an appreciative approach. One group member had been unsuccessful in a promotional interview and was unable to contribute positively. What was unexpected was that this spread across the group, even though the topic was something the group members felt positively about. This wasn't a *Lord of the Flies* situation, but there was something in the dynamic here which created a negative atmosphere. The leader opted to keep to plan but completed as soon as possible. The group member who had, in effect, sabotaged the session apologised the next day. What a lot of precious time wasted when an unexpected emotional reaction led to a spiral of negativity.

SLTs are not experienced in dealing with this type of group dynamic – and nor should we. It doesn't often 'go wrong,' and a clear structure and ground rules can help avoid any groundswell of negativity. There should be an expectation that we are emotionally intelligent in our approach, keep to the ground rules, and value the time together.

Stuck in Supervision

Sometimes a supervisee or supervisor realises that the supervision isn't productive. Where there is choice it is easier. The supervisee can work towards changing supervisor or the supervisor towards closing the relationship in a positive way, e.g. signposting to a colleague with a different skillset.

This is one of the reasons why it is good to have a system for supervision in place which includes a contract and structured reviews of 'how it is going.' It's important to recognise when supervision is going stale and make some changes.

When I meet a new supervisee I mention the eventual ending of the relationship in the first conversation. I am possibly applying my learning from Malcolmess' *Care Aims* (2005) about the importance of mentioning closure right at the beginning. From Gestalt theory (Schultz 2021) we know people feel more secure knowing there will be an end point. Supervisees need to feel comfortable saying when it is time for them to move on to another supervisor. Having a conversation to say this is eventually expected helps.

Difficulties are most acute when a supervisee has been allocated a supervisor and nothing seems positive. For whatever reason the relationship is stuck in a dismal swamp.

The only option may be to engage in the sessions, while 'knowing' this is not a 'good fit,' although options like raising this with a manager or a grandparent, if there is one in the supervision model, may be considered.

 REFLECTIVE LEARNING

What are the top three games people play which you have noticed?

Negative contagion was covered in Chapter 12. It arises again here. Have you experience of one person's attitude spreading through a group?

CAMEO – HAYLEY TACKLES SERIAL CANCELLATION OF SESSIONS

Hayley was supervising Jude who was habitually cancelling two out of three supervision meetings. There was no continuity, and Hayley's impression was that Jude did not value supervision. Jude's cancellations tended to be workload related. 'I'm snowed under. You know what it's like' she would say. This had happened too many times, and Hayley felt Jude either needed to engage with supervision and use the time to explore why she was 'snowed under' and what to do about it, or to end the relationship.

When the next meeting finally happened, Hayley suggested they begin with a review of the contract and a conversation about how supervision was going. Hayley was able to use this to mention the number of sessions attended (and missed), and Jude realised she was never prioritising supervision and seeing it as time which could be most easily re-allocated to clinical work. Hayley suggested they might use the time to talk about casework and how Jude felt overstretched. They agreed that supervision should not be so easily cancelled, and Jude needed to carefully consider any future cancellations. The review of the contract helped resolve a situation the supervisor was struggling with, allowing the relationship to continue.

14 | Coaching in Supervision

"Are we nearly there?" Alice managed to pant out at last.

"Nearly there!" the Queen repeated. "Why, we passed it ten minutes ago! Faster!"

Alice's Adventures in Wonderland

Key Themes

- Links between supervision and coaching
- 4D appreciative coaching
- Simply coaching
- Goal setting
- Mentoring

Currently there is a trend in the NHS to widen access to coaching. It is easier to train to be a coach within an organisation. This seems to be driven by learning and development departments. It is a positive and reinforces the importance of progression over time with specific goals to aid this process. Coaching is extending in clinical teams and has a groundswell of support.

Links between Supervision and Coaching

Let's look at how supervision links with coaching and then visit mentoring. The NHS Leadership Academy describes coaching as *"a method of deploying techniques embedded in artful questioning and appreciative inquiry to help leaders unlock their full potential to achieve personal and professional*

DOI: 10.4324/9781003226772-15

success." Coaching often has most value when a practitioner wants to focus on their current position while hoping for development in the medium term. Coaching is usually time limited. It creates clarity and direction and is valuable from early career to senior leadership.

In clinical supervision, a coaching approach is increasingly popular. Supervision is a developing skillset and has so far drawn predominantly on techniques from counselling and psychotherapy. The addition of coaching skills to the skillset of the supervisor gives a structured future-focused dimension.

Wallbank (Chapter 12) suggests different types of support depending on how engaged and motivated someone is at work. If a practitioner feels overwhelmed then active listening is needed. When someone is energised, contributing pro-actively, and ready to move on in their career then coaching is possible.

If we follow the NHS Leadership Academy's lead in promoting an appreciative approach then the starting point in coaching is going to be exploring "*what's working, what's going well and what should we do more of.*" David Cooperrider's (2005) development of appreciative inquiry (Chapter 9) focuses on ways to build on these positives. Artful questions might begin with exploring achievements and proud moments.

Ask for Exceptions

Sometimes supervisees are so stuck in the dismal swamp of difficulties and frustrations that it seems they will be navigating through this swamp forever. It can be difficult even imagining what a different future might look like, let alone focusing on goals to reach it. One strategy which can be helpful in these situations is to talk about exceptions: exploring times or situations where the problem isn't such a severe issue.

An example might be Maisie who struggled with working relationships. In supervision her descriptions were always focused on the way in which colleagues treated her. There was little awareness of how her own behaviour might complicate and compound the difficulties.

After a 'stale session' I jotted down some possible directions. Did Maisie have any relationships without these issues, or where it was less severe? Maisie could talk about very productive relationships with clients.

This was positive and was explored further by brainstorming a list of words which described her style with these clients. The clinch question was about whether there was anything different in interactions with clients and peers. By re-framing the situation Maisie began to realise there were some significant differences in how she interacted with peers and clients.

This was the glimmer of possibility, a possible pathway out of the dismal swamp. By working through the description with a coaching supervisor Maisie began to view her style of communication with peers differently. When Maisie looked interested in what was said, listened and commented, or asked questions she had successful relationships. Her anxiety and vulnerability with colleagues in the office was affecting her style of interaction, and colleagues did not find her warm and approachable.

Insight was gained about the contrast between the difficult relationships with peers and positive relationships with her clients. The positive was used to begin changes in the way Maisie worked on relationships with colleagues in the team.

Coaching involves goal setting. A gifted coach will listen, ask questions, and encourage moving forward in terms of goals for self and career development.

Appreciative Coaching in the 4D Style

The NHS Leadership Academy advocates appreciative coaching. The 4D model is used as the basis of coaching. The process begins with *discovery*, where a topic is explored in depth; then *dreaming* where ideas for future directions and creating this positive future are considered; then *design* discussions about any changes in style, behaviours, and who might be supportive in helping reach this position. Then finally *delivery*, where small steps are planned, moving in the direction of the desired changes. What can someone do today, and 'do more of' in order to move towards achieving the dream?

Sometimes a supervisee knows where they want to develop. This might be a service project like the child development centre example below. It might be a personal quality or new clinical skill. If the direction is known then this can be explored using this 4D process.

Sometimes a supervisee arrives at a coaching session with no fixed ideas. They have signed up for coaching with a general feeling that it is time to do something differently but are not sure about direction. This is when a general appreciative coaching conversation with specific questions can be helpful in identifying direction. General appreciative questions don't relate to any specific topic. As the supervisee considers the questions, new ideas for future directions usually emerge – providing the agenda for the next session.

General appreciative questions:

- You at your best – supervisor encourages supervisee to tell a story about a time they were in flow, felt positive, creative, successful, and enthusiastic. How was this a special experience? Who else was involved? Describe the event as a detailed story
- Success factors – what are your values, strengths which give you successful days at work?
- What things do you most value about yourself as a practitioner?
- What do you recognise as your core values?
- Oh for a magic wand, three wishes: what three wishes would you make to improve your job?

Personal Reflection

When I attended a session with Diane Whitney it was inspiring. The focus was on service development and making changes for more effective service delivery. The concept is simple but powerful. One example given was of a multi-professional team at a child development centre (CDC), beleaguered by long waits and splintering of multi-professional working, as each professional service became a silo, focused on its own waiting times. The practitioners in this scenario were tired and clearly not achieving anywhere close to effective service delivery.

The practitioners attended an away day to address the issues and improve things. The facilitator took an appreciative inquiry approach and coached the team through the 4D Cycle. The key difference was that instead of problem solving and putting in strategies to prevent further deterioration the emphasis was on "What do you do well?," "When do you get it right?," "When are things working well?," "How does that look?," "Let's pinpoint the specifics and find out what it is that you need to do more of as a team." In appreciative inquiry the expectation is that if we focus on the positives and do more of what is working then there will be a groundswell of success which will overcome the old negative patterns. In terms of the CDC there was a need for courage to move away from the service model which had evolved over the years and was failing.

In modern service delivery it is no longer possible to put in place a service model which will be unchanged for several years. With changing landscapes, complicated by a pandemic, it is necessary to look at what's needed, what's working locally and nationally in similar settings, and implement something which deals with the needs of clients in the system and those waiting for access. The need is for a responsive, solution-focused approach to waiting lists and ongoing care.

Appreciative coaching is possible for a team or individuals. Here are some examples of the sort of questions which might be used while working through the 4D process.

Exploring the Current Landscape ("Discovery" Stage)

- What's already working well?
- What do you contribute to this working well? What are your special abilities (superpowers) which are making a difference here?
- What is it that makes you feel positive and motivated at work (energised)?
- Tell me about a time when things went really well and you felt you'd made a particularly positive impact on a situation or for a client
- What do you wish you could do more of?

Imaging a Future Where Things Are Going Well ("Dream" Stage)

- What's the biggest dream for yourself? If all the problems and difficulties had miraculously disappeared how would your job look? What if anything were possible and there were no barriers to getting to this position?
- What would X (someone you admire) do to get to this future place? This could be a real person, an admired professional, or someone imaginary such as a superhero
- Pause and consider the future you want to move towards. This is an imagined future
- Consider barriers in the landscape which are preventing change – imagine yourself in a helicopter hovering over the barriers. Can you see anything differently when looking at things from a different position?
- Picture yourself in ten years' time when you are receiving a national award for creating your imagined new future. What might others

notice about you which is different? What qualities stand out? What roles did you play in this story of achieving your dream?

"Design" and Development Stage

This stage is about choosing a specific direction. It's more rooted in reality:

- How would you design this future working life? New service improvement? Dynamic team?
- What do you need to help you develop and focus your ideas, actions, or new personal style?
- Who do you work with who might be supportive?

"Delivery" Stage

- Where do we go from here? Is there any part of this dream which is already happening today?
- What first steps could you take this week/this month/today/tomorrow to actually move towards making it happen?
- How will you know when you've got to where you want to be?

Going through this process with a small-scale project can be a very effective work-based learning project for a practitioner keen to develop leadership skills. A team project shows the importance of analysing a situation, developing ideas for the future, and looking at the practicalities of moving forward and implementing change.

Simply Coaching

In a coaching supervision there is often evaluation at the beginning of the block. This might be a 360-degree feedback questionnaire. I might ask a supervisee to complete an online signature strengths survey and share the results. Talking through strengths in the first session before focusing on goal setting gives a positive boost to the session (Niemiec 2017).

Some coaches will use a Myers-Briggs questionnaire before the first session and then discuss strengths and any desire to change style. Often coaching is about style, but this isn't necessarily the case and a goal-based coaching approach also fits well with competency frameworks, for example, coaching for a newly qualified practitioner completing RCSLT competencies, or an assistant practitioner completing competencies in the Assistant Practitioners' Professional Framework (APPF).

Coaching supervision fits into the developmental function (Procter's model). After evaluation at the first session or online prior to the first meeting there is a conversation about direction and how to use the time available. Coaching supervision is usually time limited, e.g. we will meet six times in the next three months.

When taking a coaching approach I like supervisees to have some sort of tracking paperwork between sessions. The supervisee will have goal-based paperwork and they might keep brief notes, a log, or a series of mind maps.

Coaching can be a very appropriate model to choose in supervision. There would need to be discussion where there is an existing supervisory relationship using a different approach. The supervisor can't just launch into a goal-based approach. There is a change in dynamic when goal setting becomes part of supervision.

Here is a guide about what to cover in a coaching-based supervision session:

The Beginning

There is a 'check-in' finding out what's been happening since last time. This may include "What's gone well? What have you achieved?"

In the very first session there will be some admin around contract and ground rules for working together. I would, at this point, give some information about what usually happens in a session and how it is important to feel at ease. I use words like 'space, place' and 'Thinking Space' (from Nancy Kline).

After this the focus is on deciding the direction of the session. In simple terms "What do you want to think about in supervision today?" There is divergence here from reflective supervision as the focus in a coaching-based session is on a goal and may pick up where the previous session left off.

The supervisee gets an opportunity to think through the direction in more depth while the supervisor listens and begins to grasp the key features of the supervisee's situation.

The Middle

The supervisor guides the conversation into specifics. Perhaps this is a focus on what's going well despite the difficulties. It might be focusing on the problem and exploring the situation and the relationships involved in more depth.

Sometimes it's being curious about what might be possible if a new approach were tried. There might be re-capping and going over the topic again and something different, something overlooked emerges.

The supervisor keeps the conversation going, asks questions to clarify, and offers insights. The aim is to help a supervisee find new direction and give encouragement, guidance, and appreciation. A coach can give examples of something, e.g. a story from their own practice which relates to the topic.

This is coaching though, and the nudge is gently towards a practical goal plan linked to the topic.

Closing

Usually in a coaching session there is some practical action for the supervisee. Often the goal I set is around simply noticing things and experimenting with a different style. This sounds simple, but it is actually one of the hardest things we do.

The key difference with other approaches is that there is often reference to ongoing goals and new mini goals may be set at the end of each session. There is probably some evaluation about whether there is anything to do differently in the next session.

Then it is booking the next session. If it's the last session in a block then there is probably reflection on the block, what's been covered, and celebration of learning points.

Goals and Goal Setting

Goals and goal setting are part of coaching-based supervision. There is lots of information available about SMART goals. I struggle a little as I feel I am using a similar template for colleagues as that used for clinical goal setting. Nevertheless, advocacy of SMART goals is strong and it is appropriate. I tend to talk in terms of RAW goals: realistic, achievable, and worthwhile. The wording is more appreciative with a description of the desired outcome rather than a strict "if this happens then this will be the outcome and it will be achieved in this timescale and demonstrated by this change."

Here is SMARTish goal setting:

SMARTEN UP – What ... How ... When?

- Specific
- Measurable
- Achievable and appealing
- Realistic
- Timed
- Enthusiastic
- Natural
- Understood
- Prepared

Taken from Purdie *Life Coaching for Dummies* (2010)

I recommend Stephen Covey's (1989) approach to goal setting. Much information on goals is dull, but Covey has a roles with goals approach. The use of a weekly planner integrates goals into everyday life.

Personal Reflection

When taking a module on my master's programme the other students came from wide ranging backgrounds. There was a manager of a children's hospice, a police officer working with families, a senior nurse from a kidney dialysis unit, a modern matron in maternity services, and the manager of a hospital portering service. We were focusing on self-development through reflective practice and were guided through Stephen Covey's work on roles and goals. The discussion was about identifying the differing goals in our lives – parent, child, professional, trainer/teacher, gardener, five-a-side football player. This was not just about roles at work but a holistic life approach. Then we considered each role and what we hoped to achieve in that role in the next year.

I look back on that room in Leeds on a late autumn day and see it clearly now, because it became unexpectedly emotional. Two men in the group shared how they realised they did not put the same amount of thought and energy into home roles that they did into work roles.

The time for family was often squeezed as demands at work took priority. There followed a productive discussion in pairs about roles and new goals to go with these roles. It is a very simple tool but putting the roles and goals down on paper led to quite a rollercoaster of an emotional session.

After that Leeds day I used Covey's weekly planner with work and home goals together, e.g. preparation for a project meeting, complete five reports plus buying a birthday present or looking at holiday ideas online. This isn't for everyone, as some people choose to keep work and home very separate. For me, it helped to plan this way to re-build a work-home life balance. I no longer use the Covey planning template, but I still think in terms of roles and goals. I've gone back to it at times when work was 'taking over' home life again.

It's possible to divide up our roles at work in this way too. You might be a clinician, a pathway co-ordinator, a safeguarding champion, a supervisor, and so on. You might be a learner, building your skills in a new clinical area, or embedding some training on video interaction into your clinical work. When considering goals at work it can be helpful to spill all these roles onto paper (and there will be more than you expected) and jot down ideas about what you hope to achieve in each role in the months ahead. It might be as simple as making sure you book meetings with your supervisee and ensure there is a room available for those dates/times. It might be around re-designing team meetings so they are more productive. It doesn't matter, the model fits with all roles. Covey devised this approach as part of his *7 Habits of Highly Successful People* (1989) and by using a wider role-based goal approach we are more likely to move forward in all aspects of our job role.

Covey's eight characteristics of successful, principle-centred supervisors:

1. Continually learning (we never stop learning)
2. Service oriented (the service is the purpose of days at work)
3. Radiate positive energy (and probably hide on the days when it is dark and dismal)
4. Believe in other people (and this can be hard work at times)
5. Lead balanced lives (and work hard on this)

> 6. See life as an adventure (work isn't boring either)
> 7. Seek synergy (know how to bring things together and forge partnerships)
> 8. Know about self-renewal (looking after ourselves)
>
> *Principle Centred Leadership* (Covey 1999)

In goal setting it is crucial to believe and trust that supervisees are motivated and want to progress. Once the direction (goal area) has been set then goal planning begins. Often the goal is strengthening a quality or skill like time management, reflective practice, assertiveness, stress management, or leading meetings.

When having conversations about setting a goal it is important to consider evaluation. The supervisor will give feedback, but this is not a grading progress. When setting the goal have a clear idea of what success looks like. The win-win is encouraging a supervisee to evaluate their own progress in the goal.

> **When goal setting for self-development Covey (1999) gives a five-step process:**
>
> - Knowing the desired result/destination – what will success look like?
> - Discussing who needs to be involved – can the supervisee proceed on their own initiative?
> - Clarify assumptions – so it's clear what is possible
> - Time available – checking it is practically possible
> - Reporting back about progress – set a time and place

We can lose sight of goals in everyday work, and so it is important they are realistic and embedded into daily routine. How goals are recorded is an individual decision. It is often a chart with a place to record the goal and plan for achieving it. Sometimes there is a need for detailed steps or sub goals, and timescale. It can be helpful to jot down the positive factors available to boost success and any barriers which might slow down progress.

A coach needs positive expectations (high hopes) about success. Positive expectations are powerful, and with confidence in their abilities supervisees often stretch to extend capability.

The supervisor will be being curious, communicating with empathy, and fostering an environment with creativity, trust, and communication about hopes and dreams or the future.

184

One of Covey's most useful concepts is 'sharpening the saw' by learning and developing. It is impossible to cut wood with a blunt saw. We can keep trying but it takes a long time and we don't get very far. But by putting effort into sharpening the saw, by engaging in supervision and continual professional development, we keep sharp and agile in our professional thinking.

Goals cannot always be achieved speedily, so it is important to celebrate milestones along the way, anticipate setbacks en route, and accept *"that gridlock and deadlock aren't disastrous, if you think of keys to unlock them."* The key is described succinctly by Ann McGee-Cooper (1994): *"Celebrate any progress. Don't wait to get perfect."*

Utilising a coaching approach to supervision gives structure and goals are more likely to be achieved if a supervisee has a planned, organised route to success. Carefully crafted goals support professional and career development. In the words of Covey this is *"because the process plumbs the depths of the individual brilliance and talents of people."*

Mentoring

Mentoring is a supportive relationship which exists to develop people either within their current role or looking to the future.

What is the skillset of a good mentor? One of the larger NHS Mentoring Hubs in the Northwest region pinpoints this as:

- Having an interest in your own learning and development (back to sharpening the saw again)
- Being a good listener
- Being critically reflective on own practice
- Being curious

The difference between coaching and mentoring isn't always clear. In coaching there is focus on the specifics of the job or personal style (communication, action tendencies, and attitude). In mentoring there is more of an overall career focus, looking beyond current job to career progression.

A mentor is someone who is sharing knowledge, skills, and experience to facilitate development. A coach provides support for job goals. In the mentoring literature there is a focus on broadening horizons and how we need to change our style to progress to new and different roles.

There is a progressive structure to mentoring.

Once the mentoring relationship is agreed there are usually four phases:

- Preparation
- Negotiating
- Enabling growth and development
- Closure

These phases are sequential, building on each other, and can vary in length. As with coaching there are timescales – mentoring is not usually long term. It might be for six months or a year but is not an open-ended arrangement.

Clutterbuck (2004) suggested ten mentoring competencies:

- Self-awareness
- Communicating
- Interest in developing others
- Goal clarity
- Sense of proportion/humour
- Understanding others
- Conceptualising
- Professional/business savvy
- Committed to own learning
- Relationship management

This list is a good list of qualities for anyone supporting and developing others, whether that is through clinical supervision, coaching, or mentoring. I like the sense of proportion/humour and know that is a critically relevant skill for all types of support. Reaching right back into literature and Jane Austen in *Pride and Prejudice* (1813), there is something very important about being able to laugh at ourselves and not take everything too seriously in our working lives. I reflect here about why I bring Jane Austen into this and realise it is because her work is about people, their relationships, and their interactive styles with others. The dialogue is frequently conversational discussion between two characters about dilemmas and difficulties followed by episodes of reflective thinking and writing. It seems Austen was an acutely reflective practitioner!

The other skill highlighted by Clutterbuck is a little different and is professional and business savvy, which is especially important in independent practice or NHS commissioning. Perhaps most important is to have an interest in developing others. There are supervisors who have been told to supervise someone because it is part of the expectation in their grading. I know of no evidence, but I think we all know intuitively if our supervisor is interested in our work and what we are saying. If you know your supervisor is disinterested there may be little which you can do about it if that supervisor has been allocated to you and you have little choice; but in that situation, I'd advise you focus on extending your wider supportive network and quietly working for a change in supervisor.

This leads into Hay's (1997) focus on different styles in mentoring. Again, this fits for clinical supervision too.

Hay's mentoring styles are:

- Controlling
- Nurturing
- Logical
- Adaptable
- Spontaneous

Hay points out that the best mentors have *"all 5 styles in good working order."* Our thinking style influences our approach to problem solving and decision making. At first glance there might be some apparent contradictions. Why would we want a controlling mentor? Wouldn't a nurturing mentor be stifling? But, if we consider a typical session, we want someone with warmth, who encourages us; we want someone who will take back control of a session if it is drifting; we need someone who can adeptly move from discussing a complex case to an issue we are having around completing our discharge admin. We need someone who can spontaneously think on their feet and give us guidance when we are struggling, but we also need logical thinking around risk in our caseworking. Phew, I hope that this illustrates the need for a range of different personal qualities in a successful supervisor/mentor/coach.

For those who work in children's services this is beginning to resemble the styles of parents interacting with children in the Hanen approach (The Hanen Centre). Hay also identifies five working styles and suggests most are strong in one or two of these.

Hay's Five Working Styles

- Hurry up
- Be perfect
- Please people
- Try hard
- Be strong

So, reflect for a second or two about your own style in Hay's simple framework and see what you recognise. Are you bogged down in perfectionist detail? Are you always rushing around? Are you resistant to saying what you really think as it might make a relationship with a colleague difficult? Viewing ourselves within this type of framework can be a helpful aid for reflective thinking.

Personal Reflection

I had a moment while writing this book, which was one of those uncomfortable reflective realisations. For many years I have seen myself as not having perfectionist tendencies. I am one of those clinicians who does what's needed and doesn't get bogged down in the detail. That's true. Yet when reading again about decision making and accompanying dilemmas, I realised that in some ways I am a perfectionist. I spend hours choosing holiday venues and apply endless criteria in this decision-making process, a tranquil place, a certain sort of breakfast, plain walls in muted shades with no patterned wallpaper, plenty of windows to let in light. When I read about this very thing as an example of perfectionist decision making it struck a chord. I was very resistant to the suggestion that when making such decisions we should choose one criterion only, the most important criterion, and make that the basis of our decision. My reaction about taking one criterion of garden view and so having small windows and garish wallpaper was interesting. I clearly am a perfectionist regarding my holiday choices.

Mentoring widens our horizons and is an alliance with a more experienced colleague which looks to the future. It is usually outside of the team and may be someone from another organisation. During conversations the mentor uses reflective tools but tends to share their own relevant experience.

Coaching is closer to the 'here and now' with change through specific goal planning. There is, of course, overlap. Life coaching seems closer to mentoring than job-based coaching in taking a holistic perspective, looking at balance, hopes, and how to move towards a different future.

 REFLECTIVE LEARNING

Exception Questions

This is a slightly different type of question, enquiring about any times or situations when the issue being considered isn't such a problem. These can be incredibly useful in supervision. You are searching for glimmers/golden nuggets to highlight and help plan. Try asking an exception question.

Appreciative Coaching Questions

Look through the generic appreciative coaching questions and try some out. Write your own versions.

Try out one of the questions in relation to yourself, e.g. *oh for a magic wand and three wishes: what three wishes would I make to improve my job?*

SMARTEN UP a Goal

Have a go at writing a goal using the SMARTEN UP cues.

4D Coaching Trauma

Look through the 4D appreciative coaching questions. Choose the ones you are most likely to put in your Supervision Toolkit.

CAMEO – COACHING COMES INTO SUPERVISION

Beckie had been establishing herself as an experienced clinician in her team. She was looking to apply for a highly specialist post within the next two years. She felt that colleagues perhaps still looked at her as the

189

'newbie' as it was a team with very little staff turnover. In supervision it emerged that she wanted to change perceptions of herself, so she was seen as an emerging specialist and not an early career therapist.

Her supervisor used solution-focused questioning to clarify how she hoped the future would look. How would people see her? How would a new student coming on placement see her in comparison to others in the team? What would be different? What did she need to do to make this happen?

Then the supervisor brought in a coaching approach with clear goal setting. The first goal was around developing a small area where Beckie could show enthusiasm and gain a higher level of specialist expertise. Beckie knew that there was a lack of enthusiasm, knowledge, and skills in technology in therapy and this was one of her interests. The supervisor used expressions like 'changing how colleagues perceived her' and 'upping her profile in the team.' Beckie had ideas about how she could share information, produce resources, and potentially offer to present a case where technology had made a difference.

Beckie was ready to move forward in her career. The coaching and goal setting described here could have been with a manager, a clinical supervisor, or a coach external to the team. It worked well as part of clinical supervision.

15 | Top Themes in SLT Supervision

"Well! I've often seen a cat without a grin, but a grin without a cat! It's the most curious thing I've ever seen in all my life!"

Alice, *Alice's Adventures in Wonderland*

Key Themes

- Most common topics that occur in supervision
- Thinking contextually

What Are the Common Themes?

This is a chapter drawn from practitioner experience and the limited literature around themes in supervision. If we ask practitioners to write a list of what they find stressful, which situations they mull over afterwards, there are clear themes. It is often not about what to do next with a client. If we have a clinical dilemma, we tend to seek out advice quite quickly. We might save up clinical queries to check out at our next supervision or puzzle out why something isn't going to plan, but we are unlikely to wait if we are struggling clinically. I've never read any research on this, but I truly believe that as a professional group we are actually very good at giving each other quick advice in ad hoc conversation in the office.

It's easier if you have colleagues around you to tap for ideas and offload quickly. If you work in an isolated role in a school or as sole practitioner in an independent practice then it is necessary to seek email support and teleconferencing. In my supervisory practice I offer packages including scheduled meetings plus email support between supervisions, and the reason I do this

DOI: 10.4324/9781003226772-16

is because I feel that an isolated clinician misses out on accessing this quick advice. It is critically important as part of offloading mental grime.

> **When supervisors compare notes on themes in supervision these topics inevitably arise:**
>
> - Juggling (workload)
> - Balance in caseworking
> - Time and energy
> - Giving more/overextending till there is no time left
> - Navigating difficult relationships at work
> - Case management in complex scenarios
> - Dissatisfaction between expectations and reality of provision.
> - Individual needs requiring divergence from a care pathway
> - Working environment and power
> - Feeling inadequate and worrying what others think

Little needs to be written to describe these top topics. Whatever our clinical specialist area these are themes across the profession. Most practitioners, whatever their grade or role, will be juggling workload or 'prioritising priorities' every week. As an NHS manager I knew when I looked at the submission linked to the waiting list at the end of each week, that some of the team had worked longer hours than they should on phone calls and other duties and left the data inputting for the following week. I would be under pressure around this, but it is easy to understand that as practitioners we tend to put people first. However, the fact remains that many AHPs (I know from experience OTs and physiotherapists are no different) struggle with paperwork, including writing timely reports and completing discharge processes. Traditionally in speech and language therapy the reviews would slip back a month. With modern care pathways it might be something else which is impacted to give headroom.

The first four items on the list have common roots and are topics which should be explored in supervision. It's important to reflect on our style and our action tendencies at work. I was never the therapist who could complete my travel expenses every day, but I know some colleagues found that very easy. However, with determination I found ways of organising my time so that the pressures of paperwork piling up could be considerably reduced. I'm one of those people who works better in blocks of time. I'm more effective writing several reports together. I also learnt to work with my energy patterns, and I might wish I was an early bird but I'm not. Strangely I work better between 12 noon and 3 pm – I don't know a name for this. Once I worked out energy and time management patterns, I learnt to cope effectively balancing clinical and management roles.

Giving a client more, sometimes called overproducing or overextending, is something which is a strong theme for independent practitioners. Many do not cover all their overheads in their pricing (e.g. pension, insurance, videoconferencing). Some are too accessible, especially since the pandemic changed working practices and messages from clients might arrive on a Sunday afternoon. It can be a challenge not to respond. When businesses were struggling during the pandemic many were undercharging, giving more than the contract with the family covered. A conversation with a nursery worker might last longer than the allocated ten minutes; an additional report or conversation with a paediatrician is needed. Few clinicians work to an exact 'billable hours' model yet feel frustrated that they continue to provide more than was initially anticipated. Sometimes in independent practice there is an element of supervision around professional business dilemmas.

My own approach to training in supervision considers situational supervision. We are looking at a multi-faceted situation. It might be clinical; it might be around relationships with carers or other professionals involved with the case. We might be aware of dissatisfaction with what we can offer and expectations. We are looking at a complex 3D situation. We are also considering our own role in events and whether what we do is influencing things and whether we should change anything. Speech and language therapy is a relationship-driven profession. So, with the many relationships which we develop and extend in our working lives there is going to be some occasional friction.

Case management in complex scenarios is always a top topic. These are cases which benefit from time spent standing aside and reviewing the decisions, events, relationships. We bring a case to supervision which has a complex background; probably those 3D relationship factors.

One of the wonderful things about our profession is that we work embedded in an evidence base, but no two cases are ever quite the same. Even two children with similar moderate phonological impairment in the early years will have different personalities, different levels of family support, or different concerns in nursery. Their response to therapy can be vastly different, and this is why however many care pathways we devise as clinical leaders there will always be a need for decision making at each step of the pathway.

Considering Cultural Context

Awareness of cultural context is a topic always present in supervisory conversations. Kenneth Hardy and Toby Bobes (2017) use the term 'thinking contextually' for the process of developing deeper understanding of ourselves and others. Thinking contextually *"enables us to view multi-layered realities, perspectives and experiences that are overlapping and interconnecting."* Conversations about cultural context should look beyond the immediate situation and consider the complex multiple influences which impact on any situation.

The need is to shift from considering an individual to that individual within a wider context. A key theme of this book is to consider the wider context in situational supervision.

It is strongly suggested in the literature that it is the responsibility of the supervisor to create the safe space and offer an 'invitation to talk' about cultural context with willingness and interest in engaging in conversations, if the supervisee chooses to (Connie Jones & Laura Welfare et al. 2019). The suggestion is that a supervisor mentions this commitment to cultural inquisitiveness as the relationship begins, expressing hope there will be an opportunity to learn and understand about each other's cultural backgrounds, with awareness that their experiences and perspectives will be different. Supervisors need to introduce conversations about cultural identities *"because supervisees, particularly supervisees from marginalized or minoritized identities, may understandably be reluctant to do so."* The supervisory relationship can be strengthened when a culturally competent supervisor introduces conversation about cultural identities (Haskins et al. 2013; White-Davis et al. 2016; Ancis & Marshall 2010; Inman 2006).

Hardy and Bobes use the terms *culturally* and *contextually* interchangeably when referring to *"the role contextual variables play throughout our lived experiences"*: how we see ourselves, how we see others, and how they perceive us. They give a list of *"domains of interest"* to facilitate contextual thinking for supervisors to use and bring cultural sensitivity right into the core of their work.

Reflective supervision is about viewing situations differently, with changed perception, considering our own role in situations and empathising with the perspectives of others. The supervisor guides the conversation into considering different stories about the same events.

The suggested domains of interest (and the list is not exhaustive) to promote contextual and cultural thinking include ethnicity, class, gender, race, religion, sexual orientation, nationality, age, ability, and regionality.

Hardy and Bobes feel that contextual thinking *"is optimally achieved when this list, these variables are comprehensively considered, especially in relation to each other. The domains of interest can be shared and visible to give a prompting structure for considering cultural contexts."*

Guiding a reflective conversation towards *"cultural similarities and differences with genuine, respectful inquisitiveness is an important supervisory skill."* Day-Vines and colleagues (2013) suggest the term 'broaching' for this. Jones and Welfare provide suggestions around wording when 'broaching.' They stress their prompts are not prescriptive and just suggestions for inviting conversation.

An example of broaching:

> *One of my favorite things about my work is that I am always learning new things about myself and others. I think of every relationship as intercultural. Let's watch for opportunities to talk about our own identities in our supervision, okay?*

Supervisors can easily adapt the different reflective models (Chapters 6 and 7) to include opportunities for exploring cultural context. Considering context fits in the cultural conversational cell of the Triangle (Hewson), and in Gibbs' model during step 2 talking about thoughts and feelings. In Boud et al.'s (1985) loops model, context can be considered both as part of reflective processing and also in outcomes when looping back to the experience and re-evaluating aspects and seeking new perspectives.

When guiding a conversation using these models there is opportunity for cultural consideration in the reflective processing and learning/actions steps. Johns' model could easily integrate context-related questions. Phase 5 can be extended to include:

How has this experience changed my knowledge in the following ways – cultural context.

Also

How am I more able to realise desirable practice in terms of considering cultural context?

Consideration of cultural context might be about the practitioner's cultural 'lived experience' and how factors relating to this might be relevant in this situation. It might also be linked to the cultural context of a client and their family's experience and access to therapy. Cultural context needs consideration with practitioners being curious, for example, about how the cultural context might affect communication, engagement, and choice/preference of strategies in a case.

There can be discomfort in discussing cultural context and a supervisee may choose not to talk about this. The essential thing is for the supervisor to broach context and signify their own cultural curiosity and the hope that there will be insights and learning points in the supervisory journey. As practitioners we are gradually feeling more confident about broaching and exploring cultural contexts.

Other Top Topics

I've added another top topic in the last few years, and this is when an individual's needs diverge from a set care pathway. In my last NHS Trust each clinical leader developed an evidence-based care pathway. Care pathways vary, but in my organisation, practitioners could diverge from the pathway with justification. It can be helpful to take these cases to clinical supervision to re-cap dilemmas and decision making and build confidence.

I'd also strongly advocate there is more conversation about positive cases where things have gone well. This is underused in supervision and come to think of it, I need to suggest this more in my supervision groups. Let's feel positive about our practice sometimes.

We move on now to feeling inadequate, with low levels of clinical self-esteem and worrying what others think of us. Last year I attended an Acceptance and Commitment Therapy (ACT) course. The idea of ACT was something I'd struggled with in the context of therapy for adult fluency. I utilised mindful thinking, but not ACT. The course was helpful in re-framing my thinking about this approach.

It's useful for accepting that sometimes we are unable to change things. We can't always change how people view us. Sometimes other people might think we are not the amazing therapist we would like to be, but we know we are doing as good a job as we can and investing in our own development, by engaging in appreciative, reflective supervision. We can accept how we feel, be kind to ourselves, and not dwell overly on what we can't change or change quickly. When self-esteem is low, then thinking 'what would a good friend say to me about this' is helpful. A friend would often be kinder to us than we are to ourselves.

The working environment can be a significant topic. When you have a good working environment then it doesn't factor into supervision. When it is a problem then it can become a problem which drains and pre-occupies thoughts.

And finally, power. This is never to be underestimated. A supervisory relationship is uneven in power. When we work in a team some people have more power than others. Some guard and use their power strategically. Sometimes in a team it isn't the obvious person in charge who holds the power. In terms of case scenarios there can be carers/colleagues who have power and influence over whether the therapy is successful. The important thing is to be aware of the importance of personal power and influence; often something connected to power underpins a difficult situation.

The top topics in supervision change over time. As mentioned above, when we work in a setting where it is impossible to book rooms for therapy or for quiet meetings then it is a significant barrier to successful service delivery. When the accommodation is good then this doesn't feature. Topics can vary, but coping with the demands of caseworking, unusual situations, and tricky relationships always features. When we are deciding what to take to supervision we should identify anything which 'keeps us awake at night.' Well, there really ought not to be anything about work which gives us insomnia, and so I'd prefer to word this as 'those things which stay with us after the session or conversation.' Something is puzzling, a little different, and the way forward causes us to think outside of our usual professional autopilot.

 REFLECTIVE LEARNING

Reflect on your own top topics which you take to supervision. Are there themes? Have these themes changed over time?

If you are a supervisor do the themes in this section 'ring true' for you? Anything to add?

Power

It's always interesting to watch and notice who 'holds the power' and 'who is reluctant to give up any power.' Power is usually there; we're just usually too busy to notice it.

Positive Perspectives

None of us tend to take positive scenarios to supervision. Even HCPC suggests we do that more. Consider what positive achievements might be topics to take to supervision.

CAMEO – TOO MUCH TO DO, TOO LITTLE TIME

Kaitlin worked part time as a highly specialist therapist. The team was continually under pressure taking on new clients, and her admin backlog was building up. Kaitlin always needed to leave exactly on time due to home commitments. She kept thinking there would be time to catch up with admin the following week and there never was. Now she had a week's leave rapidly approaching and the idea of time away from work was making the stress much worse. She felt she had to complete everything before her leave. To make matters worse a parent had rung up and asked to speak to her manager, Claire, and enquire about how much longer she would need to wait for a report (the assessment had been four weeks ago). It was beginning to feel like a 'stress mess.' Kaitlin had always liked her job and prided herself on meeting professional deadlines. She had always been the one who had a calm approach, and colleagues came to her for support. Now she just didn't want to come in the door on her days in work. She'd felt like snapping at a colleague that morning and looking back there had been no need to be so irritated.

Claire had listened to the parent and needed to feedback the conversation and what she had agreed with Kaitlin. She had already noticed that Kaitlin seemed low and stressed when she was in the office. She suspected it wasn't going to be an easy conversation. Claire also remembered that the two last times Kaitlin had taken a holiday there was the same pattern of stress building up and overspilling into irritable interactions with colleagues. Her colleagues knew what was happening and empathised; they were worried about her.

The de-briefing conversation was indeed difficult. Kaitlin was initially defensive and then burst into tears. Claire knew this was where her training on restorative reflective supervision was relevant and just listened and commented. When Kaitlin was calmer and could listen Claire gently broached how this was something she had noticed before as Kaitlin prepared for leave. Claire felt this was not a case of burnout, but a specific situation linked to leave.

From the conversation it emerged that Kaitlin had in the past used a couple of late evenings a week and the half term holidays for report writing. She wasn't someone who could just sit down and write a report and preferred to have a block of time when she could work through reports. This had worked well for her previously, but now she had no flexibility for working later and needed to take leave when it was half term. Her headroom for admin had totally disappeared.

So how to move forward? It wasn't appropriate for a conversation that day, but Claire knew that a different structure to Kaitlin's working month might help. If Kaitlin needed focused time to write reports, then an admin 'mini-block' could be scheduled in. Kaitlin had also disclosed that she found her colleagues' positivity about half term and potential catch up on paperwork 'jarring' and that wasn't fair on colleagues but had made her feel snappier.

Claire had a dual role as manager and supervisor and planned to talk about whether a different person as clinical supervisor might work better. In fact, this didn't happen. Perhaps because at this point Kaitlin could not face scheduling in another meeting with another person. Kaitlin's stress levels did reduce once she re-structured her time at work to allow for report writing and received restorative resilient supervision sessions. Kaitlin had the flexibility to organise her own diary, and of course this isn't always possible.

<table>
<tr><td>

16

</td><td>

Supervisors Giving
SUPER-VISION

</td></tr>
</table>

"When you can't look on the bright side, I will sit with you in the dark."
Hatter, *Alice's Adventures in Wonderland*

Key Themes

- Becoming a supervisor
- What makes a good supervisor?

Learning to Be a Supervisor

At some point someone suggests a practitioner might like to be a clinical supervisor. Our first experience in supporting others in their development is probably as a placement educator. It is when we begin to supervise colleagues that structured clinical supervision begins. It can be an exciting prospect as it reinforces that we are seen as experienced and capable of being a supervisor. It would be positive if, at this point, some training around the supervision process was offered. The reality is there may not even be supervision for supervisors. The training accessed by most new clinical supervisors is probably around student education. There is overlap, but the emphasis for students is on educative function and direct feedback. This isn't the model advocated for supporting colleagues.

We often learn from our own supervisors. We notice styles and know our preferences and in the early days probably copy 'good supervisors.' We do all have experience as supervisees! We focus on what we need to be a supervisor, but Ghaye and Lillyman (2007) pointed out the crucial importance of learning to be a good supervisee. Indeed, the first training I facilitated for a

DOI: 10.4324/9781003226772-17

team was about reflective clinical supervision with emphasis on being a good supervisee.

With supervisees who have been trained in supervision and know what to expect and how to prepare and engage in a reflective conversation, taking on the role of the supervisor is much easier.

It is hoped that at some point there will be some training on supervision, e.g. an internal or external course. If it is difficult to locate a course then often Safeguarding Supervision training, which is more widely available, covers the basics of the interpersonal skills, like active listening, challenging, summarising, and supporting reflection.

So, what makes a good supervisor? There is an activity often included in speech and language therapy training courses about what makes a bad conversation. Participants role play sabotaging a conversation by interrupting, looking away, talking away from the topic, and fidgeting a lot. It is powerful in reinforcing the features of bad and good conversations. It is helpful to spend a few minutes considering the same in terms of supervision. What makes a bad supervision session? You are likely to have no difficulty coming up with a list of words to describe this. When we recall a bad experience of supervision it gives clear pointers about what **NOT** to do. I am used to being positive and wondering whether to choose a different word here, but some supervisors really are in the wrong role and are just not very skilled.

Characteristics of Effective Supervisors

There is broad agreement about the qualities needed in a good supervisor. Figure 16.1 shows an adaptation of Clutterbuck and Lane's (2004) view of the skills required. The following list is drawn from several sources where supervisees in healthcare professions were asked what they valued most in a supervisor. In speech and language therapy Helen Catherine Mataiti (2008) identified it was more about interpersonal knowledge and skills, personal values, and attitudes and less about clinical skills and capability.

Most Important Values in a Supervisor

- Mutual trust and respect
- Ability to form supportive relationships
- Having relevant knowledge and competencies
- Being committed to providing supervision
- Having good listening skills
- Interpersonal knowledge and skills

- Personal values
- Positive personal characteristics
- Making a supervisee feel safe and supported
- Respecting confidentiality
- Flexible, bringing in different approaches as appropriate
- Experienced in conflict resolution
- Still interested in learning

Interestingly, there was no significant difference between those characteristics valued by experienced and less experienced practitioners. The common denominator across studies is that basic trust needs to be in place for an effective supervisory relationship.

Encouragingly Mataiti's findings also suggest that whatever their level of experience all practitioners were still learners. She goes on to say that *"this means clinicians across all different levels of experience require support from clinical supervisors, to learn reflectively from experiences in the workplace."* The study showed that qualities linked to professional knowledge and identity were actually least valued. A supervisor's interpersonal insight, skills, and personal characteristics were much more valued than their clinical competence, professional knowledge, and identity.

Oratio et al. (1981) found that interpersonal skills, respect, and empathy were most important for effective supervision. Tang (2005) found the greatest differences between effective and ineffective supervisors related to interpersonal relationship and personality characteristics.

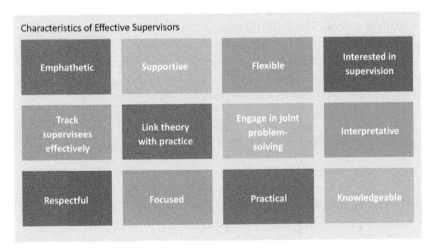

Figure 16.1

Sloan (1999) found that, when rating a good supervisor, community health nurses valued *"the ability to develop supportive relationships (encouraging trust, empathy and mutual regard) and to provide an environment where the supervisee felt comfortable enough to discuss limitations."* Much more importance was placed on personal qualities and interpersonal competence *"over and above any specific qualification."*

There is a pattern of agreement across all these studies that when a safe, respectful environment is in place, supervision is likely to be most effective. Goodyear et al. (2007) found that the relationship was paramount and that in a positive environment practitioners are more likely to feel able to discuss their errors or mistakes. Edwards et al. (2005), suggested *"supervisees were more able to discuss confidential or sensitive issues when they had high levels of support, trust and rapport with their supervisor, particularly when clinical supervision took place away from the workplace."*

So, although there are still very few studies, it is clear that it is the relationship which is valued most highly as the foundation for growth and development in supervision. When there is a positive relationship and a safe space to talk then more effective supervision occurs.

Mataiti concludes that practising clinicians need clinical supervision that *"is less related to professional practice issues and more focussed on individual wellbeing and supporting experiences in the workplace. As such, practising clinicians' restorative needs must be taken care of before clinical issues are addressed"* (see Chapter 12).

Sloan investigated perceptions of good supervisors using thematic content analysis and concluded that *"supervisees viewed their supervisor as a role model, someone who they felt inspired them, whom they looked up to and had a high regard for their clinical practice and knowledge base."* The supervisor also needed the ability to form supportive relationships and to have good listening skills. Expressing commitment to and enthusiasm about supervision was also important. Having a supervisor who was an expert in the field added to credibility, but this was secondary to trust.

A good supervisor will encourage a practitioner to think through situations and devise solutions through discussion. Supervision is a learning process which gives a safe space to consider options and make decisions with support. As has been highlighted previously a key factor in all studies was a relationship based on mutual trust and respect.

HCPC suggests that supervisees might be *"offered a choice of supervisor with regard to personal match, cultural needs and expertise."* A supervisor should be competent in supervision, as well as diversity issues, the supervisory relationship, evaluation, feedback, and ethical, legal, and regulatory matters.

 **REFLECTIVE LEARNING**

Effective Supervisors

- What do you find helpful or unhelpful in a supervisor (from the perspective of supervisor or supervisee)?
- What makes an effective clinical supervisor (for you)?

What Makes a Super Supervisor?

- Who is the best supervisor you have had?
- Who was the worst supervisor you have had?
- What qualities make the difference between the best and worse supervisors?

Strengthening Skills as a Supervisor

How can you be a more effective supervisor? We can all improve … so what would you need to strengthen to be as effective as you can be in the role?

CAMEO – IMPORTANCE OF TRUST

Andrea thought her supervisor Courtney was good. She found the sessions valuable and always left the session feeling more energised and positive. Courtney was supportive but challenged her thinking. Recently she had been involved in a very complex case with joint working across professions. Andrea thought this had been difficult but was proud of her achievements. She had been assertive with a clinical psychology colleague who had initially challenged her advice, but after talking with Andrea had understood her treatment approach, so despite her anxieties around standing her ground clinically there had been a positive resolution. Andrea and the clinical psychologist were planning a joint meeting with the client and family.

However Andrea was stunned when her manager mentioned this situation to her and asked if she needed any further support in liaising with clinical psychology. She was a clinician who didn't tend to discuss her cases in the office. She tended to save up her queries and take these to supervision. There was nothing in this case which had been discussed in the office or with a colleague. The only person with whom she had discussed it was Courtney, her supervisor. The likelihood was that Courtney must have mentioned this case to Andrea's line manager. The supervision contract specified that discussions were confidential unless there was a legal or safeguarding issue. Yet the only explanation which Andrea could think of was a break in trust. For her trust in her supervisor was critically important. She really didn't need this stress. Should she speak to her supervisor and check whether there had been some conversation between her supervisor and manager? Or simply ask for a change in supervisor without mentioning why?

In the end Andrea did raise this with her supervisor. Courtney was thoughtful and said that she had spoken with Andrea's manager in the last month. She had complimented Andrea without using names or identifying information about her management of her difficult case. Andrea had not asked her manager how she knew about the case as she had been shocked. It turned out that after the supervisor had complimented Andrea to her manager, her manager had worked out which case this was and was trying to be helpful. There were learning points for everyone involved in this scenario.

Sharing Perspectives, Group Supervision

"It's always teatime."

Cheshire Cat, *Alice's Adventures in Wonderland*

Key Themes

- The basics
- Group structure and dynamics
- Potential issues
- Ground rules
- Functions of group supervision – Proctor
- Online groups
- Peer supervision and inter-professional supervision
- Reflective group supervision

Group Supervision, the Basics

Individual clinical supervision is normally the default offer. From being newly qualified in their first job practitioners are used to having one-to-one supervision with an experienced clinician. The availability of group options varies but the increase in videoconferencing has made group supervision more accessible.

There are several types of supportive group. Action Learning Sets and Quality Circles follow a set process, often driving forward a service improvement. Peer case review or case support groups are 'advice shops' where SLTs take a case and colleagues give suggestions.

DOI: 10.4324/9781003226772-18

A clinical supervision group is something else entirely. This is a safe space, created jointly by the facilitator and supervisees in the group. There is an agreed structure through which the group navigates each time. Rebecca Goldberg (2015) gives an excellent description when she says *"an integral factor of effective group supervision is having a cohesive group of supervisees who are willing to work collaboratively together to craft a dynamic, interpersonal supervision experience in which all participating parties benefit from the interaction."* There is in-depth discussion of professional situations presented by supervisees, usually where there are some dilemmas about direction/decision making or things feel stuck. After listening to the clinical story the group uses a framework such as reflective conversation or solution-focused inquiry to explore the case together and give their insights to the supervisee.

The 'go to' reference for group clinical supervision is Proctor's *Group Supervision: A Guide to Creative Practice* (2008). Shohet and Shohet (2020) have even removed a chapter on group supervision from their book and instead signpost readers to Proctor. Proctor is worth visiting if you have an enthusiasm for group supervision. It is in depth, written from a counselling perspective, whereas sometimes what we need is readily accessible information. This chapter contains key points in relation to supervision groups in speech and language therapy. This includes some information highlighting both positives and challenges of a group approach.

Goldberg (2015) writes that group supervision provides supervisees with *"numerous perspectives to consider when engaging in case conceptualization."* It is possible that direct advice might be given occasionally, e.g. yes you really do need to ensure there is a referral to a paediatrician, specialist in adult neurology, local mental health team, etc. However advice giving should be exceptional and not routine, whereas in a case review group the onus would be to give advice.

Group Structure

There is usually a group facilitator/supervisor who guides the group through setting the agenda and moving through the items on the agenda, summarising discussions, highlighting transition points, and drawing the group to a close. In some groups one person is always the facilitator, in others the role rotates between members.

When a new group forms there needs to be time for supervisees to get to know each other. Often everyone gives a short presentation. Suggest each member contributes something which will help everyone to remember them, e.g. a clinical story in which they are at their most interesting as a practitioner. If this is a new group, where members do not know each other, then the task of the facilitator is to enable group members to know something about each other as quickly as possible, leaving time for supervision.

It is critically important that the dynamics work positively. I'd go so far as saying this is when knowing how to be a good supervisee really comes into play. In speech and language therapy supervision groups I have not noticed the process of Tuckman (1965) with forming, storming, norming, and performing.

Few SLTs or assistant practitioners have time to go through a lengthy group forming, storming before functioning and performing together. Every supervisee knows the purpose of the group and respects colleagues, and it is just necessary to monitor their own behaviour and get on with it. Any storming is unnecessary and a group needs to be productive and is not a place to play out competitiveness. If there is any storming before forming it needs to happen so quickly that no one notices it! It can still be six months before a group is stable enough to allow 'closed' membership. After that a group tends to remain productive, dependent on commitment to attendance.

The group members need a place for mutual support and to share ideas and views. A practitioner joins a group knowing there is a slight risk of more challenge with the need to justify judgements and decisions to more people.

The role and competencies of the supervisor are different in group supervision. The supervisor has to be facilitative in approach – and indeed is often called a facilitator. In one-to-one supervision there is a wider choice of styles. One-to-one supervision, for example, can be very focused, with each powerful question building on the previous question. In group supervision this would become a dialogue between two people with everyone else as onlookers. A group cannot become a series of individual supervisions. The facilitator has to consider group coherence as a priority and ensure everyone is involved at some point. The facilitator keeps the group focused, maintaining structure and signalling the stages of the session to the group. The facilitator ensures the structure is known, reinforced, and re-visited.

The challenge is to ensure everyone has the opportunity to participate. The key to a successful group seems to be that each person needs to find something of value in attending.

The supervisor will ask clarifying questions and make summaries, but the style is *facilitation* and less intense than some styles used individually. The facilitator may use frameworks like Kolb to encourage reflection and movement (not getting 'stuck').

A good supervisor will consider group needs as a whole and be determined to 'keep the show on the road.' This facilitator will know it is essential to create the group as a place of safety. They are watchful of patterns of hierarchies forming and other potential leaders marking their position, e.g. monopolising time. There is a slight danger that by trying to avoid conflict the group becomes too cosy with a tendency towards agreeing and validation of each other without challenging.

Some feel that having a rotating peer facilitator means it is more likely the group will lose focus and be too supportive. I can see this point, and yet sometimes this is the only way to implement supervision. When there is a rotating supervisor, the whole group needs to keep to a clear structure and even agree a framework for bringing cases, circulating a summary of any cases beforehand, and keeping to ground rules.

The positives of groups outweigh negatives. Some of my own most valued supervision has been in a group setting. For example, a group with six SLTs with various levels of experience, facilitated by a mental health nurse. What were the features of this supervision group which make me value it to this day? I think it was the style of facilitator who created trust, combining curiosity and tentative questioning with humour.

- The facilitator did not lead from a position of superiority (power) and used a solution-focused style of being interested and curious about speech therapy and our workloads. He knew nothing about the profession when the group commenced

- There was a clear structure, but a warmth and informality. The group was held monthly for just over an hour

- Drinks were allowed, and it was not necessary to be serious all the time

- Each person was asked what they were bringing to supervision that month and then there was negotiation about priorities for that session. Usually two cases or situations were discussed

- A case or situation was presented as a story with lots of details. Sometimes the supervisor clarified further during the story

- After the presentation, we could all make comments or ask questions as we started to make sense of what the wider aspects of the situation involved. This was not just about the treatment plan, but the levels of satisfaction, relationships, decisions, and dilemmas, and the perspective of other professionals involved in the case

- After group exploration the case holding therapist reflected a little further and considered some of the comments and suggestions

- Then the facilitator would give insights and summarise discussions before concluding

- We moved on to the next case

Structure of a Session

This is the basic session format:

- Informal welcome/news sharing
- Discussing (brief outline) of what supervisees have brought to supervision
- Agreeing an agenda
- Case presentation 1
- Reflective conversation: the group comments and share things which cross people's minds (reviewing/reflective). "Let's go round and see what your different thoughts are"
- Presenting therapist considers options
- Case presentation 2
- Summary of key points from today's conversations
- Closing session

Personal Reflection

I can clearly see the bemusement on the face of my supervisor on one occasion, regarding a case I had just presented.

The child was making progress but had considerable, enduring difficulties, and rumbling dissatisfaction about the number of school visits. There was a meeting approaching where I was a little concerned that I was going to be questioned again about why more therapy was not being provided. I knew the care planning was appropriate, and it was the wider context and 'how to' approach the meeting which I'd brought to supervision.

The group supervisor had been 'puzzling out' the profession and was beginning to get an idea of the SLT role and scope of practice. Suddenly he said 'you lot are not appreciated, you are sometimes downtrodden in fact ... Get that banner out and hold it in front of you ... you know speech and language therapy matters and others should have that level of respect too. Have you thought of having your own meetings? You always seem to be attending other people's where you have less influence.'

It was positive to hear this rather passionate response and I've remembered that phrase about 'getting that banner out.'

I didn't call a meeting for this case. I can report, though, that there was a learning process and these comments and challenges permeated into my thinking. I didn't sew a banner but some months later I began to offer Communication Planning Meetings when I was working with a child with long-term needs and friction around differences in opinion about the amount of time and style of therapy. I was a lead clinician with the leeway to set up this sort of meeting. I followed a person-centred approach and brought the child as communicator into sharp focus. What were the child's strengths and needs? Through discussion we identified potential goal areas for the future. This was recorded visually throughout the meeting. It worked well and seemed to strengthen my relationship with families. I believe it helped families realise I was committed to their child's care. I spent time explaining my evaluation and suggesting directions and they valued being involved in the process in a true 'parents as partners' model.

I attended many courses in my specialist fields of complex developmental needs. Looking back at this, my first clinical lead post, access to this small supervision group gave me a truly fantastic learning experience. I was already realising that successful support is about far more than the care programme and is around communicating, valuing others as partners, listening to the hopes of families, and taking these into account in the planning process.

Since then, I've been involved in many supervision groups and led many too. I still find this structure works best (and I have tried other models and approaches). Getting the relationship and dynamic established, agreeing an agenda at the beginning of the session, listening attentively and asking curious questions, giving insights before allowing the presenting practitioner to reflect again on the case and advice given works very well indeed.

Key points for group supervision:

- As with any supervisory relationship the most essential rule is to promote a safe space with mutual respect and trust
- An identified facilitator should always guide the group. This might be the same facilitator each time or rotating
- The focus can be on individual cases, wider casework, relationships, service development, or barriers to change

- Group members need to be committed to attendance and keeping to ground rules
- There is the expectation that group members will think about supervision and prepare beforehand
- Within this safe space everyone should commit to contribute (no one should be hiding by saying that they have nothing to bring to supervision)
- As part of strong commitment to the group each supervisee needs to work hard to ensure the group process works positively
- It is actually quite easy to disrupt a group with lack of contributions, stonewalling, or not joining in or asking questions or making comments
- It is important there is awareness and agreement that this is not sequential one-to-one supervision with an audience. The group works together to give 3D depth and colour to the cases presented
- A clear structure with an agreed way of deciding the agenda, e.g. 1 long case (40 minutes) + 1 short case (10–15 minutes), 2 cases (20–25 minutes each), 3 to 4 cases (10–15 minutes), with time allocated to each discussion
- The recording style should be agreed. There needs to be an identified way of recording the session. This can be an anonymised summary. It might be the supervisor notes the key themes and any actions/resources
- An email summary can be sent as follow up with a reminder of the next group date

The group needs to develop a definite *shared identity*. Over time supervisees get to know what they have in common, shared interests, strengths, and action tendencies. As a group evolves usually a level of caring and concern develops between group members who have shared knowledge and respect for each other as practitioners. Sometimes a group becomes a wider supportive network, a community of practice.

Group Dynamics

The aim of the facilitator is to keep the group focused and functioning. It is harder to address a specific individual's need in a group setting. Sometimes a supervisor may need to follow up something with a group member individually after a session, but this should be an exceptional occurrence.

The needs of the individuals are less important than the needs of the whole group. The supervisor needs to work hard to ensure that everyone attending feels there was value in attending.

The group is a place to bring issues for support in problem solving. It is possible that there are no solutions to a case/situation being discussed in a group, so there will be cathartic as well as problem solving conversations. Where a relationship or situation has no easy solution, then the very act of sharing this difficult case with supportive colleagues can be cathartic. Where there is no solution, this is more about dealing with emotional reactions or frustration connected to the situation. As the discussion starts there can be recognition that this is going to be a cathartic conversation, reducing the weight of the case on the practitioner and potentially providing ongoing support.

Repeatedly venting on the same topic is not constructive, but a one-off offload can be helpful.

The facilitator can guide the group to consider "How much of this situation is under our control? Is it possible to do something about it?" If it is, then the group moves towards problem solving mode.

Sometimes a group is set up specifically for practitioners at a certain level of experience, e.g. newly qualified, early career, established, or specialist practitioners. For a group designed for less experienced practitioners the group is going to fit into a developmental function of supervision and the facilitator might utilise templates for preparation prior to the session.

For early career practitioners a group can resemble the sheltered practicum (safe, sheltered learning space) advocated as ideal for professional learning by Argyris and Schön (1995). Group members share stories of practice, supported by colleagues asking reflective questions such as "What if?," "Was there anything positive?" They learn what to take to supervision, e.g. "I'm sharing this because I couldn't stop thinking about it after the session."

A reflective or solution-focused group can easily choose a framework to structure the conversation (see Chapter 7).

Kolb works well in groups as it moves very simply through four stages:

- Talking about the practical, "concrete" experience
- Standing back, pausing, and reflecting on the event
- Learning from the experience, any insights, making conclusions
- Thinking ahead with "active experimentation," considering 'best fit' options, putting learning and ideas into action

A group needs to decide whether the stories of practice presented should be longer or shorter. Longer stories give some 'back story' with details about motivation, any links with previous events, strategies which have been tried previously and failed. Shorter stories give a sharper presentation of key points.

I find a longer clinical story helpful as often in complex cases there is a recurring pattern of dissatisfaction within a long-term relationship with the service. I also feel the skill of telling a clinical story pulls on self-reflection and the very act of talking through the sequence of events can throw up some solutions. Others, however, would totally disagree with this viewpoint and prefer a more succinct summary of current issues and a total focus on the future.

The group interaction needs to be structured so there is an exchange of ideas and gentle challenge, but no fear of adverse criticism, which on rare occasions can be a form of attack. Occasionally a practitioner enjoys challenging to such an extent that another group member dreads the questions after presenting a case.

The facilitator can model words or phrases which are positive after a presentation. When challenging carefully choose vocabulary such as "I wonder," "That's really interesting, I'm curious about what you were thinking when X happened?" On occasion I have dealt with this type of scenario by suggesting that after listening I think it might be useful to take a solution-focused approach in this case. This change moves the emphasis to focusing on what's working, working well, and so validating the supervisee.

Exploring and facilitating through questions is very important. Thinking out loud in a tentative way is a very effective technique. That 'I wonder' tool is powerful. I talk with supervisees about how I track what is being said, and that while I am listening often thoughts, images, and links with previous events and experience comes to mind. When there is a pause in the conversation and if it is appropriate then I might share these impressions as part of sensemaking. In a group I ask if there are any thoughts, ideas, if anything crosses anyone's mind about this situation to stimulate discussion.

After a case or situation is presented then group members should ask questions and share their experience, reflecting together as a group. Group members give each other ideas and insights and ways of adapting practice in complicated cases. Less experienced members learn through experiencing the group and beginning to contribute to case problem solving.

Issues Which Might Arise in Group Supervision

- One of the group is struggling or has low mood and there is negative contagion; the group mood plummets and it is hard for the supervisor to inject any positivity
- The group becomes an offload session, without any reflective learning
- There are unrealistic expectations from one member that it is possible to bring several items to the session with lack of insight that others share the time
- The need to avoid overloading anyone who is clearly stressed and in need of restorative supervision with reduction in any "why don't you?" questions or receiving suggestions which make their To Do list grow
- Balance between feeling comfortable and trusting the facilitator and colleagues with some reflective questioning and challenge. There should be no fear/no attack
- This is a sheltered practice space, but it shouldn't become so cosy that there is never any challenge
- Wellbeing is part of every group. This can be discussed between members, and ways of strengthening support through the way the group functions might emerge. Sometimes there is a decision to focus on a theme such as over-committing ourselves at a session
- The number of supervisees in any group is tricky. Too many and the group dynamic becomes more difficult to manage with fewer opportunities to present cases. *I prefer about six members as this allows for one or two absentees and still leaves a functional group*
- Over time as group members leave the group there needs to be conversation about new supervisees joining
- Group members need to decide if it is an open or closed group and the process for inviting new members when existing members leave
- Keeping a group going is a challenge; people leave due to job changes, differing supervision needs, and timing. Dynamics change with every new group member. Having a structure in place for agreeing the agenda and how long is spent discussing each case can help integrate a new member more speedily
- It can be important to have a static or closed membership for a time so a group gels. When closed membership is agreed, and someone

leaves, it is important for group members to discuss together how to find new members

- A string of apologies arriving at the last minute can be tricky – avoid a situation with one supervisee and facilitator and no time to cancel
- Ground rules can be forgotten and need re-visiting at intervals
- In any supervision it is possible that someone is struggling with life outside of work as well as at work and needs wider support. In one-to-one it is easier (not easy) to broach this and talk with a supervisee about how we look after ourselves when other things in life are happening. It is also about ensuring a supervisee's emotional state is not affecting their practice. There can be something in the ground rules to cover this as it is more frequent than we realise. It is likely that a supportive one-to-one conversation between group member and supervisor is needed outside of the session

Two Facilitators Is Too Many

Next on to a tricky situation. It can be quite usual when a new group is formed for there to be someone who is not the facilitator but acts as though they have this role. It is unlikely that anyone would show outright hostility to the facilitator in a drive for dominance! It is more likely that one person is 'jumping in' with solutions from their experience when the group is supposed to be reflective and not advisory. Sometimes this is an expert practitioner with a wealth of knowledge and experience who is just used to dispensing advice.

Strategies which might help in this type of situation are:

- Reviewing the ground rules where the approach is clear (not directive or advisory)
- The facilitator giving interest and respect to the supervisee who seems determined to challenge the facilitator's position
- One approach is to continue calmly marking the points of transition, identifying the sections, and sensitively but firmly continuing to facilitate the group
- Of course, there is the option for a facilitator to bail out and leave the group if one of the supervisees is continually vying for dominance. I can think of one occasion where I have considered doing this

Once when facilitating a group which had met for several sessions I noticed a supervisee talking about their skills and experience continuously and dispensing advice. I didn't think of this in terms of vying for power and just became concerned that the group experience was changing from a reflective conversation to an advice shop and I seemed powerless to prevent it. In the end I concluded that this colleague had this style in any situation. The technique of shifting to a solution-focused approach in the next session was incredibly helpful. After that, two things helped:

- Using a framework which was circulated prior to the session, e.g. Gibbs' Model
- Firmly leading through the sequence of the session, summarising positives at the end of the session

---

Switching to a Solution-Focused Question Approach

- Take us through what you feel you have done right so far
- What have others found helpful in similar situations?
- Let's turn this on its head. Let's focus on what's happening, what people are doing now which stops things getting worse
- Let's each think of something positive about how X is navigating through this difficult case
- Has this made anyone think they might do things differently in their own caseworking in the future?

Some people think leadership and support are always directive. Some are acting from a position of expert knowledge and seem to need to affirm with a group that they have this.

An exception is around the needs of newly qualified practitioners when it can be helpful to give advice. This is a stage when advice is needed, wanted, and appropriate.

Ground Rules

One supervisee might tend to monopolise time and bring more than their share of items for supervision. This is OK on one occasion, but if it is a tendency it is going to disrupt the group.

If group facilitation is successful, then all the group will benefit from a productive, positive learning environment. It can be helpful to have something in the ground rules about everyone needing to expect the author-ity of facilitator, e.g. in moving conversation on if it is going round in circles and others need to present: "that is interesting but we don't have time to consider it today, we could plan some work around it next time."

Making sure that ground rules cover group functioning and style, e.g. we listen without interrupting, we hold back advice unless it is requested, can pre-empt a lot of difficulties.

Operational Ground Rules/Contract

- Facilitator will ensure there is clarity in structure and process
- Mutual respect 'by all for all'
- Timekeeping is the responsibility of everyone
- Striving for time keeping – starting and finishing on time and not overrunning when presenting a case or situation
- Seek opinions, actively listen, respect opinions
- Ground rules can cover style of feedback, but it usually isn't necessary
- Everyone commits to preparing and contributing
- Fairly sharing time – not everyone can contribute every time
- There will be an agreed number of cases discussed, e.g. one in-depth or between two and four shorter cases each time
- Confidentiality
- As groups are forming ground rules should be circulated to high-light their importance
- Some supervisors suggest ground rules are read out loud every meeting. This seems to me like precious time draining away. Referring to ground rules during the session reminds everyone they exist. They are there for reference with a set schedule for reviewing them as a group (see Chapter 21 for contract template)

Functions of Group Clinical Supervision

Supervision groups tend to fit into the developmental function with some restorative function around emotional issues. The mutual support which develops once the group has formed will, as a by-product, give an element of restorative resilience. Being a member of a regularly scheduled supervision group acts as an antidote to isolation and supports confidence. There will be some normative discussion about how a situation fits with policies and pathways. Below are some themes linked to the three functions which are relevant to groups.

Developmental Function in Groups – Themes

- Checking with others about best practice approaches
- Practically adapting approaches for individual clients' needs
- Problem solving – next actions
- Cathartic consideration of case
- Talking about challenges – a challenge I overcame this week
- Support on negative feelings about clients/carers
- Sharing resources and information
- Update on previous case discussion

Normative Function in Groups – Themes

- Case discussion with quality and standards learning points
- Ethical dilemmas
- Considering a new technique/strategy
- Discussion of a different approach to an unusual situation/problem
- Bringing an article/video clip or policy document for discussion

Restorative Function in Groups – Themes

- Sharing antidotes to isolation
- Validating confidence – checking something out
- "What went well" – something to be proud of
- Workload juggling for balance
- Time and energy management
- Dealing with emotional response to a complex situation

Sometimes a group can be an opportunity for practical training in the skills of group facilitation. Learning to facilitate can be easier in a group you know, where the other supervisees are aware you are keen to develop your skills and will support you in that. Occasionally, I've set up groups where training to be a facilitator is part of the group's purpose. Supervisees take turns at being facilitator and reflect on the experience.

A group can cover different models and frameworks in a planned way, with supervisees learning theory in this practical setting. What better way to learn about different models of reflective practice than in exactly the type of setting advocated by Schön – a safe and sheltered place to try out and extend skills with support from experienced practitioners.

Basic Facilitator Skills

The facilitator is tracking and adjusting depending on contributions of supervisees. In the early stages of becoming a facilitator the following can be helpful.

- Monitoring own body language to ensure signals given are positive
- Turning head and making eye contact
- Keeping eye contact going throughout
- Turning purposefully towards others
- Track the content and dynamics
- Bring in each supervisee – any thoughts/anything to add?
- Add own experience/reflection
- Avoid the group becoming one-to-one sequential supervision
- Mark transition points/summarise
- Track energy levels
- Maintain momentum and vary pacing
- Summarise impressions and achievements and close
- Keep on time

Online Groups

The research around online therapy is generally positive (RCSLT and ASHA Guidance 2021). There was already a move to online options, e.g. fluency services in Australia and Hanen Parent Programs, before acceleration due to the pandemic. I work predominantly online now and generally find little difference and some positives online. There are some aspects of direct therapy which would not work online for me, although it may be different for a colleague.

Clinical supervision has followed a similar pattern to therapy. There was already a move towards online, due to cost efficiency, convenience, and environmental reasons. Certainly the choice of supervisors has increased dramatically with the advent of online supervision.

There are challenges around technology and variability of signal and bandwidth. There seems to me, and it is a subjective impression, that there is no difference in the topics and content of reflective conversations. There is perhaps less incidental 'chatting' as would happen at the beginning or end of face-to-face supervision. I value informal communication and so having an informal catch-up at the beginning of a session, sharing news, goes onto my agendas.

It is difficult to specify the positions of professional bodies here as the landscape has changed dramatically and it seems unlikely there will ever be a return to face-to-face supervisions as default.

The supervisor does perhaps need to work a little harder to ensure things go to plan and to create that safe space online. The facilitator needs to work at structuring the group, and some visual reference points can be helpful. There is also more continual focus, with fewer breaks – briefly gazing out of the window happens less during online supervision.

Peer or Co-Supervision

There are widely different viewpoints about peer supervision. I cannot imagine my progression in speech and language therapy without endless conversations with peers, pulling apart cases, responses to therapy, and interpersonal relationships in the case. I experienced excellence in learning.

Sometimes peer or co-supervision does not have the same acute questioning and challenge. In simple terms it could be too comfortable and cosy. It is possible to envisage a situation where practice remains unchanged or static because both practitioners are keen to keep things the same and work within their existing comfort zone.

It can work well with structure and a reflective questioning framework. This definitely provides support. Those involved just need to recognise potential pitfalls and ensure there is reflective learning taking place.

Inter-Professional Supervision

This is inter-professional supervision in services where clinicians from different professions work in an integrated team, e.g. in adult neurology settings or pre-5 complex needs or services with overlapping caseloads where there are opportunities to plan in tandem with colleagues.

For my last eight years in the NHS I was leading Integrated Children's Teams with SLTs, physiotherapists, OT, and special school nursing. It is a

221

difficult task to pull together different professions, find points where there is common ground, and form an integrated team, rather than different professionals just happening to sit in the same office. Tools such as integrated care pathways and shared meetings help.

One tool which the practitioners took and implemented was group supervision (both clinical and safeguarding). The different professions considered cases together and challenged and supported each other.

Inter-professional supervision was beneficial in practitioners getting to know each other and respect clinical knowledge. There was an incidental cost-effective aspect as well, as through case discussions duplication in case management became obvious. There is little written about inter-professional supervision, but there seems to be definite advantages for clinicians working closely together with similar caseloads in forming stronger working relationships.

Kristiina Hyrka and Kaija Appelqvist-Schmidlechner (2002) looked at team supervision as a way to develop collaboration in multi-professional teams. They found that *"communication had become more open in the teams. Team members had learned to know each other."* However, although joint decision making had developed, more conflicts were actually noted! Reading the study, I am unsure if this was actually conflict or more that as clinicians got to know each other they felt more confident in challenging. The conclusion was that the supervision was valuable but also a challenge for the facilitator!

There is a recent development around multi-professional supervision in primary care with investment in the development of a new model of supervision. The project linked to Future NHS Collaborations (2020) has developed a model of supervision. *A Core Model of Supervision for Multi-Professional Teams* has been published to support general practice nurses and other health professionals in a collaborative approach to care. This was about *"building capability to support improved and innovative approaches in delivering health and wellbeing."* An e-learning programme has been developed alongside in partnership with NHS England, NHS Improvement, and Health Education England to complement the core model and provide further resources

A Group in an Inter-Professional Setting

Fleur Griffiths (2002), an educational psychologist, researched collaborative working in a nursery assessment unit. All the children had complex needs, and one of the team was an SLT. It interested me as a clinical lead as part of transforming practice. Griffiths aimed to narrow the gap between theory and practice through group supervision. The model the team used was grounded in play-based, interactive support with progress tracked over time.

Sometimes the team would meet and talk about the children in unstructured conversation. However, sometimes they met formally and used a framework to guide the conversation. This was based on Birkeland (2001) who classified stories of practice into types. Birkeland based this framework on Critical Incident Technique (Tripp 1993) and Katz' (1995) work on 'Critical' or 'professional predicaments.'

Griffiths brought this creative story-based technique for reflective practice into a group setting. Practitioners took turns to tell a story about their practice in a supportive atmosphere. The stories take a situation such as something going well (a sunny or turning point story), and these labels give a metaphor or visual identity. The stories gave focus to reflective conversations. Griffiths was seeking to extend collaborative good practice through a reflective group approach. During the research project the team had a transformational experience and became strong reflective practitioners. The SLT abandoned formal assessments in nursery.

The story types:

- Sunny stories
- Success stories
- Turning point stories
- Blunder stories
- Routine stories
- Something new

Critical Incident Technique Works Well for Group Conversation

Reflective practice began in the teaching profession. Schön (1983) and Dewey (1910) before him put forward *"reflection"* as a way in which professionals construct new interpretations and knowledge to guide their actions.

David Tripp (1993) was an advocate of reflective practice in teaching but knew that some found it difficult to identify which situations to take to supervision for reflective learning. Tripp devised an approach based around *"critical incidents."* This more structured approach would, he hoped, give practitioners a route into reflection for professional development. He adapted Critical Incident Technique, developed for de-briefing pilots after an incident in flight.

A critical incident can be any event and does not need to be significant or complex. In this model critical just means a relevant event. The approach generally asks practitioners to tell a story about an experience which was 'a little troubling,' e.g. students finding it difficult to settle and focus on work again after lunch.

The incidents are analysed in conversation with colleagues. A practitioner tells a story about a recent critical incident. Any decisions or judgements made during the event, the sequence of events, the other people involved, and any systems and processes are considered.

Story structure is used to add depth and dimension to the reflection. The reflective conversation is systematic and analytical. The following aspects of the event are discussed sequentially.

Format for Critical Incident Analysis

- The cause and context of the incident
- Describe the incident with detail
- Your feelings and perceptions; how significant was it for you?
- Your thoughts/feelings during the event
- Your actions taken during the incident

Daniel J. Ayers (2013) writes a helpful description, saying

The process of generating a critical incident begins with a straightforward, descriptive account of an event. The account, or record, can be generated through diary writing, jotted notetaking, or a reflective journal entry. Critical incident analysis depends on a thorough initial record of an event, a detailed description of your experience.

But what to write about? Start by noticing particular events, and your reaction to them. For example, you may find something unsettling, confusing, rewarding, or cheerful. Perhaps the event was unexpected. Perhaps it was something that went almost unnoticed.

Wider Thinking Strategies

Tripp suggests that we consider

- All the positive/negative/interesting points about the situation
- Alternatives/possibilities/choices which were also available
- Alternate viewpoints/perspectives/opinions possibly held by others involved

Group reflection on the story leads the group into discussing potential ideas and solutions. Practical ideas for improving the situation in the future are discussed, e.g. making a clearer transition between lunch and learning, playing a musical cue, etc.

Decisions, and the decisions of others are considered from an objective standpoint, a better position to uncover the motivations, values, and beliefs which underpin actions. This is reflective learning based on real situations with practitioners strengthening their professional judgements and decisions. If the group meets together over time, then the scenario can be brought back for tracking and evaluation.

Group supervision can be a very beneficial experience. The facilitator structures the session, steering through time keeping, and noticing and responding to group dynamics. Some frameworks used in individual supervision are transferable to groups. The storytelling models based on Critical Incident Technique can work well.

 REFLECTIVE LEARNING POINTS

Small Group Experiences

You will have been part of many small groups. Spend some time thinking back to your experiences.

Groups at Work

What role do you tend to take in small groups at work? Do you contribute a lot or only when you feel you need to? We all vary in how much we contribute.

Group Dynamics

Group dynamics can be powerful. Have you been involved in a group where you have noticed a colleague undermining the group leader? Did the group falter and fail?

What is the best group functioning you have been involved in at work?

Getting into the Role

Imagine you are a group facilitator – the group has already met and agreed contract and ground rules. Now it is time for the first structured supervision meeting. What do you need to do and say? Picture how it goes and what you need to do to keep the group moving forward.

CAMEO – THE IMPORTANCE OF ACCESSING 'SUPERVISION FOR SUPERVISORS'

Chris was accessing supervision for supervisors. She led a group once every four to six weeks. It was a group which was proving unexpectedly stressful. One practitioner never had anything to bring to supervision. Chris felt this was an issue as every time the agenda was set at the beginning of the supervision this group member announced she had nothing that month. Another group member had a tendency to 'jump in' and solve the issues which others brought to supervision. The first couple of times this had happened Chris had noticed it but decided to 'let it go.' Now it seemed to be habitual and this group member was taking a lot of 'airspace' with continual ideas and suggestions. Chris was increasingly aware she was holding back and just letting events take their course. Maybe this 'advice shop' approach was what the group members wanted. It wasn't reflective practice, but maybe it was 'OK.' Chris was considering relinquishing her role; she was dreading the group meeting and then afterwards spending ages dwelling on what had happened and her failures as facilitator.

Chris brought this scenario to her own clinical supervision. Chris had previously led other groups successfully. In this group she had two extremes: a practitioner who never contributed and another who seemed to want to lead and continually advise to others. The optimistic 'it will be better next time' approach hadn't worked. Here she was now in her own supervision, near to tears about her inability to change the dynamic in this group.

The conversation helped. Just describing the situation and sharing the thoughts she had experienced during the groups helped Chris begin to see this was an unusual and random situation. Most supervision groups are positive experiences with colleagues keen to listen and support each other. There were several possible ways of approaching the lack of involvement. Chris considered an individual conversation with this group member, and that could have worked, but decided against it. She began to wonder if reflective exploration of a case was something which was difficult and led to avoidance.

For Chris the most comfortable plan was to bring in group process and return to the contract, circulated and agreed when the group commenced. She regretted that she hadn't stipulated the commitment needed at the beginning, but she hadn't felt it was necessary. She realised that the contract specified there would be regular reviews in the format of a conversation between group members about 'how it was going.' If she scheduled in a review, it would give her the opportunity to go through the rules and highlight key points like the need for everyone to bring something to supervision. She also wondered about asking for a brief outline of each person's issue or case to be circulated before the meeting. She was unsure about this as it was more paperwork for everyone, but also felt it would highlight the need for involvement.

The second problem was the group member who seemed to want to take over the group. Her supervisor led a discussion around this and brought in the insight that it is not uncommon for there to be a group member who seems to want to challenge the designated leader and act this way. Several solutions, including a one-to-one conversation with this colleague, were considered. Chris took away two ideas. One was linked to the earlier conversation about the contract and to do the same and emphasise the need for reflective discussion and perhaps set everyone the objective of not jumping in to rescue colleagues with advice. The other was to suggest a structured reflective framework be tried out for a session. She could even involve the colleague who dominated the group in asking the questions in the framework. Chris retained her authority as the supervisor suggesting a specific framework, but offering others leadership of reflective conversations. The colleague would need to use the suggested structure when guiding a conversation, and there would be no place for advice giving in this reflective model.

The group continued and over the next four months became a positive experience for all involved. The situation with the colleague who dominated proceedings improved, and the facilitator brought in a structured framework and a whole group objective of not giving advice.

18 | Different Media in Supervision

"When I used to read fairy tales, I fancied that kind of thing never happened, and now here I am in the middle of one!"

Alice, *Alice's Adventures in Wonderland*

Key Themes

- Expressive writing
- Writing – self-supervision through reflective writing
- Modern media
    - Email support, telephone, instant messaging
    - Online supervision and etiquette

What follows is an overview of expressive writing before focusing on frameworks and practicalities of self-supervision through reflective writing.

Expressive Writing

The research on expressive writing for reducing stress levels is consistent and impressive and yet rarely showcased. Pennebaker at the University of Texas pioneered this research.

When people write about their emotions and thoughts this results in improvements in social, psychological, behavioural, and biological measures. Expressive writing has the advantage of low cost and easy accessibility.

It seems to be effective in minimalist form too. It is possible to jot down key words to reduce stress levels. Writing things down, even for a few moments, may be helpful in *"reducing stress and anxiety"* (Briana Murnahan

DOI: 10.4324/9781003226772-19

2010). Interestingly Murnahan expected to find that paper-based strategies (diary, journal, blog) would be more effective than email in reducing stress and this part of her hypothesis was not supported by the evidence. What seems more important is to choose a media which works for you.

The research on expressive writing is compelling, and results keep being replicated. In reflective writing we are not writing about the trauma which Pennebaker et al. (2006, 2007) covered in research. However, if it works at reducing the stress of traumatic events then logically the same is likely for stressful events of professional practice.

Let's look at an adapted version of Pennebaker's framework. This is especially useful for any events which carried a high emotional load. The sort of event which might occupy our thoughts – the 'mental grime.' This technique gives a simple, effective way of dealing with a stressful situation and any associated feelings.

The research suggested that "*completing this exercise can increase happiness, reduce symptoms of depression and anxiety, strengthen the immune system, and improve work and school performance.*" Expressive writing focuses on feelings more than events, objects, or people. It can have a story structure of beginning, middle, and end.

Framework for Writing

Write about something which had an emotional impact and load.

Find a time and place where you won't be disturbed.

Write about an event and focus on your emotional reaction, thoughts and feelings which were provoked by the event. This should be something which was an emotional challenge.

When writing it is important to explore the event and its effect on you. If this sparks any connection with previous events at work, in life, or relationships outside of work then include this in the 'stream of thought.' The suggestion is to write continuously for 20 minutes. Write only for yourself. Don't worry about structure, spelling, or grammar. No one else will ever read this.

Finally, and this is optional, write from the perspective of other people involved in the event or situation.

After experiencing a stressful event it's possible to dwell on what happened, those work issues which occasionally keep us awake at night. Expressive writing allows us to process events from a distance, considering our role and that of others. Transforming a complicated event into a storyline sequence makes it feel more manageable.

In the research participants wrote for 20 minutes a day for 4 consecutive days. Compared with a control group who wrote about general topics with no emotional load those who wrote about stressful experiences reported greater happiness levels three months later, visited the doctor less than usual during the six-week period following the writing exercise, and seemed to have healthier immune systems. It seems startling in terms of research results. However it has stood the test of time and been replicated by Pennebaker and others. The studies are often referred to as the Pennebaker Paradigm. The surprise is that this approach to helping people process and deal with events isn't utilised more.

The research supporting writing as a tool for wellbeing and stress reduction is surprisingly strong. It is a continual puzzle why such a cost-effective (free), hassle-free tool is not used more. It is there between supervision sessions, before difficult meetings, and at the end of a long day when thoughts may still be spinning around, and it is a way of quietening thoughts.

Self-Supervision through Reflective Writing

Reflective writing is certainly an underrated tool. It can be the most effective place to begin self-development as a reflective practitioner. My training began at master's level with keeping a reflective journal which was then graded as part of the course evaluation. This was the most consistently I kept a journal but I have gone back to this tool on many occasions when struggling with events at work.

We keep professional logs or journals and yet the idea of this being reflective writing is limited by the frameworks which we use when writing. It is usually a recording log, possibly with the identification of a learning point.

The RCSLT diary emphasises the importance of reflective writing about development activities. HCPC has resources for reflective writing on its website. The HCPC template gives a format of examining an event in detail, alongside aspects such as the clinician's response, interactions with others, and the learning and plan for how this will be sustained. When professionals are called for additional audit in the re-registration process there is a requirement to write an essay which shows a level of reflection on learning.

Reflective writing is a habit, and I was certainly better at keeping a reflective journal when it was a requirement for a course. I need to go back to it more often and more regularly. There are other different formats for reflective writing. These can be exactly the same ones as used for reflective conversation, e.g. Driscoll and Gibbs.

RCSLT has devised an online Reflective Writing Workshop. This workshop covers reflective practice and how this involves more than a description of events. Several approaches are covered, the frameworks of Gibbs, Driscoll, Brookfield's lenses, and the REFLECT Model. Here is a brief overview of the models in the Reflective Writing Workshop. (Chapter 7 covers reflective models in depth.)

> The RCSLT Reflective Writing online Self Study pack includes several models including:
>
> The Reflect model (Barksby 2015) gives a structured consideration of events.
>
> - Recall
> - Examine
> - Feelings
> - Learn
> - Explore
> - Create
> - Timescale
>
> Driscoll's What? So What? Now What? model explores thoughts and motivations.
>
> Gibbs uses specific question cues to unpick events and give insights.
> Brookfield's reflective lenses show different perspectives.

The HCPC template contains the following advice.

> *There is no right or wrong way to reflect on your practice. Different people learn in different ways and while one person may learn by reflecting on a positive outcome, another may find it most useful to focus on a situation they found challenging.*

This reinforces that reflecting on positive events is equally important to focusing on dilemmas and difficulties.

Email Support, Telephone, Videoconferencing

In writing this section, I'm aware that almost as soon as it is completed it will be out of date. There is a temptation to avoid writing about this altogether on the grounds that information becomes irrelevant as the technology and protocols connected with it move forward rapidly. Yet this is a high-profile topic and there are basic principles and insights which remain relevant.

The pandemic and social distancing have rapidly accelerated the use of technology in healthcare and supervision. There were moves to increase remote supervision prior to the pandemic, but it was slow motion development. Now looking back at the literature the impression is of people looking for reasons to justify an approach they preferred – a face-to-face meeting with a supervisor. So, what follows is an attempt to share some current views around remote supervision.

Pre-pandemic there were practitioners working in locations where there was no alternative who embraced technological solutions. Fluency therapy in Australia was forging ahead with videoconferencing, widening access to services. Airedale NHS Trust had devised a videoconferencing approach for adult fluency offered in prisons and secure units. Medical consultations online with specialist doctors in geographically remote areas such as the Scottish Islands was increasing. There were glimmers of outstanding practice through technology. Meanwhile in a Northern NHS Trust I was still struggling with any suggestion of adding Skype to a meeting or moving a planned supervision online.

Now a high percentage of healthcare consultations are via videoconferencing. This is the middle of change and what blended pathways and approaches will look like in future is unclear. If we add environmental and efficiency considerations to the impact of the pandemic the groundswell of change is towards the permanent use of online consultations and supervisions.

Email support has grown in supervision. Subjectively, the impression is that this tends to be at times when a practitioner feels stuck with a case or a situation and is seeking immediate advice about next steps. It helps to know someone is there to contact for clinical support when a dilemma in decision making arises – and we know the very act of writing things down may help! There is a growth in counselling therapy of clients sending a reflective email to a therapist who later replies with thoughts and impressions.

This is new and potentially fraught with difficulties around recording. My view is that this should be treated anonymously in the same way as a student case might be discussed with a university tutor. I am imagining casenotes where a therapist writes that they messaged their supervisor who suggested that this course of action was appropriate. This becomes a legally complex area.

Practitioners will be emailing each other informally for advice and support around ongoing casework. When there is an arrangement for a supervisee to contact their supervisor between sessions for additional support the communication may need to be anonymised or written knowing it could be added to casenotes.

Systems like Teams with instant messaging allow for increased communication across teams with the possibility of more than one colleague being involved in a discussion about a dilemma. These systems are end-to-end encrypted and safe ways of communicating, reducing isolation, and giving access to a supportive network. However, any message which anyone types into a messaging system (let's imagine something written quickly by a busy colleague between two therapy sessions) should be regarded as general supportive comments and not case-specific advice and not be included as part of a case record in the same way as specific supervisory telephone call might be included. All 'instant group' methods require more supervisor facilitation and structure and very clear contracting and ground rules.

As I write this I consider the advent of voice notes and have decided that this is an evolving area and policy is lagging behind technology. As with all new technology there needs to be caution and dynamic risk assessment when utilising these systems. I know I write this from a privileged position. Sometimes there is little choice and advances in technology are seized as a way of providing something that will fill a glaring gap.

In Kenya Jade Vu Henry et al. looked at enhancing supervision for community healthcare workers (CHW) using WhatsApp messaging in Kibera and Makueni. A messaging group was created for CHWs and their supervisors to support supervision, professional development, and team building. Preliminary results showed that with minimal training the group *"tailored the multi-way communication features of this mobile instant messaging technology to enact virtual one-to-one, group, and peer-to-peer forms of supervision and support, and they switched channels of communication depending on the supervisory objectives."* The change rated highly with practitioners who felt less isolated and more supported and so assuring the quality of service delivery. There was no alternative; this fitted a need and was highly successful when implemented.

In independent practice, including clinicians employed or contracted to a school, there is often more 'checking out' clinical decision making via email. There is less opportunity for a coffee break chat for many independent practitioners. Some services, including larger independent practices, are piloting the use of instant messaging groups for support and report this is enhancing the 'community of practice.' It would be interesting to see some research on this type of support. Of course, there is a need for clear ground rules, e.g. some groups have etiquette of not messaging out of working hours.

Jeannie Wright and Frances Griffiths (2010) looked at remote supervision through reflective practice, exploring the use of technology in counselling supervision in New Zealand. The study design was around two experienced counsellors and supervisors conducting a dialogue, a written conversation, spaced between supervision sessions over a year-long period.

Face-to-face supervision was their preference but involved a three-hour journey and was an impractical luxury. Initially meetings were face-to-face then continued by telephone, online email, and eventually by Skype.

I was drawn to this study by reading a finding which didn't sense check for me in stating that *"non-visual, non-instant methods encourage more reflection."* On close reading of the source this was not actually the case. This was a personal, reflective study where one of the authors preferred the space and pace of reflective writing to face-to-face meetings. She wrote

"essentially I prefer writing because it gives me time to reflect (and backspace)" and

> *one of the reasons I like writing rather than the "real time" of the phone is that I do feel more in control. I can express whatever I like on paper or on the screen and then re-read and edit before anyone else sees the writing.*

This was her personal preference with no evidence to suggest that non-visual, non-instant methods increased reflection.

What Are the Concerns Which Practitioners Mention?

It seems to be that the move to videoconferencing means sessions might be less valued, with less preparation time and less transitional time as there is no travelling to supervision. Wright and Griffiths (2010) write

> *one of the things I value about "going to supervision" is the space this creates, physically and metaphorically. I wonder whether something of this thinking time is lost when you have to switch directly out of the "busyness" of your work and onto another screen of the computer?*

A concern is expressed that when supervision is face-to-face there is a definite space, time, no interruptions, and it is possible to share difficult situations confidentially. They wonder if they might be *"less likely to pursue the kind of deep emotional content if it seemed that anyone was free to walk into the room and interrupt the session."*

These are all very valid comments. However, the same ground rules for online and face-to-face supervision should easily apply. There should be no supervision in a shared office space where someone may walk in. The need is to plan and conduct online supervision so it has the same ringfenced, special space as face-to-face meetings.

The same study discusses the pros and cons of telephone supervision. One practitioner liked this better because it was possible to make notes and refer to these which they felt was inappropriate in a face-to-face meeting. They explored what was different in telephone supervision. There was more note taking, they responded more quickly on the phone, and they were less likely to wait due to not being able to *judge the quality/timing of the silence without visual clues.* They wondered if this meant they were more advisory and less reflective during a phone call.

They say they *continue to value the immediacy ... and permission to comment on it, permission to be curious, that comes with face-to-face interactions and which remains, for them fundamental to supervision.* This logically can be created in the same way for a remote supervision. A videoconferencing supervision session needs to create a space for thinking outside of the busy day at work. It needs to be private and confidential. There should probably be a transitional buffer between another meeting on the screen and the beginning of a supervision session. In face-to-face supervision these things happen and are felt to have value and so should not be lost in an online video supervision.

As they have recently started to use Skype rather than the telephone, and they feel that the conversation is closer to face-to-face supervision, the study concludes:

> *The advantages, to me, have been the experience of real time conversation where we are each visible to the other. As a supervisor, I have found it possible to pace my comments/questions with more confidence than in telephone sessions because of what I can see of your responses.*

In terms of online supervision and etiquette there is little difference to face-to-face. The arrangements, commitment, and conversation in the session should be the same as for a face-to-face session.

 **REFLECTIVE LEARNING**

The RCSLT Reflective Writing Pack

This is an e-learning course which gives an overview of different models for reflective writing. Self-study takes about two hours.

One Word a Day for a Week!

Even in a busy working week, you might find a few moments to squeeze in a recent self-care strategy: the One Word Journal. Natalie Kogan (2018) suggests "picking a word that captures the spirit of your day—no other requirements or restrictions—if you have time you can add stickers, doodles or sketches."

Maybe if you send yourself a One Word email at the end of every working day with a word which sums up your day it might reduce stress and anxiety levels. It seems worth a try for a week!

Dismal Days

If you really are stuck in a job where you are unhappy then logic suggests this isn't going to work for you. You might end up writing the same word every day. So, if you are in this situation, instead focus on searching for glimmers, even if they are unconnected with the day job (like noticing some daffodils flowering in the car park) and jot down a word about this.

There will be glimmers in the working day, even if it is something like an administrator giving you a smile as you arrive for a meeting or finding a parking place without difficulty. This may sound a soft strategy, but as I write this I suddenly remember a time when I was unhappy at work and every day I walked down a path towards the office where there were lavender bushes planted and some days the scent wafted across the path giving me a glimmer of positivity.

CAMEO – REFLECTIVE WRITING

Zac didn't enjoy writing. He had dyslexia and used strategies which worked well for him. However, he found writing and sequencing information exhausting some days. He had been told by his manager that he needed to be 'more reflective' and the suggestion had been to keep a reflective journal. This was the last thing he needed this term.

In the end he found two ways of writing which meant he was able to follow this suggestion (well it was more than a suggestion as it had been written into a formal objective). He found an online journal format where he could use the font and texts he preferred. Then he used a string of words (a sort of stream of consciousness approach) to describe difficult situations (sessions/meetings/conversations). It was anonymous and would make no sense to anyone but him. After writing this he wrote a word for how he had felt in this situation and a short phrase for any learning or action points. He added emojis/photos sometimes. After a couple of months he felt his ability to reflect on events and learn in the job was much stronger.

Alongside this he tried out the One Word a Week approach (One Word a Day was too much and he would forget). Once a week (on Friday afternoon or if time ran out on a Monday morning) he spent a few moments reflecting on the last seven days and then chose a word to sum up the week. He wrote it in an email and posted it to himself. He could have saved it and not sent it but the very act of clicking send seemed to 'complete the week.'

Looking at Things Differently, Creative Supervision

"You know what the issue is with this world? Everyone wants some magical solution to their problem and everyone refuses to believe in magic."
Hatter, *Alice's Adventures in Wonderland*

Key Themes

- Creative approaches
- Using metaphor
- Art and crafting supervision
- Visual models
- Mindful supervision

Creative Approaches to Supervision

Using creativity and imagination to imagine a better future and work towards it.

(Butterworth 1998)

This chapter is different in that it is very much a reflective summary of my own experience of creative approaches to supervision, bringing in some references from work by more artistically gifted people along the way. I have become more confident in bringing metaphor, imagery, and storytelling into my supervisions; however I am still quite reticent and also aware many of my supervisees have the same reluctance. Bringing in visual reference points or recording sessions differently using mind mapping with different coloured ink is within my comfort zone. Creative supervision can certainly enhance supervision and add depth to a supervisory conversation.

DOI: 10.4324/9781003226772-20

Using creative techniques in supervision is very much personality driven and not for everyone. There is little in the literature about creative supervision outside of psychotherapy, art, and dramatherapy. I recall when doing a small research project that I read about supervision being linked to making a patchwork quilt. I can see that there is some imagery around connecting different pieces (patches) to give a different picture. I admit that I enjoy sewing and have in fact made patchwork cushions in the distant past, but I would personally find it inappropriate to introduce this type of media into my supervisions.

There are however ways in which we can enhance supervision using visual reference points which would be within the comfort zone of the average practitioner. We are used to using visual support with our clients and recognise the value. I might draw on a piece of paper while talking and use markers to highlight features such as the distance or barriers between people.

Kinaesthetic or tactile learning involves actions. There are approaches to supervision which are more kinaesthetic and involve visual referents, e.g. placing pebbles to demonstrate close or distant relationships. Pebbles, shells, bricks, and counters can visually represent situations.

Metaphor can be powerful in supervision. Certainly, metaphors occur to me while I'm listening and I reflect and share these with my supervisees. Often these are metaphors for practitioners feeling overwhelmed, perhaps stuck in a place where they feel unsupported or are finding it difficult to deal with a tricky relationship at work. I recently drew on metaphor linked to a stream with flowing water, different speeds, depth, rapids, turbulence, and getting stuck at the side of the riverbank. I tend to enjoy metaphor, and it certainly is possible to use a comparison and build the metaphor together and gain further Insights into a situation.

Lahad (2002) feels that creative supervision using art materials brings in the right hemisphere and visually demonstrates the sequential steps of the conversation, and any barriers or difficulties the supervisee is facing can be highlighted. Metaphors linked to weather, water images such as rivers, lake, or sea, might be brought in and have enough variability to add other perspectives and insights to the conversation. Another approach is to label feelings and use symbols or colours to highlight the emotional content.

Asking how a supervisee feels when discussing the difficulties, whether there are any images the supervisee feels are relevant in relation to the situation being discussed, can extend and add depth.

I believe there is a place for the 'walking supervision.' From positive psychology literature we know that being in an environment interspersed with open spaces, trees, and water can be calming and encourage a positive outlook. I used a local park close to the office. Some clinicians found a conversation while walking round the park helped them to talk more easily about difficulties in their job. We can underestimate the stress some feel about a supervision session. My walking supervisions tended to be for management rather than clinical supervision, but it would work just as well for clinical supervision.

Using Talking Mats

Rachel Woolcomb (2019) wrote an interesting article about *Talking Mats* in clinical supervision from an occupational therapy perspective. Talking Mats is a well-known tool in several branches of speech and language therapy. It gives clients who need support in expressive communication a focus and space to think and communicate feelings.

In 2019, the Royal College of Occupational Therapy produced guidelines aimed to provide clarity about the purpose and practice of clinical supervision. The guidelines specify that *"reflective practice goes hand in hand with supervision."* Reflective practice is defined as *"taking time and conserving the energy to think critically about your practice. It means stepping outside the action in order to see how to improve what takes place."*

Rachel Woolcomb took this statement and brought it to life in relation to Talking Mats, adapting the approach to create a visual focus for reflective supervision. Woolcomb reports that *"the visual representation of the thinking process on the Talking Mat can provide a focus for further reflection, discussion and decision making."* The visual scaling of *"Going Well, Sometimes Going Well, Not Going Well"* added an additional dimension.

She used two sets of Talking Mats topic cards. The learning and thinking card set provided a visual reference for reflection. The scales of *going well/not going well* were used, but the scale of *confident/not confident* could also work well. One supervisee was able to use the visuals to think about "issues of resilience and how they managed stressful events at work." They engaged in a reflective conversation about managing time differently and not putting off difficult tasks till the end of the working day.

There is potential in using tools like Talking Mats to encourage reflection within clinical supervision.

Mind Maps

A tool I often use is mind mapping (handwritten or using software). I use it for tracking and recording key points in supervisory conversations. I find mind maps helpful when planning for complex cases, especially when there are several potential directions for therapy. The very process of drawing a mind map gives insights. I feel quite comfortable drawing a mind map in a session. I tend to draw as a supervisee talks with the diagram becoming a shared reference point where actions can be noted.

I find a mind map a robust way of recording a session in a concise, visual way. It can also serve as a record of the session for the supervisee to take away, taking a photo with a smartphone and sharing it.

I use a mind map when listening at the beginning of a group supervision while supervisees discuss topics brought to supervision. I can quickly make a visual reference and use this as an agenda for the session. I keep checking it to ensure everyone has their space to talk that day.

A mind map can clarify thinking and help us to picture complicated scenarios more clearly. It can also provide a route out of the dismal swamp!

Use Your Imagination

I like to use questions which bring in the imagination, for example, asking supervisees what a difficult situation reminds them of (a thorny thicket); how things would look if the problem disappeared (sunshine and blue sky); or how an ideal working environment might look (plenty of space and facilities). It is fairly easy to introduce metaphors linked to landscapes, holiday beach scenes, park runs, or adverse weather into a conversation. Developing imagery together extends the depth of a reflective conversation.

I might mention something from literature if something in a conversation sparks an image; I'm not averse to pulling in Jane Austen or referencing *Wuthering Heights* (near to where I used to live so I'm allowed). Now I might also share my experiences of difficulties living in a country where I'm struggling to become fluent in a new language and my increased empathy around frustration when my communication breaks down. The difficulty of course is that my choices and experience in literature can be vastly different to the interests of my supervisees. If we work together and recognise this, then it is usually a positive experience.

I also encourage storytelling in supervision. The skill of telling a structured story of practice is important in reflective supervision. There is no reason why the stories can't be recorded using stick people, similar to *Comic Strip Conversation People* (Carol Gray 1994). Bringing in cartoons, such as *Dilbert* (Scott Adams), is something I've used in the past as a reference point and to give humour to a situation.

I certainly have colleagues who are gifted with art and craft in both therapy and supervision. I just feel innovative using different coloured pens in a supervision session, e.g. on a mind map. I would like to use pictures and artwork more as reference points, art of a stormy scene at sea for example, but I tend to think of ideas after a session. I am unlikely to ever bring out the glue, cotton wool, and ribbon, but it is important to say that some supervisors are very talented in creative supervision.

Mindfulness and Supervision

As mindfulness has come into prominence I've noticed the similarities with reflective practice. The concept of reflection-in-action is about 'thinking in the moment' and adapting our actions based on an awareness of our action tendencies gained from previous reflective learning. *"Mindfulness provides a foundation to promote supervisee development of self-awareness and reduce anxiety, as it focuses on non-judgment, curiosity, and expansion of insight"* (Campbell & Christopher 2012).

We have triggers which lead us to behave in certain ways in certain situations. Triggers for feelings of frustration, anger, impatience can lead to behavioural patterns which disrupt relationships. I remember when working as an NHS manager that I began to feel overwhelmed before a holiday; there is probably always a longer To Do list before annual leave. However in one particular role it became two weeks of concentrated hell of late nights and weekend work to ensure things could be left for a vacation. Once started it began to lead to changes in my behavioural patterns approaching leave and sadly that meant a concentrated period of work, beginning even earlier than the last holiday. With a mindful approach there could be more awareness and different strategies put in place to counteract my tendency of exhaustion prior to leave.

Mindfulness, for me, is about slowing down thinking. It is calming thinking and just being aware of what is happening and not being as reactive. This can be a challenge, but logically mindful thinking should connect to reflecting in action. I first discovered mindfulness when I moved to lead a different team as part of an NHS re-structure and several of the practitioners had attended mindfulness courses in work time as part of a Wellbeing at Work initiative. A wide range of practitioners, with different styles and personalities, all spoke highly of the mindfulness-based stress reduction course (MBSR) and described how it had permanent effects on the way they dealt with work. This sparked my interest. Soon after that I attended a three-day training course about therapy for adults with dysfluency, and mindfulness was one of the strategies advocated. The connections were made and mindfulness became a strong strategy in my coping at work toolkit.

When I do a search there are articles about mindful supervision in various journals. This is the beginning of research in a new area and not the calibre of research expected in clinical speech and language therapy. However there is an impressive array of wider literature in the fields of mindfulness in mental health services, acceptance and commitment therapy (ACT), and positive therapy/psychology approaches. There are also publications about mindful leadership. It is possible to project, sensibly, that someone who has a mindful approach and uses tools like mindful meditation and mindful thinking to reduce stress states is going to be able to tap into slow motion thinking, consider their actions, and adjust and make changes in the future more easily. There is some overlap between reflection in action and mindful awareness. The mindful thinking approach of Ellen Langer (1997) is slightly different and more practical and is outlined below. Langer found that mindful thinking helped individuals view situations from different perspectives. By seeing events and information through a different lens, they were able to create new potential solutions.

So, mindful supervision is not about meditating in preparation before a supervision session, or using deep relaxation and then visualising a difficult meeting considering how to pre-empt and cope with the anticipated challenges. Though anything which slows down thinking, reducing stress hormones like cortisol, is going to link with a measured, calm approach and enhance our reflection on events.

A supervisor might benefit from a mindful approach and being more aware of thoughts, inner responses, and any emotions triggered by what the supervisee is saying (Richards 2010). One of the core skills of a clinical supervisor is the ability to focus and track the content of the supervisee's contribution and to listen without disrupting the supervisee's train of thought. Moving into a more mindful listening (thinking) style sustains attention and strengthens this process of tracking what is said while simultaneously considering possible patterns and themes.

There are other approaches linked to mindfulness, such as reflective journaling or mindful meditation. Early research with teachers and student teachers shows enhanced job performance (Bernay 2014). Murphy (2017) writes that when student teachers were introduced to mindfulness techniques they reported that this strengthened their classroom management. Access to mindfulness helps practitioners step aside, consider ongoing events, and basically have greater awareness to act to reduce any potential for classroom disruption. Murphy writes of the importance of the split-second decision in a classroom situation and that through slow motion mindful thinking the gap between realising that some action is needed and choosing and implementing the action seems longer. It can't be longer, so this is about perception and thinking differently in the moment. It seems that 20 minutes a day 3 times a week spent in mindfulness meditation will result in:

- An increased capacity to give full engaged attention
- Release free thinking from patterns that are no longer relevant

Refreshing the mind this way gives new 3D perspectives on events and situations.

Mindful Thinking

In finding a flexible state of mind Ellen Langer developed a form of mindfulness which is a little different. This is about engaging a style of thinking where we focus on any differences or uncertainties in a situation and by doing this break away from our habitual fixed viewpoint. Langer's approach is about flexible thinking without absolute certainty. Things might sometimes be this way, but it isn't definite, and they won't always be this way. It is a way of thinking differently which changes perspective and has very positive results.

In finding a flexible state of mind there can be:

- Greater engagement
- Effective and enjoyable learning
- Competence
- Positivity
- Creativity
- Less likelihood of burnout
- Less illness
- And it seems increased charisma

This is a mindful approach when listening and processing incoming information in daily events. We should respond attentively, notice small changes, and actively adjust our responses as needed.

There are four characteristics to mindful thinking:

What's happening in the moment? Focusing attention on what's happening in the here and now, in the present moment; it is probably not what you expected it to be.

Noticing aspects about what's happening: focusing attention on anything which is different, unusual, or new about a situation or interaction with someone. Are there any differences, even very subtle differences? What messages are there in the intonation, the mood, or tone of voice? Is there a difference in the sequential order of events? What has been left out or added in?

> *Searching for other perspectives*: wondering what other possible perspectives there could be in this situation. Keeping an open-minded perspective. Langer says that we overestimate how often people think the same way as ourselves.
>
> *Focusing on the situation/context*: how does the background, the landscape, or the context affect the behaviour of others? Sometimes it's the background which drives behaviour.

Mindful thinking is about tracking ongoing events and thinking more flexibly. It's about reducing assumptions and any tendency to form immediate conclusions. By thinking differently, we reduce our tendency to respond automatically. We view situations differently and interpret events through a wider lens. When we're in the middle of a stressful interaction, then stepping back and thinking about the whole situation using these categories can be useful. We slow down thinking, stand back, and look attentively at what's happening. Thinking differently in this mindful style should reduce intense emotions and give perspective.

Langer advocates using conditional language like *might be, could be, maybe* instead of absolute words like *was, always, never*. Reducing words with definite meaning gives an element of uncertainty, letting us step back to view things differently. In mindful thinking there should be more pausing and less immediate reactivity.

Steven Haberlin (2020) focuses on applying different mindful methods in supervision.

Haberlin showcases some techniques such as:

- Mindful walking, where the pace is slowed, sometimes the attention is just on the steps, or breathing while walking, giving natural breaks in the conversation. Haberlin describes this as focusing fully on the here and now
- Focusing listening, in meetings and other times where we need to listen attentively
- Avoid judgemental thinking and look for ways of building positive connections
- Mindful moments, where supervisors take a moment to clear their thoughts before moving on to the next session. The five-minute pause is an underused technique

These are techniques which facilitate concentration, reduce anxiety, and lead to calm, slow motion thinking. Instead of being stand-alone techniques they can supplement existing frameworks of supervision.

 REFLECTIVE LEARNING

Choose one of the approaches described above in this chapter; perhaps Ellen Langer's mindful thinking in daily life which gives a scaffold for 'reflecting in the moment' and doing this consciously for a day.

Consider if any of the approaches are within your current comfort zone or just a slight stretch, e.g. using visual referent points; bringing in metaphor.

If you know and use Talking Mats then visit their website and read about using Talking Mats to provide a reflective thinking space.
https://www.talkingmats.com

Try out a mindful walk – it might be a one off, but the walk will do you good.

CAMEO – I CAN SEE CLEARLY NOW THE RAIN HAS GONE

Zoe was having a difficult time at work. She knew she needed to change jobs; there was an unexpected personality clash with the new Head of the school where she spent a large percentage of her working week. He had already formally complained about an OT colleague. Zoe steered clear of him as much as she could and dealt with the deputy instead, which was a positive experience.

Cameron her supervisor knew his support was around 'treading water,' coping with the situation and accepting things as they were (while searching for other jobs). Zoe was in effect grieving for the job she had enjoyed before the new Head took up post. There was a culture of fear developing in what had been a school with a positive ethos. Cameron was supporting surviving; this was a long way from thriving.

Cameron often used scaling and that wasn't quite right here, he needed something a little different. After some consideration he chose some words which could be used to describe a working day/hour/morning. He wrote out the words on a large piece of paper and then found and included artwork of the weather to link with the words; he chose lovely inspirational scenes and knew that Zoe would value these as she had an interest in art. He made a paper and e-version. During the next session he brought in this new tool. Zoe could identify with a stormy scene at sea and a frosty landscape. As he was a solution-focused enthusiast he couldn't help but introduce a search for glimmers. When something was more positive he pointed out the scene of a warm, sunny day with a lake.

This made Zoe smile and brought a little humour into the supervisions. She was able to begin using the scenes in her conversation, and Cameron realised it was a tool which was more far reaching than he had realised. It had given Zoe visual imagery which she was using to process difficult experiences, and it strengthened supervision sessions. She was able to mention moments when the sun came out (glimmers/small positives).

Zoe did have success in finding a post in an NHS Trust and the supervisory relationship drew to a close. After the last session Zoe sent Cameron a thank you email which was peppered with references to the weather scenes and expressed her strong gratitude for the supervisory support when she had been struggling to be positive.

20 | Training and Development

"Well, in our country, you'd generally get to somewhere else—if you ran very fast for a long time, as we've been doing." – Alice

"Now, here, you see, it takes all the running you can do, to keep in the same place. If you want to get somewhere else, you must run at least twice as fast as that!" – Queen of Hearts

Alice's Adventures in Wonderland

Key Themes

- Training – what are the options?
- Developing your own training
- Training in other relevant skills
- Supervision for supervisors
- Legal context across England, Scotland, Wales, and Northern Ireland

---

Training Options

What training is available for practitioners interested in being a clinical supervisor? What is the process of becoming a clinical supervisor or finding out more about clinical supervision from the perspective of a supervisee? (See Chapter 16 for supervisory skillset.)

There is little in the way of formal training in supervision skills and even less which relates directly to speech and language therapy. Some newly qualified practitioners have a better grounding in reflective practice and clinical supervision than others. The starting point is often engaging in supervision

DOI: 10.4324/9781003226772-21

as a supervisee and learning from the model provided by a good supervisor. There are training options available, but it takes time and dedication to locate them.

Here is a summary of some of the options:

In-house training: in NHS organisations there may be in-house training available. As part of a clinical supervision system there might be short courses linked to basic supervision skills, offered by experienced practitioners.

I've worked in three organisations where training was offered in house on the basics of clinical supervision. I was also privileged to be able to devise training for a speech and language therapy service of 45 staff (adult and children's services) and an integrated AHP service (children's service) of 180 practitioners (both therapists and assistants). I struggle to know how practitioners can learn the basics without guided training, or even a self-study pack. The reality is that many practitioners engage in clinical supervision with minimal training.

Safeguarding supervisor training: often covers the basic skills used in supervision. It depends on the safeguarding models used in an organisation, but initial training for safeguarding supervisors covers active listening, summarising, and reflective questioning.

External training – for healthcare workers: there are a few providers of training (face-to-face or online short courses). Very few of these short courses are specifically designed for speech and language therapists, or even AHPs. The target audience tends to be mental health practitioners.

Of course, there are always advantages to training with other professionals, and the basic skillset needed for supervision will be broadly the same. However, for some practitioners, the preference will be for a profession-specific course where the activities and stories of practice are easily recognised. There are, of course, many specialisms within speech and language therapy and the early choice of adult or child posts now gives diverse careers, but training in a profession-specific course is the preference of many practitioners.

Training organisations such as Skills Development Service Ltd (SDS) provide accessible training in basic clinical supervision and advanced clinical supervision, face-to-face or accessible online or via purchased recordings.

External Training – SLT- and/or AHP-specific training:

- Intandem is a supervision, training, and development partnership which offers foundation training, followed by more advanced training for supervision with a structured approach to training. The training is multi-disciplinary, but the leads have experience and insight into speech and language therapy and were lead authors for the current RCSLT guidance (2017). Intandem can also be commissioned by organisations to provide bespoke courses

- ARC Supervision and other similar services are offered by clinical supervisors who have an enthusiasm for providing training. ARC offers training for supervisors and supervisees in reflective practice and appreciative supervision through online short courses, and also via practical experiential group facilitation

The Helen & Douglas House Clinical Supervision Toolkit (2014):
This resource gives an overview of key tools.
Several models of reflective practice are introduced in this toolkit including:

- Shohet 7 Eyed Model
- Driscoll What? So What?
- Gibbs' Cycle
- Johns' MSR

The aim of the toolkit is to share learning and clinician experience to inspire other practitioners to *"reflect, grow and imagine the possibilities for clinical supervision"* in their own setting. The toolkit gives anyone working in the helping professions an overview of clinical supervision as a way of supporting wellbeing and best practice.

The Clinical Supervision Resource (NHS Scotland):
NHS Scotland has created a resource, divided into four units of e-learning. This resource has been created to support healthcare practitioners develop relevant knowledge and skills for participating in clinical supervision. There is a particular focus on the restorative function of supervision.

> **The four units of e-learning:**
>
> *Clinical supervision Unit 1: fundamentals of supervision*: gives a good overview for those new to supervision, providing an introduction to clinical supervision; the purpose, processes, and potential benefits.
>
> *Clinical supervision Unit 2: fundamentals of supervising others*: aimed at experienced clinicians, looking for tools to support skill development and models and frameworks.
>
> Each step of the Wosket and Page (2001) model is covered in detail. Other models are also covered with emphasis on selecting tools to meet the needs of supervisees.

> *Clinical supervision Unit 3: effective facilitation of clinical supervision*: covers the approaches, skills, and techniques needed to facilitate clinical supervision. It focuses on resilience with an overview of practical tools such as active listening, parent-adult-child model, and appreciative and strengths-based approaches.
>
> *Clinical supervision Unit 4: leadership and clinical supervision, promoting person-centred, safe, and effective practice*: about leadership and how supervision connects to the quality agenda.

Developing Your Own Training

Commissioning external provider training: if a training course is not available, then it may be possible to commission external training agencies, e.g. from Intandem/ARC.

Development of in house: it may be possible to develop a clinical excellence session or series of sessions within your team with invited speakers or colleagues researching and presenting on topics relating to clinical supervision.

> **Some basic ideas for in-house training are:**
>
> *Restorative Resilience through Supervision: An Organisational Training Manual for Health and Social Care Professionals (2015) by Sonya Wallbank*: if you are in the position of needing or wanting to provide formal training and resources are not available then the restorative resilient package (Chapter 12) forms a good basis for a group to learn together over a training day/s. The training pack *"allows an organisation to cascade the restorative resilience approach throughout their staff, initially 'training a trainer', who can then pass the knowledge on to any number of supervisors."* It comes with handouts, slides, and video clips to run the training. An accompanying book gives background, theory, and research.
>
> *Robin and Joan Shohet's book (2007, 2021)*: the book is based on their training programme and experiences/reflections of participants. The content of the training is covered and even includes recipes for cakes linked to each module.

Suggested Contents of Internal Training

My own approach has, wherever possible, been to widen training to include all practitioners in a team and offer training in "*What makes a good supervisee?*" as well as skills needed to supervise effectively. This idea came from Tony Ghaye's (2001) work on reflective supervision.

At a basic level training might involve:

- Spending time as a team looking through the RCSLT Guidelines
- What makes a good supervisee?
- Becoming a supervisor – the transition
- Going through a reflective package together such as the RCSLT Reflective Writing Pack
- Considering:
  - What is clinical supervision?
  - What is NOT clinical supervision?
  - Developing an understanding of supervision models and practice
  - Frameworks to use to structure a session
  - Tools to encourage reflective conversation
  - What factors create a positive supervisory relationship?
  - Recording supervision

Training in Supervision-Related Skills

Training in counselling skills: although the functions of supervision and counselling are very different, the strategies used in supervision draw upon counselling, e.g. active listening. My own training began this way with a short course on counselling skills for SLTs. It was a good foundation to extend in the future. Some who attended the short course went on to train with Relate or The Samaritans as they wished to contribute to those organisations and strengthen their skills. Many local universities and colleges offer counselling courses, but it is a weighty commitment if you don't have a specific interest in counselling.

Reflective practice: knowledge about reflective practice and the models which can be utilised in conversation gives a strong foundation. There are now videos on YouTube posted by experts such as Daphne Hewson giving insight into using these practically.

The RCSLT Online e-Learning Course on Reflective Writing: gives a grounding in several models of reflective practice. *"This course covers a more in-depth look at what reflective practice is, as well as looking at several different models to aid your reflective practice"* (RCSLT).

The Reality of 'on the Job Learning'

The reality is that many clinical supervisors have had limited formal training. Competence is gained through an eclectic mix of 'on the job learning' from experienced colleagues, local courses, and increasingly e-learning. *"Competence depends on habits of mind, including attentiveness, critical curiosity, self-awareness, and presence"* (Epstein & Hundert 2002).

Considering the importance of clinical supervision across the UK there is a distinct lack of training opportunities outside of those provided locally by NHS organisations.

Personal Reflection

My own training had a similar eclectic path. I certainly accessed local courses in two health trusts and engaged in structured group supervision with a gifted supervisor. I believe that watching my supervisor listen, focus, and contribute insights which provoked further thinking about situations was invaluable training, how he skilfully managed the dynamic of the group and guided supervisees in 'what to bring to supervision.'

Following this I studied an MA in Professional Training and Development, expecting to focus on formal training and instead discovered reflective practice. How we learn in practice situations and through conversation with others was a revelation. I realised that I could dwell on difficult experiences/encounters in my job, and I regularly sought out advice around clinical direction for a case, but I rarely pressed the pause button and considered my own actions and contribution to events. This clicked into place with the support of a tutor who supported my reflective journaling and gave feedback, strengthening my skills in reflective practice.

Having to write a reflective journal taught me to interrogate my actions and extend my practice. In writing I could zoom in on what went into my decision making and use reflective models to consider what was happening in complex cases. From reflecting-on-action I gradually became more astute at reflecting-in-action. Extending my reflective skills further happened over time, strengthened by attendance on short courses on emotional intelligence, positive psychology, and appreciative leadership, alongside advanced skills in facilitating supervision groups and online supervision.

However, it was Sonya Wallbank's restorative resilient approach which gave me the greatest insight into myself as a supervisor (Chapter 12) (Bishop and Sweeney 2007; Wallbank 2010).

I realised that someone who is overloaded and approaching burnout cannot take on advice or additional actions, even when suggested in a helpful way. This learning crossed between both clinical and management support.

Eventually I felt experienced enough to provide training for SLTs as well as OTs, physiotherapists, and assistant practitioners. Initially the training was based upon reflective practice and empowering speech and language therapists to reflect and recognise work-based learning. This was later fine-tuned to reflective clinical supervision training. The training focused on situational supervision to emphasise that supervision covers far more than case-specific support.

Learning from the training feedback showed that specific case support was readily available and was called supervision, but it was usually advisory support.

For assistant practitioners there was an additional session on reflective practice. Qualified practitioners commented that this would have been valuable for them too as they had received little formal training on the theory and models of reflective learning. They felt stronger in their confidence around counselling skills such as active listening than they did in reflective models.

Assistant Practitioners

Speech and language therapy assistant practitioners need to access clinical supervision, and this is included within the RCSLT guidelines. The supervision needs of assistant practitioners can sometimes be seen primarily in relation to specific case supervision. Yet an assistant practitioner needs the same access to workload-wide supervision as a qualified speech and language therapist. The daily situations experienced, decisions made by assistants 'out in the field,' and complex interactions with clients, families, and other professionals give more than sufficient material to take to clinical supervision.

Assistants are as much in need of restorative space to reflect on the demands of their work as SLTs. They need access to wider workload supervision as well as support and supervision for delegated care plans. For some this is not happening and is a gap which needs addressing.

Developing from Individual to Group Supervisor

Leading a group supervision session requires different skills to individual supervision. Chapter 17 covered successful group supervision. I feel that a group supervisor needs a combination of the skills of air traffic controller and diplomat, alongside the usual tools of active listening and reflective learning.

Often the best way of learning is to occasionally 'stand in' for an experienced supervisor in a group you attend. This sheltered environment is an opportunity to try out skills in a supportive setting: standing in for a colleague in a group which is set up and functional. It is possible to try out fledgling skills such as scanning, ensuring all group members get the opportunity to bring something to supervision and feel that their time has been worthwhile.

There are occasionally training courses on leading group supervision, but these are rare. This sparsity of training is surprising. When I attended a course which covered group supervision it was valuable in enhancing my awareness of group dynamics and strategies for making the group supervisory experience positive for supervisees.

Supervision for Supervisors?

There is increasing recognition of a need for supervision for supervisors. This is obvious when we think about it but is not widely available. Milne (2009) notes that *"the supervision of supervisors is the most deficient area in the whole enterprise of clinical supervision."*

Henderson et al. (2014) wrote about how there had been little discussion between practitioners about what needed to be provided by organisations for supporting and developing supervisors. Bernard and Goodyear (2004) concluded that *"far less attention has been paid to the development of supervisors than has been devoted to those receiving it."* Until the research catches up with practice then a common-sense approach to this situation is the way forward. It is sensible and reasonable to expect clinical supervisors to access supervision for supervisors to support and strengthen skills.

Legal Framework

Across all nations in the UK there is a legal framework which is supportive of supervision.

Health and Social Care Act 2008 (Regulated Activities) Regulations 2014: Regulation 18

The intention of this regulation is to make sure that NHS providers deploy enough suitably qualified, competent, and experienced staff to enable them to meet all other regulatory requirements. To meet the regulation, staff must receive the support, training, professional development, supervision, and appraisals that are necessary for them to carry out their role and responsibilities.

The RCSLT Supervision Guidance gives an overview of the legal frameworks for each country. There common themes are:

- *Training and development needs should be evaluated at the start of employment and at regular intervals through the course of employment.*
- *Providers must meet supervision and leadership requirements, in order to meet the skills required to support the needs of service users*
- *Regular, ongoing supervision should be received throughout the period of employment.*

(RCSLT 2017)

In Scotland a post-registration framework specifies supervision requirements according to different levels of career stage and provides resources, such as practical tools for implementing supervision effectively. In Wales the Care Council provides guidance for effective supervision. In Northern Ireland the Regional Supervision Policy outlines the approach to supervision and support for AHPs. It includes ensuring that *"appropriate induction, preceptorship and supervision are in place to support transitions along the career pathway."*

The RCSLT Supervision Guidelines state that to meet the regulation, practitioners *"must receive the support, training, professional development, supervision and appraisals that are necessary for them to carry out their role and responsibilities."*

There are currently a limited range of training options for those who wish to become clinical supervisors. The impression is that in the nursing profession there is a greater focus on reflective practice and clinical supervision for nurses in training. In speech and language therapy there needs to be either more coverage of clinical supervision at undergraduate level or a wider range of post-graduate opportunities to build and develop skills as a clinical supervisor. With the change in service provision due to the impact of the pandemic there is now wider acceptance of online platforms for training, and so it is probable that more options will become available in the medium term.

 REFLECTIVE LEARNING

Leading small groups (supervision or meetings). This is a skill which can be needed from early career through to experienced practitioner. If you are new to this, it can be daunting. If you are experienced, then you know it can still all go wrong and learning is never complete. What are your strengths in taking the lead in a small group of colleagues? Any skills you wish to consolidate or develop?

Imagine a small group of different celebrities or cartoon characters. You are the facilitator. How do you cope with this challenging group? What competencies do you need to keep the group on track and make sure everyone has a 'fair slice of time'?

Have you ever had any guidance about what makes a good supervisee? Probably not. Consider the role supervisees have in making a group effective … what makes a good supervisee?

Reflect back on your own training over time as a supervisor. What has been the most valuable training? Courses? Work-based experience? Individual study?

CAMEO – DEVELOPING SKILLS THROUGH ONLINE GROUP SUPERVISION

Jamie was trying to develop into a leadership and/or management role after being a specialist clinician for several years. He worked in a team covering a wide geographical area and didn't have much contact with colleagues, except at the monthly meeting. This was now on Teams. He wanted to progress in his career but felt isolated. He talked about this in one-to-one supervision and realised he was frustrated at 'standing still' and not moving forward. Everyone was busy and seemed weary and pre-occupied. He spent some time drafting some ideas and then sent an email to his immediate manager saying he hoped she agreed this was a need in the team and resource (time) could be given to try it out. His manager was supportive.

So, Jamie set up an online supervision group. The plan was to meet once every half term and Jamie would set this up and facilitate initially; but others could take on the facilitator's role in the future (if the group was successful). It went OK. There were a few learning points about setting the agenda and time keeping. Colleagues were supportive and seemed keen to meet again.

He asked if next time the group might be recorded so he could watch, reflect, and look to improve his own skills. Everyone agreed; they also offered to give him gentle feedback and support his quest to develop his skills as a group facilitator. They also told him to feel positive about his skills as this was an initiative which would help reduce the isolation of working in a large geographical area.

21 | Paperwork and Practicalities

"The hurrier I go, the behinder I get."
White Rabbit, *Alice's Adventures in Wonderland*

Key Themes

- The supervisory contract
- Scheduling, recording, reviewing, and confidentiality
- Accessible resources
- Supervision policy
- Evaluation

This chapter is all about the practicalities of organised clinical supervision. This ranges from a contract between two practitioners to a supervision policy operating in a larger speech and language therapy team.

What is available to help evaluate the impact of supervision? How often should supervision be reviewed, and when should you change supervisor? Do you need different supervisors within your individual network of support? What needs to be included in a supervision policy?

The Supervisory Contract

The strong suggestion is to always have a supervision contract, even within an organisational system. Often this is quite routine and a matter of approving something sent by your new supervisor. However, it can be the opportunity to discuss how the supervision will work in practice and even the style which supervision will take. Hawkins and Shohet state that *"In an*

DOI: 10.4324/9781003226772-22

individual clinical supervision situation, the contract represents a working agreement between the participant and the facilitator and in addition reflects the expectations of the organisations and professions involved" (2012). The other advantage is that the contract can be part of reviews about 'how supervision is going.'

So, at minimum, the contract should include:

- Overall aims/aspirations
- Frequency
- Length
- Venue or online arrangements
- Acceptable reasons for cancelling
- Acceptable notice for cancelling (with exception of unavoidable personal crises such as illness, car breakdown, or internet issues)
- Record keeping
- Confidentiality and when confidentiality could be broken, e.g. safeguarding
- Review schedule
- How the relationship will close

Cassedy (2010) also suggests that "*Contracting in individually arranged supervision could also consider:*

- *the style*
- *the framework and models used*"

The HCPC website contains a very useable Supervision Agreement Template. An example of a group contract is given at the end of the chapter.

Scheduling

For no reason based in research the usual schedule for clinical supervision is every four to six weeks. The inevitability is that with holidays and cancellations this is likely to average less than 12 meetings a year. The Allied Health Professions have chosen not to follow counselling and clinical psychology and advocate more frequent meetings with a much more directive supervisory oversight of all cases. The approach chosen more closely resembles that of nursing. Monthly or half termly sessions are usual and can work well. The risk is that the supervision drifts and sessions are not booked or cancelled and re-scheduled and it turns into a session once every three months.

There is often some flexibility in NHS services. If a practitioner is new to a post or specialism, then the scheduling might increase for an agreed period of time. There is a set schedule (RCSLT) for NQPs of weekly supervision for six months and then a monthly schedule.

If restorative resilience is being implemented, then initially some sessions will be closer together initially until a safe platform of resilience has been reached and frequency reduced.

Record Keeping and Goal Setting

Recently I changed to keeping brief notes about the topics and themes discussed in clinical supervision. My supervisees know I tend to draw mind maps or diagrams to track key points in a conversation. Sometimes if the supervision is funded by an educational setting there is specific paperwork. For online group supervision I compile a short summary of themes and action points and share with attendees.

There should be a record of the date/themes and any action points. I increasingly encourage supervisees to keep their own notes as part of their CPD log. RCSLT's Reflective Dairy allows for clinical supervision to be recorded as part of learning and development.

In a larger NHS organisation, the paperwork may well be fixed as part of a wider supervision policy. There will be local variability about who has access to the notes and in some cases with a 'Grandparent Model' the notes may be shared with the grandparent at agreed intervals.

What I am clear about is that recording supervision is not the same as describing a clinical session. We are not writing about our colleagues in the same way we write up our casenotes. Casenotes have grown longer over time, and it feels uncomfortable and unnecessary to write this amount about a session. If more information is needed, then the supervisee could write a Reflective Diary sheet about the session.

Both Power (1999) and Driscoll (2006) suggest that a very brief record of each session is kept: the date, times, names attending, and a general, brief note of issues raised and discussed. This is there as a written reminder or 'aide memoire' for the supervisor/supervisee.

If the clinical supervision is based on a coaching approach then there will be paperwork about goal setting. Again, this needs to be appropriate and not the same SMART goal setting sheet which is used for clients.

The HCPC website also provides a Supervision Recording Template.

Sharing Records/Confidentiality

This needs to be transparent with agreed safety and security of the information. Who will records be available to? Are there any circumstances where sharing is appropriate? Is there any third party outside of the supervisor and supervisee/s who could have access, e.g. a grandparent? This is unlikely in speech and language therapy, but there are systems where someone senior is identified as mediator if any issues arise in supervision.

Dimond (1998) suggests organisations should receive *"the minimum necessary information for effective monitoring to take place."* This might be the dates recorded and a collective summary of themes across practitioners.

Records can be accessed for legal reasons, e.g. a court subpoena. If there is a disciplinary process then there is an argument, mentioned by Dimond, that because the supervision took place in working hours the records are the property of the organisation and so accessible. This approach is unlikely to be taken by organisations, but I have been involved in a case where supervision records were requested as part of a human resources process.

Standards for Continuing Professional Development

Supervision is a great way to demonstrate your CPD, and the notes that you take during your supervision can be used to highlight development. It is of benefit, therefore, to keep an accurate record of your supervision activities, including themes discussed, feedback received, and reflective notes about applications to practice.

Reviewing

At agreed intervals it can be helpful to talk about how the supervision is going, what the positives have been, and whether anything needs adjusting.

I worked for a while with an excellent supervisor who would always summarise the session as it closed and note any learning points or ask what she had done which was especially helpful.

If clinical supervision is linked to a programme developing the supervisee's supervision skills, then it is helpful to talk about different approaches and the style and structure of the session. For example, there might be a contrast between a session with a reflective cycle one month, followed by a solution-focused approach the next.

Practical/Accessible Resources

The intention was to give examples of paperwork and templates in this book, but HCPC templates are freely available. There are examples of contracts and recording sheets which are basic, but very user friendly.

Driscoll gives an example of contract headings and a specimen contract. The following contract is adapted from this example. This starts by specifying that the contract will complement the service's policy and guidelines on supervision. An independent service could also reference the RCSLT Guidelines.

Names/designations
of those involved

Venue

Frequency/time

Review arrangements for supervision, e.g. six months

Joint responsibilities:
To honour the contract
To maintain the boundaries of the supervisory relationship (Content, Time, Space and Confidentiality).

Clinical supervisor responsibilities:
To provide supervision as per guidelines
To record each client discussed
To record the date and time of each session

Supervisee's responsibilities:
To accept supervision as per guidelines
To prepare any material in advance
To consider and select situations/clients for presentation

Housekeeping:
Sessions will only be cancelled due to sickness or if making the session becomes impossible for either party
If a need for supervision arises outside of the contracted sessions, the supervisor will accommodate the supervisee as soon as possible for an additional session

Confidentiality
The boundaries of confidentiality within supervision are anything which is illegal, that breaks professional code of conduct, or that infringes the service's disciplinary process

---

Howard (1997) proposed a 12-point supervision agreement checklist. This is rather formal in its terminology and comes from the counselling profession.

Points included in Howard's supervision agreement checklist:

Purpose: what's the purpose?

Professional disclosure statement: informing supervisee about your professional background and limitation of this supervisory relationship. *This is not usually included in speech and language therapy supervision contracts*

Practical issues/matters: where, when, how, how often?

Goals

Approach and evaluation

Responsibilities and accountability

Confidentiality and documentation

A statement of agreement: this is **a document summarising agreed expectations**. Anything different or significant from usual supervision contracts can be highlighted here as 'special conditions'

Problem resolution: is there a process, e.g. grandparent arrangement?

Dual relationships: specifying what will be different if the supervisor is also the supervisee's manager

A Supervision Policy

In a larger organisation these are organisation-wide policies way above team- or service-level policies. At times, e.g. in a larger independent practice, it can be necessary to have a clinical supervision policy.

The key needs in a policy document would be:

- The title, date written, author/s
- Date of next review
- The background and reason for the policy
- A brief description of the approach to be taken and any preferred frameworks/models
- The contract and any 'set' aspects of the contract, e.g. schedule, length of session
- What to do if there are disputes
- Any resources such as templates or websites with frameworks, etc.
- It is helpful to number each section for easy reference, e.g. 1.1, 2.3, etc.

It is a case of describing in clear language what is happening in supervision and the expectations of everyone employed in the service as far as clinical supervision is concerned.

RCSLT Guidance gives clear direction:

- *A clear, up-to-date supervision policy, with practice that supports the policy (speech and language therapy/organisational).*
- *A clear system of supervision (managerial and professional) for all staff.*
- *Effective training of supervisees and supervisors.*
- *Evaluation and monitoring of actual supervision practice, frequency and quality.*

(RCSLT 2017)

Group Supervision

In a group there is often more focus on ground rules to enable the group to function efficiently. Ground rules can cover frequently encountered difficulties like interrupting, someone never bringing material for supervision, or lack of apologies/sporadic attendance.

The contract will specify when the group needs reviewing. This can be informal and low key; everything is going well and there is no need to go through re-formulating the contract. It can be a very useful to check whether the group style is working and whether anything might change. For example, a preparation sheet before a meeting may no longer be required, or there is a decision to introduce one. It is individual!

Sometimes there is an agreement to bring in different styles of supervision for CPD purposes, e.g. using different reflective models each time or using solution-focused questions. It may be working well, but how can it be the best supervision it can be?

Formal Evaluation

There is little in the way of formal evaluation paperwork. Hewson and Carroll (2016) provides a simple review sheet in the Reflective Toolkit. It is very general with the most useful aspect probably plotting on a graph whether a supervisor has been high challenge/low support or vice versa with discussion about whether this ought to change.

The re-branded Manchester Clinical Supervision Scale (MC-SS 26) measures supervisees' perception of the effectiveness of supervision..

The MC-SS 26 has seven subscales:

Trust/rapport
Supervisor advice/support
Improved care skills
Importance/value of supervision
Finding time
Personal issues
Reflection

Examples of items linked to subscales:

- Supervision gives me time to reflect
- Work problems can be tackled constructively during clinical supervision sessions
- It is important to take time for clinical supervision sessions
- It is difficult to find the time for supervision sessions
- I learn from my supervisor's experiences

It is used as a quantitative outcome measure for research. You will see from the examples that the items (there are 36) are very easily linked to everyday supervision. It would be possible to use the subscales as a framework for a review conversation about 'how supervision is going.'

A number of reliability and consistency issues were noted by Buus and Gonge (2013). These are interesting because they are due to the tool being based on *"a broad conception of supervision,"* ranging from formal supervisions to frequent ad hoc sessions. The suggestion was to refine the concept of supervision and focus on fewer types of supervision. Logically though this criticism suggests it might be a good tool of measuring general support and how well practitioners feel supported in a service.

REFLECTIVE LEARNING

Consider how you make notes or record/log your supervision (whether supervisor or supervisee). Do you have a consistent system? Do you record broad themes or more in-depth information?

Look at the HCPC website and the paperwork provided. Is there anything different to what you are using? Do you need to make any changes?

CAMEO – EVIDENCING SUPERVISION

Agnetta was in a total panic. She had received notification that she had been chosen for HCPC audit of standards as part of the bi-annual re-registration of therapists. Despite re-assurances that there was nothing to be concerned about, her CPD had been regular and implemented in practice, she was anxious. She realised that she had not kept a log of dates when she had received individual and group supervision. She had recorded her attendance on courses or Journal Clubs in her RCSLT diary but not her supervision. She wanted to talk about her learning from supervision in her essay submission for HCPC. It didn't take too long to trawl through her diary and retrieve dates. However, she is now recording dates in a log and considering noting key themes discussed in her RCSLT diary.

An example clinical supervision contract:

Clinical Supervision Contract

Supervisor

When taking the role of clinical supervisor, I take responsibility for:

1. Ensuring an organised sheltered environment for supervisees to discuss their practice in their own way
2. Facilitating supervisees to explore, clarify, and learn from their own thinking, feelings, and perspectives regarding their practice
3. Giving and receiving open, thoughtful, and constructive feedback
4. Sharing with the supervisee information, experiences, and skills appropriately
5. Challenging professional practice in an open and supportive manner
6. Keeping brief notes of themes and circulating for CPD records

Supervisee

As a supervisee, I take responsibility for:

1. Identifying issues for which I need supervision and taking time to share/ consider them
2. Becoming increasingly able to share stories of practice in supervision
3. Identifying and communicating the type of response which is useful to me
4. Becoming aware of my own role and scope and its implications for myself and the organisation and profession for which I work
5. Thinking about supervision during the weeks between sessions and 'jotting down' ideas for 'things to take to supervision.' These won't all be taken to supervision, but the very process of making these brief notes helps trigger our reflective thinking
6. Being open to others' feedback
7. Noticing when I justify, explain, or defend before listening to feedback
8. Keeping a record of my supervision arrangements

Supervisee and Supervisor

We shall take shared responsibility for:

1. Arranging when, where, and how long each ensuing supervision session will take place
2. The frequency of supervision session
3. The limits to and maintenance of confidentiality (safeguarding)
4. Reviewing regularly the usefulness of supervision every three months
5. Knowing the boundaries of the clinical supervision process
6. Making the group a positive, supportive experience for ourselves and others
7. Looking after myself as a clinical practitioner

Housekeeping

- Prioritise attendance whenever possible
- Let the supervisor know if you can't attend so the session isn't delayed while waiting for you to Zoom in
- Groups to start 'on time' and if you are late joining then quietly join the conversation as there probably won't be opportunity to re-cap anything you have missed
- Please give specific apologies before the session. The reality is that we all have unexpected events at home and work which mean we cannot always attend supervision

Example of a Clinical Supervision Record

The HCPC templates and many service templates for recording themes discussed are excellent. Here is a different format adapted from Ghaye and Lillyman (2007).

Clinical Supervision Record – for Individual
(Completed after each session, not for sharing.)

Reflection on content of session:

Points for personal action:

Points for professional development to be considered further:

Date: Signed:

---

22 | Final Reflections

> *"How funny it'll seem to come out among the people that walk with their heads downwards!"*
>
> Alice, *Alice's Adventures in Wonderland*

Key Themes

- Optimum conditions for effective clinical supervision
- Effective supervisors
- Wider benefits
- Professional responsibility
- Supervision for supervisors
- Situational supervision – avoiding rabbit holes

It's time to draw some thoughts together and make some conclusions.

What Are the Characteristics of Effective Supervision?

In 2019 HCPC commissioned a review of the literature on the characteristics of effective clinical supervision in the workplace. This was carried out by a team from Newcastle University, Charlotte Rothwell, Amelia Kehoe, Sophia Farook, and Jan Illing.

This was wider than speech and language therapy, but the findings are relevant to the profession. The team summarised the key characteristics of effective clinical supervision.

DOI: 10.4324/9781003226772-23

The supervisory relationship should be:

- Based on mutual trust and respect
- Choice of supervisor offered where possible, *"with regard to personal match, cultural needs and expertise"*
- Shared understanding of the objectives of supervisory sessions, based on an agreed contract
- A focus on support through *"sharing/enhancing of knowledge and skills to support professional development and improving service delivery"*
- Regular and based on the needs of the individual
- Ad-hoc supervision should be provided in cases of need
- Supervisory system based on the needs of the individual, e.g. one to one, group, internal or external, remote, or a mix
- An employer who *"creates protected time, supervisor training and private space to facilitate the supervisory session"*
- Training for supervisors
- Ensure all staff have access to the sessions, regardless of working patterns
- Provided by several supervisors for a team
- Training in the overlapping responsibility as both line manager and supervisor

What Are the Qualities of an Effective Supervisor?

We know when we have a good supervisor. We know when our supervision is working positively. There are different styles and approaches. There are common factors when considering what makes good clinical supervision.

Common factors for good clinical supervision:

- A compassionate/empathic supervisor
- Genuine and says what they think when needed
- Listens, not just 'waiting to talk'
- Can draw on different models and approaches
- Guided reflective conversation
- Appreciative, strengths based
- Safe space

- Protected time
- Focusing on wider casework, e.g. relationships, barriers, coping with stress
- Warm towards supervisees; positive regard and respect
- Understands the difficulties experienced
- Sees supervision as CPD
- Values improved experience and outcome for clients

Driscoll (2006) gives a succinct summary of the key characteristics of effective facilitators. This is relevant to supervisees as well as supervisors.

Driscoll's key attributes are:

- An ability to work collaboratively
- Integrity
- Honesty
- Sensitivity
- Self-awareness
- Credibility
- A sense of humour

What Are the Benefits?

With a positive supervisory relationship practitioners feel supported and experience less stress and burnout, feel less isolated, and need less sick leave. Clinical supervision can be considered part of self-development, extending clinical competence through work-based learning.

CQC (2013) guidance states it helps practitioners in managing the personal and professional demands created by *"the nature of their work."* It is a space to consider skills and receive feedback separate from the management line. CQC highlights that clinical supervision is

> *particularly important for those who work with people who have complex and challenging needs – clinical supervision provides an environment in which they can explore their own personal and emotional reactions to their work. It can allow the member of staff to reflect on and challenge their own practice in a safe and confidential environment.*

RCSLT states that *"All organisations need to make a positive, unambiguous commitment to a strong supervision and reflective practice culture."*

Supervision forms 'an essential component' of a good quality service. Supervision enhances quality by:

- *Ensuring accountable decision making.*
- *Enabling identification of risk.*
- *Facilitating learning and professional development.*
- *Promoting staff wellbeing.*

(RCSLT 2017)

What Is My Responsibility as a Speech and Language Therapist?

RCSLT is specific and clear in guidance that at service level there has to be commitment to both supervision and reflective learning. Additionally the individual practitioner needs to take *"personal responsibility for fostering a strong supervision culture, by ensuring that they access regular supervision and training related to this."*

We have a responsibility to be reflective practitioners accessing clinical supervision and ensuring skills remain sharp. In summary RCSLT says:

> *A commitment to consistently evaluating knowledge, skills and practice in the context of supervision is essential and requires honesty and professional integrity.*

Situational Supervision – Avoiding Falling into Rabbit Holes

Clinical supervision is about far more than case-based support. The crucial thing is to know what supervision involves and have confidence in building positive and productive supervisory relationships, whether as supervisor or supervisee. When a case or situation is discussed there is a need to consider the whole scenario in depth, a multi-faceted, technicolour 3D situation. Reflective practice along with other techniques from the supervisory toolkit allows dynamic conversation about the events, the clinical stories which practitioners bring to supervision.

This reflective journey draws to a close by going back to Alice and her rabbit holes and looking glass. I hope that by utilising reflective practice in clinical supervision that you will avoid falling down too many rabbit holes, but when you inevitably do, that you find a looking glass nearby to guide you back to the surface again.

"*Every adventure requires a first step*
Not all who wander are lost."
"*Only a few find the way. Some don't recognize it when they do, some don't*
ever want to."

Cheshire Cat, Alice's Adventures in Wonderland

Cameos
Putting It into Practice in Professional Situations

All the cameos have their roots in professional scenarios, but they have been fictionalised, blended, mixed up, merged together so nothing is recognisable. All are designed to bring real life into theory and give a flavour of 'therapy life.'

JESSICA OVERCOMES 'THE OVERLOAD'

Working with Jessica was a positive process. The focus was initially on casework with Jessica working out the strategies which most helped her cope in a busy clinical role. She hoped to be a Band 7 in the next two years and knew she needed to extend her organisation and leadership skills alongside her clinical competencies. Jessica was always positive and looking for solutions for the times when she felt 'overload' creeping in. We explored what the 'overload' consisted of and the times when it was strongest and when she was less aware of it.

The feeling of being overwhelmed by admin became known in our conversations as 'on the overload.' The overload resembled a mist or fog creeping in and wasn't always noticed till it had filled the room.

Once we had worked through ways of pre-empting overload and pushing back the encroaching mist it felt like a safe platform had been reached. Next the need was to enjoy the job again after a difficult period. The focus changed to coaching in supervision: what Jessica needed to do in order to increase her chances of promotion, either in her team or other organisations. Jessica had objectives in her Performance Development Review, but these were not specifically focused on her career progression and dream job.

In the end a focus on leadership skills and an intention to be pro-active about innovation in clinical work and governance in her team

DOI: 10.4324/9781003226772-24

made a difference. Jessica wanted to show colleagues and her manager that she had developed and was ready for new challenges.

This was a journey from supervision focusing on practical ways of dealing with 'the overload' to a solution-focused (doing more of what works well) coaching approach to support wider development.

RESTORATIVE BEFORE DEVELOPMENTAL SUPERVISION

Anna was working in a large NHS Trust. She had moved to a different team focusing on Adult Re-hab with a multi-disciplinary team approach. This wasn't going well. Anna had thrived in her last role and welcomed this move as a positive opportunity. She was, however, missing her colleagues who had become friends over time and felt less enthusiastic about this new role. Her new manager had suggested she access additional supervision to support her in this transitional period. Anna had been reluctant and felt this was a sign of failing in her performance but agreed to more frequent schedule of supervision with a supervisor outside of the team.

The first two meetings were cathartic. They were scheduled close together as the reality was that there was not enough time to complete everything Anna brought to the first meeting. The supervisor listened and booked in a second meeting the following week. This was unusual, but felt to be necessary. Due to calendar complications the second meeting was arranged as an online teleconference.

The first meeting there had been a cathartic 'offload' of regrets, anxieties about failure in the new role, and a very miserable picture. As per restorative resilient supervision the supervisor listened, summarising to check her understanding of the situation. The first session had ended with simple validation by the supervisor that this change was difficult and for Anna to know she had been exceptional in her previous role and those skills were still there.

Towards the end of the second meeting the supervisor felt able to do more than listen. It was possible to begin to ask questions and use a reflective model to begin a structured exploration of what Anna was experiencing. The supervisor facilitated Anna in choosing two or three particularly stressful situations in the new role and exploring reactions, feelings, and any common patterns. There were also the beginnings of a search for glimmers (small positives). This continued into the third session (the following week) where relationships, strengths, and gaps were considered.

The supervisor made the decision to schedule weekly sessions knowing there was time, availability, and support for this. This is not possible for every practitioner.

Anna began to network in the wider team more. She built relationships based on joint working with the assistant clinical psychologist and OT. Her relationship with an especially dogmatic senior colleague improved over time, but the difference in values and beliefs about how to approach therapy meant Anna felt she was always 'working hard' to maintain the relationship. Eventually Anna left to work in a similar post in a neighbouring department. Interestingly she stayed in this specialist area and maintained contact with her supervisor.

THROUGH THE LOOKING GLASS – SEEING OURSELVES DIFFERENTLY

Stacey had been receiving supervision for several months. It was positive. Her supervisor listened to what she brought each time to supervision and then there was some joint problem solving which usually seemed helpful. Yes, this might possibly resemble 'tick box' supervision, but Stacey was confident in her work and the supervisor wasn't noticing any need to challenge.

Then Stacey spent a period of time away from her team on special leave. This had been unexpected and taken at short notice. On her return things didn't seem to be going quite as well. Stacey was proud of herself for coping and settling back into her work. It hadn't been an easy time personally and it still wasn't easy. She began taking more sick leave or calling in and booking leave at very short notice. Her manager had said this was no longer possible as there had been several expressions of dissatisfaction from clients who had been re-scheduled. When her manager spoke with the clients it had been apparent that there had been more cancellations than anyone realised and clients were less happy with the service.

When she arrived at the next supervision session Stacey was angry. She was disappointed that her manager and team were not supporting her at this time of difficulty in her life. The supervisor's impression was of genuine distress with this overlay of irritation and anger with colleagues. As Stacey talked, the supervisor perceived the perspectives of others. Colleagues had covered Stacey's workload at short notice and had accepted and done this in a supportive way. There seemed little in the way of thanks for their efforts. This was still happening and although there was still support, it was clear that colleagues were tired of covering and beginning to question if this was always necessary. Resentment had surfaced. There were very different viewpoints and perceptions of this situation.

The supervisor was struggling with the direction to take. The last session had ended with Stacey feeling a little better 'in herself,' but the supervisor could see that there was a lack of awareness about the load her colleagues were taking. The low-level friction, which with one colleague was verging on passive aggression, was likely to continue. There was also the possibility of performance management on the horizon.

Stacey asked for an additional ad hoc supervision. Her manager had broached the possibility of more structured support for her performance at work in the context of the dissatisfied clients which had caused her considerable shock. The supervisor began by listening and decided this was not stress linked to burnout and was more an inability for Stacey to perceive that there might be some foundation to the attitude of colleagues. It felt like a complicated, tangled web, and the supervisor was unsure if she could approach this without causing more distress and perhaps damaging the supervisory relationship.

The supervisor decided to change the format of the session and bring in a more structured reflective model. This proved to be very helpful as it gave some formal distance to the questions, which came out of the model. Stacey could see the reflective cycle and associated questions and the direction of the conversation. In effect the supervisor moved to a more formal type of reflective practice. The advantage was the questions enabled Stacey to gain insight and see how her last-minute cancellations and general disengagement from the team impacted on others. The structured model allowed her to see the situation from different perspectives.

Stacey began to offer help to colleagues in a more reciprocal way. When she felt able to she volunteered for a clinical governance co-ordination role. At the last session her manager had suggested a laptop and more remote options for working which was a valued win-win solution.

CHANGE IN MANAGER LEADS TO CHANGE IN ROLE AND REMIT

Jonathon had been working in a mainstream school service. He had been a support assistant in school prior to taking on the role of assistant practitioner. He had received in-house training and support and was committed to his role. There had been a change in leadership in his service and care pathways were being updated and modernised. There was a strong commitment to norming practice across the service so care was equitable. Jonathon appreciated this was necessary and mostly welcomed it and had been excited to know that the role of the assistant practitioner would be recognised and specified in the new pathways. Then the first pathway was presented to the team. He had experienced shock and disappointment during the presentation and felt unable to express this. The problem was that he had developed a specific role and what he regarded as expertise in supporting children in the classroom. He had used his educational background to enhance and strengthen the clinical approach of his team.

He saw his role as working both with, and alongside the qualified therapists in delivering innovative targets and outcomes. He was not qualified and knew he did not want to follow that route, but he felt had a clearly defined and distinct role which he enjoyed very much. It did not seem to exist in the new care pathway. He felt his role had been axed and no one had spoken to him about it. He no longer wanted to go to work and felt very let down by his team.

His supervisor listened and tried to work out what was happening. Jonathon was clearly very bruised emotionally by events in his service. The supervisor thought it likely that the practitioner who had devised the new care pathway was totally unaware of the implications for Jonathon and other assistant practitioners. The supervisor decided to begin to ask questions to check out her theory about what was happening. Then she decided this was one of those occasions where advice was needed. The supervisor could have listened further and supported Jonathon through his angst at a changed job role. However, she felt that some direct communication might actually change the direction of the pathway changes.

After exploring several options Jonathon decided to talk to other assistants in the team and share with the service leadership their need to be involved in the process of producing the changed pathways. They needed their knowledge, experience, and different perspective to be valued. He also knew that he needed to talk to the therapist who had devised the care pathway which had caused the distress, and he acknowledged that she had asked for feedback about the pathway. The supervisor noted that this was a team which was modernising and dynamic but had some learning to do about including all practitioners in decision making and there was a problem to be addressed if the assistant practitioners were not confident in expressing their opinions.

FREEZE FRAMING AND FAST FORWARDING EVENTS

Nadia was working with consultant medical colleagues in a joint clinic. She had a highly specialist role and felt generally confident in her decision making. What was happening though was that she was holding back from giving her opinion in planning conversations with a specific colleague. She worked with one consultant with no difficulties, but the style of the other consultant meant she was not communicating effectively.

The supervisor used some appreciative inquiry questions and it was clear there were few perceived positives on which to build. So, the supervisor changed to a reflective model and brought in the idea of looking at events through different lenses. This wasn't quite Brookfield's lenses as the supervisor thought that this would be 'too much.' However the idea of standing back and then looking at her role and contribution at a safe distance as if through a lens helped. The supervisor used 'streaming' imagery to add depth to the discussions. When a specific interaction was freeze framed this really helped Nadia to reflect, rewind, and consider what had been in her thoughts and why she had held back from challenging her colleague with her slightly different opinion about what the client needed.

After the freeze frame analysis the supervisor brought in more fast forward with reflecting on what might happen next time, what might Nadia say differently and 'rehearse' and feel confident saying it. The combination of the freeze frame and fast forward gave opportunity for reflection on events plus anticipatory reflection. Nadia reported that she had begun to use this technique just before the joint consultations to plan and prepare. She also noticed that she was beginning to pause within the situation and adjust her contributions 'in real time.' This sounded like reflection in action which can be really hard to do. Things weren't perfect as her colleague was difficult to work with, but the joint consultations no longer felt like the dismal swamp.

BETHAN APPROACHING BURNOUT

Bethan was a team leader who generally enjoyed her work. A management re-structure and a new focus on waiting list targets was beginning to have an impact on her team. Her new immediate manager was not an AHP and was unable to appreciate why more children could not be seen within the target waiting time.

This was resulting in considerable anger in the team who felt clinical standards for ongoing care might be compromised if more children were seen for initial assessment. A duty of care would be established and workload problems compounded.

Bethan was not sleeping and finding it more difficult to cut off from work. She felt her attention span was reducing when listening to people. What had changed was that she no longer felt comfortable going to work and was dreading one-to-one meetings with her manager and her staff.

Bethan had cancelled two supervision meetings. She asked for the next one to be online as she didn't want to spend time travelling. Her supervisor immediately noticed that Bethan had changed since the last meeting; she looked and sounded flat and defeated and on top of this had begun to book in and see additional cases herself to try to improve the waiting times. During the session she talked while her supervisor listened. Her supervisor was able to comment that it was no surprise she felt this way, it was a very difficult situation to experience and to be compassionate and gentle to herself. Bethan was blaming herself and her personality for feeling low about her job.

Her supervisor suggested taking some time off work, perhaps consulting her general practitioner. Bethan did not feel she wanted to do that at this point, but accepted that she needed to do something. She acknowledged she was stuck in a quagmire. She agreed to ask for immediate annual leave and take time accrued and step aside from work for a few days.

Her supervisor knew there were reflective conversations about standards, risk, and staff wellbeing ahead but knew that today it was a case of actively listening. She suggested scheduling a session immediately after Bethan's leave. Her supervisor also suggested, as she was aware this was possible, that Bethan contact her manager and explain she felt run down and needed a break from work and also made it clear that the tensions in her team resulting from the waiting list concerns were impacting on her wellbeing at work and to request counselling via Occupational Health. Her supervisor felt this might reinforce the message that things were very difficult. Bethan needed to be authentic and say how things really were in her team. However distant the immediate manager they should become aware of risk in this situation and reflect on the situation themselves.

This scenario had a positive outcome. This would not always be the case in this type of situation. On her return from leave Bethan met her immediate manager who then explained she was new to her role and had not anticipated the impact of her directive to reduce waiting times on the team. She was under pressure to produce results (lower waits) herself and now had more awareness of clinical risks involved. She was concerned that if the situation regarding waiting lists did not improve then the tendering process for the contract might be more difficult with a potential loss of the contract. It helped Bethan to know more of the wider context and to feel like her manager was human.

The outcome was a team planning session led by Bethan, which the senior manager supported, which focused on the service provided and any innovative ideas to improve waiting times.

Throughout this difficult time her supervisor increased the frequency of the sessions. There was a further session after Bethan's leave where her supervisor merely listened and validated how Bethan felt. This then moved into reflective practice with active consideration of how to approach conversations or emails with her manager and how to interact with her team and re-gain her confidence as a manager.

CONFLICTING DEMANDS – A SPIKE IN WORKLOAD AND TIGHT DEADLINES

Cathy arrived at supervision feeling overloaded with requests from colleagues. She worked as an assistant practitioner in a team with 14 therapists and 4 assistants. That month had been particularly difficult as she had received several requests to prepare resources with very little notice and a short deadline as these were all 'urgent.' In conversation it emerged that she also felt that one of her colleagues wasn't taking on a fair share of the workload. To make matters worse one of the therapists had been sharp with her about her not making the deadline for completion of resources. Cathy knew the therapists were often late completing their work and this really didn't seem fair. She usually enjoyed her job but was increasingly going home still dwelling on inherent unfairness. She was feeling more and more apart from her team.

Her supervisor was part of this team and listened to Cathy's story. She realised that there was an unfortunate set of circumstances which had resulted in a spike in work for the assistants and more support could have been given by the team. Her supervisor knew that there was a training project around creating a Total Communication Environment underway and this was happening in one of the busiest months of the year.

There were a number of issues here: learning points for the team as a whole around planning more specifically for a special project; looking at a system to share out resource requests more fairly; and making sure workloads were tracked and monitored centrally. With Cathy's permission she felt some of these could be addressed directly. This was an unusual step and the supervisor thought carefully before suggesting it, but it seemed necessary to act to resolve a situation which was around poor process in the service. Cathy could and would be encouraged to talk about her frustration about what had happened the previous month, but her supervisor had a senior role in the clinical team and could see there needed to be immediate change.

Cathy felt better for talking through what had happened. She also was able to identify what would improve the situation and avoid this overload happening again. She had not said 'no' and kept absorbing work and in her own words 'festering and fuming' about it. She welcomed the supervisor's suggestion about some support around suggesting changes in team process and felt empowered to go and have a conversation with her team about her own situation and the need for things to be done differently in future.

And Finally

The cameos throughout this book spotlight the wide variety of situations which can be brought to supervision in speech and language therapy. The common denominator in all the scenarios is focused listening with summarising or asking further questions to check understanding of what is being described. A clinical supervisor can draw on their experience to give advice to a less experienced colleague who is struggling with a clinical case. They might also share stories of practice and strategies and solutions which have worked in the past. There needs to be a positive supervisory relationship with mutual trust and respect. There is usually an element of reflective conversation with guided prompts to view and re-view events and work out how to approach and do things differently.

At its best clinical supervision should be restorative, support resilience, safeguard standards, and put work-based learning right at the centre of continuing professional development.

"Begin at the beginning ... and go on till you come to the end: then stop."
The King of Hearts, *Alice's Adventures in Wonderland*.

Bibliography

Adams-Webber, Jack, Research in Personal Construct Psychology. In: Fransella Fay (ed.) *International Handbook of Personal Construct Psychology* (Wiley, pp. 51–58, 2003).

Adams, Scott, *The Dilbert Principle* (Boxtree Ltd, Reprint Third Printing edition, 2020).

Aguilar, Elena, *Onward: Cultivating Emotional Resilience in Educators* (Jossey-Bass, 2018).

Ancis, J. R. and Marshall, D. S., Using a Multicultural Framework to Assess Supervisees' Perceptions of Culturally Competent Supervision (*Journal of Counseling & Development*, 88, pp. 277–284, 2010).

Argyris, Chris and Schön, Donald, *Organizational Learning: A Theory of Action Perspective* (Addison Wesley, 1978).

Argyris, Chris and Schön, Donald, *Organizational Learning ll: Theory, Method, and Practice* (FT Press, 1995).

ASHA Telepractice, *The Telepractice Evidence Map for Pertinent Scientific Evidence, Expert Opinion, and Client/Caregiver Perspective* (2005) Website: asha.org.

ASHA Telepractice, *Services and Coronavirus/COVID-19* (2021) Website: asha.org.

Association of Speech and Language Therapists in Independent Practice ASLTIP. Website: https://asltip.com.

Austen, Jane, *Pride and Prejudice* (1813).

Australian College of Midwives (ACM), *Position Statement 'Clinical Supervision for Nurses and Midwives'* (The Australian College of Midwives, 2019).

Ayres David J., *Critical Incidents in Teaching* (University of East London, 2013 & 2017) Blogpost discussing David Tripp's approaches to the analysis of incidents, and how the practice can help teachers to develop their professional judgement.

Barksby, J, Butcher, N and Whysall, A, A New Model of Reflection for Clinical Practice (*Nursing Times*, 111(34/35), pp. 34–35, 2015).

Baughan, Jacqui and Smith, Ann, *Compassion, Caring and Communication: Skills for Nursing Practice* (Routledge; 2nd edition, 2013).

Beddoe, Liz, Surveillance or Reflection: Professional Supervision in 'The Risk Society' (*British Journal of Social Work*, 40(4), pp. 1279–1296, June 2010).

Beddoe, Liz and Davys, Allyson, *Challenges in Professional Supervision: Current Themes and Models for Practice* (Jessica Kingsley Publishers, 2016).

Beddoe, Liz and Davys, Allyson, *Best Practice in Professional Supervision, A Guide for the Helping Professions* (Jessica Kingsley Publishers; 2nd edition, 2020).

Bernard Janine, M. and Goodyear, Rod, *Fundamentals of Clinical Supervision* (Allyn & Bacon; 3rd edition, 2004).

Bernay, Ross, Mindfulness and the Beginning Teacher (*Australian Journal of Teacher Education*, 39(7), January 2014).

Bernay, Ross, Esther Graham, Esther, Devcich, Daniel A., Rix, Grant and Rubie-Davies, Christine M., *Pause, Breathe, Smile: A Mixed-Methods Study of Student Wellbeing Following Participation in an Eight-Week, Locally Developed Mindfulness Program in Three New Zealand Schools* (Advances in School Mental Health Promotion, 2016).

Berne, Eric, *The Games People Play: Psychology of Human Relationships* (London: Penguin, 2010).

Berne, Eric, *The Games People Play: The Psychology of Human Relationships* (Penguin Life, 2016).

Birkeland, L., *Storytelling and Staff Training in Kindergarten*, paper presented at EECERA Conference, Alkmaar, Holland (2001).

Bishop, V., Sweeney. In: V. Bishop (ed.) *Clinical Supervision in Practice* (Palgrave-Macmillan; 2nd edition, 2007).

Biswas-Diener, Robert, *Practicing Positive Psychology Coaching: Assessment, Activities and Strategies for Success* (Wiley; 1st edition, 2010).

Bolton, Gillie and Delderfield, Russell, *Reflective Practice: Writing and Professional Development Paperback* (SAGE Publications Ltd; 1st edition 2001, 5th edition, 2018).

Bond, M. and Holland, S., *Skills of Clinical Supervision for Nurses: A Practical Guide for Supervisees, Clinical Supervisors and Managers* (Open University Press; 2nd edition, 1998).

Borton, T., *Reach, Touch and Teach* (Hutchinson, 1970).

Boud, D., Keogh, M. and Walker, D., *Reflection: Turning Experience into Learning* (Kogan Page, 1985).

Briggs, Myres, *Gifts Differing: Understanding Personality Type* (Davies-Black Publishing, 1980). British Association of Counselling and Psycotherapy (BACP) website.

Bronte, Emily, *Wuthering Heights* (1847).

Brookfield Stephen, D., *Becoming a Critically Reflective Teacher* (Jossey-Bass, 1995).

Brunwasser, Steven and Gillham, Jane, A Meta-Analytic Review of the Penn Resiliency Program's Effect on Depressive Symptoms (*Journal of Consulting and Clinical Psychology*, 77(6), pp. 1042–1054, 2009).

Burns, Kidge, Ten Minute Talk: Using a Solution Focused Approach in Supervision (*Solution News*, 3(3), December 2008).

Burns, Kidge, *Focus on Solutions: A Health Professionals Guide* (Solutions Books; Revised edition, 2016).

Butterworth, Tony, *Clinical Supervision and Mentorship in Nursing* (Nelson Thornes Ltd; 2nd edition, 1992 & 1998).

Buus, Niels and Gonge Henrik, Translation of the Manchester Clinical Supervision Scale (MCSS) into Danish and a Preliminary Psychometric Validation (*International Journal of Mental Health Nursing*, 22(2), pp. 145–153, 2013).

Byron, Katie, *A Mind at Home with Itself: How Asking Four Questions Can Free Your Mind, Open Your Heart, and Turn Your World Around* (HarperOne, 2017).

Byron, Katie and Mitchell, Stephen, *A Thousand Names for Joy: How to Live in Harmony with the Way Things Are* (Rider, 2007).

Calkin, Sarah, Nurses More Stressed Than Combat Troops (*Nursing Times*, January 2013).

Campbell, Jennifer and Christopher John, Chambers, Teaching Mindfulness to Create Effective Counselors (*Journal of Mental Health Counseling*, 35, pp. 213–226, 2012).

Capito, C. et al., Professional Midwifery Advocates: Delivering Restorative Clinical Supervision (*Nursing Times Online*, 118(2), pp. 26–28, 2022).

Care Quality Commission, *Supporting Information and Guidance: Supporting Effective Clinical Supervision* (Care Quality Commission, 2013).

Carlson, Richard, *Don't Sweat the Small Stuff: Simple ways to Keep the Little Things from Overtaking Your Life* (Hodder Paperbacks, 1998).

Carroll, Lewis, *Alice in Wonderland Collection: Alice's Adventures in Wonderland & Through the Looking-Glass: And What Alice Found There* (Macmillan Collector's Library; Main Market edition, 2016).

Carroll, Lewis, *Alice in Wonderland/Alice through the Looking Glass* (1865 & 1871).

Carroll, Michael and Margaret Tholstrup (eds.) *Integrative Approaches to Supervision* (Jessica Kingsley, 2008).

Carroll, Michael, *Effective Supervision for the Helping Professions* (SAGE Publications Ltd; 2nd edition, 2014).

Cassedy, Paul, *First Steps in Clinical Supervision: A Guide for Healthcare Professionals* (McGraw-Hill Education, 2010 & Open University Press, 2010).

Chesner, Anna and Zografou, Lia (eds.) *Creative Supervision Across Modalities: Theory and Applications for Therapists, Counsellors and Other Helping Professionals* (Jessica Kingsley Publishers, 2013).

Chien, Chin-Wen, Analysis of Design and Delivery of Critical Incident Workshops for Elementary School English as a Foreign Language Teachers in Community of Practice (*Education 3–13*, 46(4), pp. 1–15, April 2016).

Chopra, Taraasha, All Supervision is Multicultural: A Review of Literature on the Need for Multicultural Supervision in Counseling (*Psychological Studies*, 58, pp. 335–338, 2013).

Clibbens, Nicola, Ashmore, Russell and Carver, Neil, Group Clinical Supervision for Mental Health Nursing Students (*British Journal of Nursing*; Mark Allen Publishing, 16(10), pp. 594–598, May 2007).

Clutterbuck, David, *Everyone Needs a Mentor: Fostering Talent at Work; Series: Developing Skills* (Kogan Page, 1991 & 2014).

Clutterbuck, D. and Lane, G., *The Situational Mentor: An International Review of Competences and Capabilities in Mentoring* (Gower Publishing Ltd, 2004).

Cogher, L., The Use of Non-Directive Play in Speech and Language Therapy (*Child Language Teaching and Therapy*, 15(1), pp. 7–15, 1999).

Coles, Colin and Fish, Della, *Developing Professional Judgement in Health Care: Learning Through the Critical Appreciation of Practice* (Butterworth-Heinemann; 2nd edition, 1997).

Cooperrider, David L., *Prospective Theory: Appreciative Inquiry: Toward a Methodology for Understanding and Enhancing Organizational Innovation* (NRD Publishing, 2021).

Cooperrider, David L. and Diane, Whitney, *Appreciative Inquiry: A Positive Revolution in Change: A Positive Revolution in Change* (Berrett-Koehler Publishers, 2005).

Cooperrider, David L., Diane, Whitney and Stavros, Jacqueline M., *The Appreciative Inquiry Handbook: For Leaders of Change* (Berrett-Koehler Publishers; 2nd edition, 2008).

Covey Stephen, R., *The 7 Habits of Highly Effective People: Restoring the Character Ethic* (Simon and Schuster, 1989).

Covey Stephen, R., *Principle Centred Leadership* (Simon & Schuster UK; Reissue edition, 1999).

Covey Stephen, R., *The 7 Habits of Highly Effective People: Revised and Updated: 30th Anniversary Edition* (Simon & Schuster UK; Reissue edition, 2020).

Crockett, J. and Hays, D., The Influence of Supervisor Multicultural Competence on the Supervisory Working Alliance, Supervisee Counseling Self-Efficacy, and Supervisee Satisfaction with Supervision: A Mediation Model (*Counselor Education & Supervision*, 54, pp. 258–273, 2015).

Cullen, A., Burnout; Why Do We Blame Nurses? (*American Journal of Nursing*, 95(11), pp. 23–28, November 1995).

Cummins, Keena, *VERVE Child Interaction: Video, Endorse, Respect, Vitalise, Eyes* www.vervechildinteraction.org.

Cutcliffe, John R., Kristiina, Hyrkäs and John, Fowler, *Routledge Handbook of Clinical Supervision* (Routledge Handbooks Online, 2010).

Dana, A. Deborah and Porges, Stephen W., *Anchored: How to Befriend Your Nervous System Using Polyvagal Theory* (Sounds True Inc, 2021).

David, Susan, *Emotional Agility: Get Unstuck, Embrace Change, and Thrive in Work and Life* (Avery Publishing Group, 2016).

Davidson, Richard and Kabat-Zinn, Jon et al., Alterations in Brain and Immune Function Produced by Mindfulness Meditation (*Psychosomatic Medicine*, 65, pp. 564–570, 2003).

Davys, Allyson and Beddoe, Liz, *Best Practice in Supervision: A Guide for the Helping Professions* (Jessica Kingsley Publisher, 2010).

Day-Vines, N. L. and Holcomb-McCoy, C., Broaching the Subjects of Race, Ethnicity, and Culture as a Tool for Addressing Diversity in Counselor Education Classes. In: J. West, D. Bubenzer, J. Cox and J. McGlothlin (eds.) *Teaching in Counselor Education: Engaging Students in Meaningful Learning* (Association for Counselor Education and Supervision, pp. 151–165, 2013).

De Haan, Erik and Nieß, Christiane, Critical Moments in a Coaching Case Study: Illustration of a Process Research Model (*Consulting Psychology*

Journal: Practice and Research, American Psychological Association, 64(3) pp. 198–224, 2012).

De Shazer, S., *Clues: Investigating Solutions in Brief Therapy* (WW Norton and Company, 1988).

Dewey, John, *How We Think* (D.C. Heath and Company, 1910).

Dickson, Anne, *A Woman in Your Own Right* (Quartet Books Ltd; Later Printing edition, 1983).

Dimond, B., Legal Aspects of Clinical Supervision 1: Employer vs Employee (*British Journal of Nursing*, 7(7), pp. 393–395, 1998a).

Dimond, B., Legal Aspects of Clinical Supervision 2: Professional Accountability (*British Journal of Nursing*, 7(8), pp. 487–489, 1998b).

Division of Clinical Psychology (DCP), *The British Psychological Society, Continuing Professional Development Guidelines* (British Psychological society, 2010).

Douglas, H. and Ginty, M., The Solihull Approach: Changes in Health Visiting Practice (*Community Practitioner*, 74(6), pp. 222–224, 2021).

Dreison, K. C., Luther, L., Bonfils, K. A., Sliter, M. T., McGrew, J. H. and Salyers, M. P., Job Burnout in Mental Health Providers: A Meta-Analysis of 35 Years of Intervention Research (*Journal of Occupational Health Psychology*, 23(1), pp. 18–30, January 2018).

Driscoll, John, *Practising Clinical Supervision: A Reflective Approach for Healthcare Professionals* (Bailliere Tindall; 2nd edition, 2006).

Duncan, B. L., *Handbook of Solution-Focused Brief Therapy* (Jossey-Bass-Wiley, 1996).

Dunkley-Bent, J., A-EQUIP: The New Model of Midwifery Supervision (*British Journal of Midwifery*, 25, p. 5, 2017).

Edwards, Deborah, Hannigan, Ben, Fothergill, Anne and Coyle, David, Factors Influencing the Effectiveness of Clinical Supervision (*Journal of Psychiatric and Mental Health Nursing*, 12(4), pp. 405–414, August 2005).

Epstein, Ronald M. and Hundert, Edward M., Defining and Assessing Professional Competence (*JAMA: The Journal of the American Medical Association*, 287(2), p. 226, Feb 2002).

Evans, Kenneth Roy and Gilbert, Maria, *Psychotherapy Supervision* (McGraw-Hill Companies Inc, 2000).

Fialkov, Claire and Haddad, David, Appreciative Clinical Training (*Training and Education in Professional Psychology*, 6(4), pp. 204–210, 2012).

Fish, Della and Twinn, Sheila, *How to Enable Learning Through Professional Practice: A Cross-Profession Investigation of the Supervision of Pre-Service Practice: A Pilot Study Report* (West London Institute of Higher Education, 1989).

Fish, Della and Twinn, Sheila, *Quality Clinical Supervision in Health Care: Principled Approaches to Practice* (Butterworth-Heinemann, 1996).

Fisher, Roger and Ury, William, *Getting to Yes: Negotiating an Agreement Without Giving In* (Random House Business; 1st edition, 2012).

Francis, Dawn, The Reflective Journal: A Window to Preservice Teachers' Practical Knowledge (*Teaching and Teacher Education*, 11(3), pp. 229–241, May 1995).

Fransella, Fay (ed.) *The Essential Practitioner's Handbook of Personal Construct Psychology* (John Wiley & Sons Ltd, 2005).

Fransella, Fay, PCP: A Personal Story (*Personal Construct Theory & Practice*, 4, p. 39, Centre for Personal Construct Psychology, University of Hertfordshire, 2007).

FutureNHS Platform; FutureNHS is a Collaboration Platform that Empowers Everyone Working in Health and Social Care to Safely Connect, Share and Learn Across Boundaries. Website: https://www.england.nhs.uk.

Gabrielsson, S., Engström, Å. and Gustafsson, S., Supporting Recovery Through Reflective Practice; Evaluating Reflective Practice Groups in a Mental Health Context: Swedish Translation and Psychometric Evaluation of the Clinical Supervision Evaluation Questionnaire (*BMC Nursing*, 18, p. 2, 2019).

Gaffney, Maureen, *Flourishing: How to Achieve a Deeper Sense of Well-Being and Purpose in a Crisis* (Penguin Life, 2012 & 2015).

Gander, F., Proyer, R. T. and Ruch, W., Strength-Based Positive Interventions: Further Evidence for Their Potential in Enhancing Well-Being and Alleviating Depression (*Journal of Happiness Studies*, 14, pp. 1241–1259, 2013).

Gannon, Judie and Haan de, Erik, The Coaching Relationship. In: T. Bachkirova, D. Spence and G. Drake (eds.) *The SAGE Handbook of Coaching* Ch 11 (SAGE Publications Ltd, pp. 195–218, 2017).

Gardner, Fiona, *Being Critically Reflective: Engaging in Holistic Practice, Series: Practice Theory in Context* (Red Globe Press, 2014).

Gates, Barbara, Margaret Cullen, Margaret and Nisker, Wes, Interview with Richard Davidson, Daniel Goleman & Jon Kabat-Zinn: Friends in Mind, Friends at Heart (*Inquiring Mind*, Spring, 25(2), 2009).

Ghaye, Tony, *Teaching and Learning through Reflective Practice: A Practical Guide for Positive Action* (Routledge; 1st edition, 1998; Latest edition; 2010).

Ghaye, Tony, Reflective Practice (*Faster Higher Stronger*, 10, pp. 9–12, 2001).

Ghaye, Tony and Lillyman Sue, *Effective Clinical Supervision: The Role of Reflection* (Quay Books, Mark Allen Publishing; 2nd edition, 2007).

Ghaye, Tony and Lillyman Sue, *Learning Journals and Critical Incidents: Reflective Practice for Health Care Professionals* (Quay Books, Mark Allen Publishing Ltd; 2nd edition, 2008a).

Ghaye, Tony and Lillyman Sue, *The Reflective Mentor, Series: Reflective Practice* (Quay Books, Mark Allen Publishing, 2008b).

Ghaye, Tony and Lillyman Sue, *Reflection: Principles and Practice for Healthcare Professionals Reflective Practice Series* (Quay Books, Mark Allen Publishing Ltd, 2nd edition, 2010).

Ghaye, Tony, Lillyman, Sue and Gillespye, David, *Empowerment Through Reflection: The Narratives of Healthcare Professionals; Reflective Practice Series* (Quay Books, Mark Allen Publishing Ltd, 2000).

Gibbs, Graham, *Experiential Learning* (Further Education Unit, FEU, 1988).

Gibbs, Graham, *Learning by Doing: A Guide to Teaching and Learning Methods* (Further Education Unit, FEU, Oxford Polytechnic, 1998).

Gilbert, M. C. and Evans, K., *Psychotherapy Supervision: An Integrative Relational Approach to Psychotherapy Supervision* (Open University Press, 2000).

Gillham, J. E., Brunwasser, S. M. and Freres, D. R., Preventing Depression in Early Adolescence: The Penn Resiliency Program. In: J. R. Z Abela and B.

L. Hankin (eds.) *Handbook of Depression in Children and Adolescents* (The Guilford Press, pp. 309–322, 2008).

Giltinane, Charlotte Louise, Leadership Styles and Theories (*Nursing Standard*, 27(41), pp. 35–39, 2013).

Glasser, William and Glasser, Naomi, *What are you Doing?* (Harper Colophon Books; 1st edition, 1982).

Goldberg, Rebecca M., Chapter Two: Individual and Group Supervision in Supervision and Agency Management for Counselors. In: A. Hauser Michael and Elizabeth O'Brien (eds.) *Supervision and Agency Management for Counselors* (Springer, pp. 21–48, 2015).

Golding, W., *Lord of the Flies* (Faber and Faber, 1954).

Goleman, Daniel, *Emotional Intelligence:25th Anniversary Edition* (Bloomsbury Publishing, 2020).

Goleman, Daniel and Boyatzis, Richard E., *Emotional Intelligence has 12 Elements. Which Do You Need to Work On?* (Harvard Business Review, Web article, 2017a).

Goleman, Daniel and Boyatzis, Richard E., *Everyday Emotional Intelligence: Big Ideas and Practical Advice on How to Be Human at Work* (Harvard Business Review Press, 2017b).

Goodyear, Rod, Barnett, Jeffrey, Cornish, Jennifer and Lichtenberg, James, Commentaries on the Ethical and Effective Practice of Clinical Supervision (*Professional Psychology: Research and Practice*, 38, pp. 268–275, June 2007).

Gradišek, Polona, Character Strengths and Life Satisfaction of Slovenian In-service and Pre-service Teachers (*Center for Educational Policy Studies Journal*, 2, p. 3, 2012).

Graves, Judy, Factors Influencing Indirect Speech and Language Therapy Interventions for Adults with Learning Disabilities: The Perceptions of Carers and Therapists (*IJDC International Journal of Language & Communication Disorders*, 42(S1), pp. 103–121, March 2007).

Gray, C., *Comic Strip Conversations: Colorful, Illustrated Interactions with Students with Autism and Related Disorders* (Arlington, TX: Future Horizons, 1994).

Griffiths, Fleur, *Communication Counts: Speech and Language Difficulties in the Early Years* (Routledge; 1st edition, 2002).

Grinder, John and Bandler, R., *The Structure of Magic: A Book About Communication and Change* (Vol. 2, Science and Behavior Books, 1989).

Haberlin, S., Mindfulness-Based Supervision: Awakening to New Possibilities (*Journal of Educational Supervision*, 3, p. 3, Article 6, 2020).

Haley Amber, S., Haile Gelawdiyos, M. and Shillingford, Ann, How to Cultivate Culturally Competent Counselors: Integrated Curiosity Supervision Model (*National Cross-Cultural Counseling and Education Conference for Research, Action and Change*, 4, 2020).

Hanen Centre, The, Founded in 1975 by Ayala Hanen Manolson, a Speech-Language Pathologist Who Saw the Potential of Involving Parents in their Child's Early Language Intervention, Website: Hanen.org.

Hardy Kenneth, V. and Bobes, Toby (eds.) *Promoting Cultural Sensitivity in Supervision: A Manual for Practitioners* (Routledge; 1st edition, 2017).

Haskins, N., Whitfield-Williams, M., Shillingford, M. A., Singh, A., Moxley, R. and Ofauni, C., The Experiences of Black Master's Counseling Students: A

Phenomenological Inquiry (*Counseling Education and Supervision*, 52, pp. 162–178, 2013).

Hawkins, P., Mapping It out (*Community Care*, 22, pp. 17–19, 1982).

Hawkins, P. and Shohet, P., *Supervision in the Helping Professions* (Open University Press; 4th edition, 2012).

Hawkins, Peter and McMahon, Aisling, *Supervision in the Helping Professions* (Open University Press; 5th edition, 2020).

Hay, Julie, *Action Mentoring: Creating your own Developmental Alliance* (Sherwood Publishing, 1997).

Health and Care Professions Council HCPC, *Standards of Proficiency for Speech and Language Therapists* (2014).

Health and Care Professions Council HCPC, *Standards of Conduct, Performance and Ethics* (HCPC, 2016).

Health and Care Professions Council HCPC, *The Characteristics of Effective Clinical and Peer Supervision in the Workplace: A Rapid Evidence Review* (Final report November 2019a) Dr Charlotte Rothwell & Dr Amelia Kehoe Dr Sophia Farook Prof Jan Illing.

Health and Care Professions Council HCPC, *Providing Effective Supervision; HCPC Research on Effective Clinical and Peer Supervision in the Workplace* (2019b).

Health and Care Professions Council HCPC, *Meeting our Standards, Supervision, Leadership and Culture, Reflect, Discuss, Develop: The Benefits of Supervision* (2021).

Health and Care Professions Council HCPC, *Supervision Case Studies and Templates* Website: https://www.hcpc-uk.org.

Health Education England, *AHP Support Worker Competency, Education and Career Development Framework* (2021). Website: https://www.hee.nhs.uk.

Health Education and Training Institute, *The Superguide – A Handbook for Supervising Allied Health Professionals* (New South Wales Australia, 2012).

Health & Social Care Professions, *Ireland, Reflective Practice Statement, HSCP CPD Sub-Group* (2017 & 2019).

Helen & Douglas House, Clinical Supervision Project Team, *Clinical Supervision Toolkit* (Oxford: Helen & Douglas House, 2014).

Henderson, Penny, Holloway, Jim and Millar, Anthea, *Practical Supervision: How to Become a Supervisor for the Helping Professions* (Jessica Kingsley Publishers, 2014).

Hewson, Daphne, Supervision of Psychologists: A Supervision Triangle. In M. McMahon and W. Patton (eds.), *Supervision in the Helping Professions: A Practical approach* (Pearson Education, pp. 197–210, 2002).

Hewson, Daphne, *YouTube: Reflective Supervision Toolkit 1, The Supervision Triangle (2018). Tool in: Hewson Daphne and Carroll Michael, Reflective Supervision Toolkit* (MoshPit Publishing, 2016).

Hewson, Daphne and Carroll, Michael, *Reflective Supervision Toolkit* (MoshPit Publishing, 2016).

Hewson, Daphne and Carroll, Michael, *Reflective Practice in Supervision* (MoshPit Publishing, 2016a).

Hewson, Daphne and Carroll, Michael, *Reflective Supervision Toolkit* (MoshPit Publishing, 2016b).

Holloway, Elizabeth L., *Clinical Supervision: A Systems Approach* (SAGE Publications Ltd, 1995).

Honey, P. and Mumford, A., *Learning Styles Questionnaire* (Peter Honey Publications Ltd, 1986a).

Honey, P. and Mumford, A., *The Manual of Learning Styles, Peter Honey Associates* (Peter Honey Publications Ltd, 1986b).

Horn, James, Personal Renewal and Professional Growth for Teachers: A Study of Meaningful Learning in an Interdisciplinary Environment (*Teacher Development*, 3(2), pp. 263–289, 1999).

Horton, Simon, Drachler, Maria, Fuller, Alison and de Carvalho Leite, Carlos Jose, Development and Preliminary Validation of a Measure for Assessing Staff Perspectives on the Quality of Clinical Group Supervision (*International Journal of Language & Communication Disorders, Royal College of Speech & Language Therapists*, 43(2), pp. 126–134, 2008).

Howard, F. M., Supervision. In: H. Love and W. Whittaker (eds.) *Practice Issues for Clinical and Applied Psychologists in New Zealand* (The New Zealand Psychological Society, pp. 340–358, 1997).

Howes, P. Ruth, *A Collaborative Action Research Project with a Team of Speech and Language Therapists; Perceptions and Applications of Reflective Practice*. A thesis submitted in partial fulfilment of the requirements for the Degree of Master of Arts in Professional Training and Development at Leeds Metropolitan University (Carnegie, 2005).

Howes, P. Ruth, *Situational Supervision; Through the Looking Glass* (Reflective Clinical Supervision Training Package, ARC Supervision, 2020).

Hughes, Lynette and Pengelly, Paul, *Staff Supervision in a Turbulent Environment: Managing Process and Task in Front-Line Services* (Jessica Kingsley, 1997).

Hyrkäs, Kristiina, Appelqvist-Schmidlechner, Kaija and Paunonen-Ilmonen, Marita, Expert Supervisors' Views of Clinical Supervision: A Study of Factors Promoting and Inhibiting the Achievements of Multiprofessional Team Supervision (*Journal of Advanced Nursing*, 38(4), pp. 387–397, May 2002).

Inman, A. G., Supervisor Multicultural Competence and its Relation to Supervisory Process and Outcome (*Journal of Marriage and Family Therapy*, 32, pp. 73–85, 2006).

Inskipp, F. and Proctor, B., *The Art, Craft and Tasks of Counselling Supervision, Part 1 – Making the Most of Supervision* (Cascade Publications, 1993).

Jade, Vu, Henry, Jade, Winters, Niall, Lakati, Alice, Oliver, Martin, Geniets, Anne, Mbae, Simon M. and Wanjiru, Hannah, Enhancing the Supervision of Community Health Workers with WhatsApp Mobile Messaging: Qualitative Findings From 2 Low-Resource Settings in Kenya (*Global Health: Science and Practice*, 4(2), pp. 311–325, 2016).

Jasper, Melanie, *Foundations in Nursing and Health Care: Beginning Reflective Practice* (Nelson Thornes Ltd, 2003).

Jasper, Melanie, *Beginning Reflective Practice* (Cengage Learning Inc; 2nd revised edition, 2013).

Johns, Christopher, Visualizing and Realizing Caring in Practice through Guded Reflection (*Journal of Advanced Nursing*, 24(6), pp. 1135–1143, 1996).

Johns, Christopher, *Mindful Leadership* (Palgrave; 1st edition, 2015).

Johns, Christopher (ed.) *Becoming a Reflective Practitioner* (Wiley-Blackwell; 5th edition, 2017).

Jones, Connie T., Welfare, Laura E., Melchior, Shekila and Cash, Rebecca M., Broaching as a Strategy for Intercultural Understanding in Clinical Supervision (*The Clinical Supervisor*, 38, pp. 1–16, 2019).

Kabat-Zinn, Jon, *Wherever You Go, There You Are: Mindfulness Meditation in Everyday Life* (Piatkus; Reprint edition, 2004).

Kadushin, Alfred, *Supervision in Social Work* (Columbia University Press, 1976 & re-print 1992).

Katz, L., *Talks with teachers of young children* (Ablex, 1995).

Kensinger, E., Current Directions in Psychological Science (*Association for Psychological Science*, 16(August), pp. 213–218, 2007).

Kensinger, Elizabeth A., Remembering the Details: Effects of Emotion (*Emotion Review: Journal of the International Society for Research on Emotion*, 1(2), pp. 99–113, 2009).

Kettle, Martin, Achieving Effective Supervision (*Insight* 30, 2015). Institute of research and Innovation in social services (Iriss) website.

Kline, Nancy, *Time to Think: Listening to Ignite the Human Mind* (Cassell, 2002).

Kline, Nancy, *More Time to Think: The power of Independent Thinking* (Cassell, 2015).

Kogan Nataly *Happier Now: How to Stop Chasing Perfection and Embrace Everyday Moments* (Sounds True, 2018).

Kolb, David A., Learning Styles and Disciplinary Differences. In: A. W. Chickering (ed.) *The Modern American College* (San Francisco, LA: Jossey-Bass, pp. 232–255, 1981).

Kolb, David A., *Experiential Learning: Experience as the Source of Learning and Development* (Prentice-Hall, 1984).

Krockow, Eva M., Stretching Theory; How Many Decisions do we Make Each Day? (*Psychology Today*, September 2018).

Kurtz, Arabella, *How to Run Reflective Practice Groups: A Guide for Healthcare Professionals* (Routledge; 1st edition, 2019).

Lahad, Mooli, *Creative Supervision: The Use of Expressive Arts Methods in Supervision and Self-Supervision, Series: Arts Therapies* (Jessica Kingsley Publishers, 2002).

Lancer, Natalie, Clutterbuck, David and Megginson, David, *Techniques for Coaching and Mentoring* (Routledge, 2015).

Langer, Ellen J., *The Power of Mindful Learning* (Da Capo Press Inc; 2nd edition, 1997).

Langer, Ellen J., *Counter Clockwise: Mindful Health and the Power of Possibility* (Ballantine Books; 1st edition, 2009).

Langer, Ellen J., *Mindfulness, 25th anniversary edition* (Merloyd Lawrence Book) Special Edition (Da Capo Lifelong Books; 2nd edition, 2014).

Lapworth, Phil and Sills, Charlotte, *An Introduction to Transactional Analysis: Helping People Change* (SAGE Publications Ltd; 1st edition, 2011).

Lawton, Barbara and Feltham, Colin (eds.) *Taking Supervision Forward; Enquiries and Trends in Counselling and Psychotherapy* (SAGE Publications Ltd, 2000).

Lewis, C. C., Scott, K. E. and Hendricks, K. E., A Model and Guide for Evaluating Supervision Outcomes in Cognitive–Behavioral Therapy-Focused Training

Programs (*Training and Education in Professional Psychology*, 8(3), pp. 165–173, 2014).

Lewis, K., Update on Developments in Behavioural and Cognitive Psychotherapies - A Personal View (*CBT Today*, 40, p. 1, 2012).

Lillyman, Susan and Merrix, Pauline, *Nursing and Health Survival Guide: Portfolios and Reflective Practice* (Routledge; 1st edition, 2012).

Macdonald, Barbara, Restorative Clinical Supervision: A Reflection (*BMJ Midwifery*, 27(4), 2 April 2019).

Malcolmess, Kate, The Care Aims Model. In: Carolyn Anderson and Anna van der Gaag (eds.) *Speech and Language Therapy: Issues in Professional Practice* (Whurr Publishers Limited, chapter 4, pp. 43–72, 2005).

Mataiti, Helen Catherine, *Clinical Supervisor Characteristics Valued by Practising Speech Language Therapists*. A thesis submitted in partial fulfilment of the requirements for the Degree of Master of Speech and Language Therapy in the University of Canterbury (University of Canterbury, 2008).

McGee, Paul, *S.U.M.O (Shut Up, Move On): The Straight–Talking Guide to Succeeding in Life* (Capstone; 3rd edition, 2015).

McGee-Cooper, Ann, *You Don't Have to Go Home from Work Exhausted!: A Program to Bring Joy, Energy, and Balance to Your Life* (Bantam; Reprint edition, 1992).

McGee-Cooper, Ann, *Time Management for Unmanageable People: The Guilt-Free Way to Organize, Energize, and Maximize Your Life* (Bantam; Subsequent edition, 1994).

Mid Staffordshire NHS Foundation Trust Public Inquiry. Independent Report (2013) Website: www.gov.uk.

Milne, Derek, *Evidence-Based Clinical Supervision: Principles and Practice* (Blackwell Publishing; British Psychological Society 2009).

Milne, Derek L., *A Manual for Evidence-Based CBT Supervision: Enhancing Supervision in Cognitive and Behavioural Therapies* (Wiley-Blackwell, 2017).

Milne, Derek L. and Reiser, Robert P., *Supportive Clinical Supervision: Enhancing Well-being and Reducing Burnout through Restorative Leadership* (Pavilion Publishing and Media Ltd, 2020).

Milnes, Tim and Nicolas, Tredell, *William Wordsworth: The Prelude* (Palgrave Macmillan, 2009).

Mohammed, Ruksana, Critical Incident Analysis: Reflections of a Teacher Educator (*Researcher in Teacher Education*, 6(1), pp. 25–29, May 2016).

Moon, Jennifer A., *Reflection in Learning and Professional Development; Theory and Practice* (Routledge; 1st edition, 2000).

Morrison, Ken, *Marx Durkheim, Weber: Formations of Modern Social Thought* (SAGE Publications Ltd; 2nd edition, 2006).

Murnahan, Briana, *Stress and Anxiety Reduction Due to Writing Diaries, Journals, E-Mail, and Weblogs* (Eastern Michigan University, Senior Honors Theses & Projects 230, 2010).

Murphy, Brittany, *Psychometric Evaluation of the Counselor Supervisor Self-Efficacy Scale* (UMSL Graduate Works, Dissertations 717, 2017).

NHS England, *A-EQUIP: A Model of Clinical Midwifery Supervision* (NHSE, 2017).

NHS England, *Professional Midwifery Advocate Model* (NHS England, 2018a).

NHS England, *A-EQUIP: Advocating for Education and Quality Improvement, England's Model of Midwifery Supervision - 'One Year On'* (NHSE, 2018b).

NHS Learning for Scotland, *The Knowledge Network: NMAHP: Supervision: Supporting Learning Environment*. Website: https://learn.nes.nhs.scot.

Niemiec, Ryan M., *Mindfulness and Character Strengths: A Practical Guide to Flourishing* (Hogrefe Publishing, 1st edition, 2013).

Niemiec, Ryan M., *Character Strengths Interventions: A Field Guide for Practitioners* (Hogrefe Publishing, 2017).

O'Connell, B. and Jones, C., Solution-Focused Supervision (*Counselling*, pp. 289–292, November 1997).

Oratio, A. R., Sugarman, M. and Prass, M., A Multivariate Analysis of Clinicians' Perceptions of Supervisory Effectiveness (*Journal of Communication Disorders*, 14(1), pp. 31–42, January 1981).

Padesky, C. A., Kuyken, W. and Dudley, R., *Collaborative Case Conceptualization: Working Effectively with Clients in Cognitive-Behavioral Therapy* (Guilford Press, 2009).

Page, Steve and Wosket, Val, *Supervising the Counsellor and Psychotherapist, A Cyclical Model* (Routledge; 3rd edition, 2014).

Parlarkian, R., *Look, Listen, and Learn: Reflective Supervision and Relationship Based Work* (Washington, DC: Zero to Three, 2001).

Pengelly, Paul and Hughes, Lynette, *Staff Supervision in a Turbulent Environment* (Jessica Kingsley Publishers, 1997).

Pennebaker, James W. and Chung, Cindy K., *Expressive Writing, Emotional Upheavals, and Health* (University of Texas at Austin, 2007).

Pennebaker, James W., Kiecolt-Glaser, J. and Glaser, R., Disclosure of Traumas and Immune Function: Health Implications for Psychotherapy (*Journal of Consulting and Clinical Psychology*, 56, pp. 239–245, 1988).

Pennebaker, James W., Kacewicz, Ewa and Slatcher, Richard, Expressive Writing: An Alternative to Traditional Methods (*Low-Cost Approaches to Promote Physical and Mental Health: Theory, Research, and Practice*, Springer, pp. 271–284, 2006).

Peterson, Christopher and Seligman, M. E. P., *Character Strengths and Virtues: A Handbook and Classification* (APA Press and Oxford University Press, 2004).

Phillips, Annie, *Developing Assertiveness Skills for Health and Social Care Professionals* (Routledge, 2013).

Pitt, Joanne, *Self-Reflection Journal for Therapists: Get the Most Out of Your Sessions with this Guided Self-Reflection Journal* (Independently Published, 2021).

Porges, Stephen W. and Dana A. Deborah, *Clinical Applications of the Polyvagal Theory - The Emergence of Polyvagal-Informed Therapies*. Norton Series on Interpersonal Neurobiology (W. W. Norton & Company; 1st edition, 2018).

Potter, Steve, *Therapy with a Map: A Cognitive Analytic Approach to Helping Relationships* (Luminate, 2020).

Powell, Jean H., The Reflective Practitioner in Nursing (*JAR: Journal of Advanced Nursing*, 14, p. 10, 1989).

Power, S, *Nursing Supervision: A Guide for Clinical Practice* (Sage, 1999).

Proctor, Brigid, Supervision–Competence, Confidence, Accountability (*British Journal of Guidance & Counselling*, 22(3), pp. 309–318, 1994 print, 2007 online).

Proctor, Brigid, Supervision: A Co-operative Exercise in Accountability. In A. Marken and M Payne (eds.), *Enabling and Ensuring: Supervision in Practice* (Leicester National Youth Bureau/Council for Education and Training in Youth and Community Work, 21–23, 1986).

Proctor, Brigid, Training for the Supervision Alliance Attitude, Skills and Intention. In: J. Cutcliffe, T. Butterworth and B. Proctor (eds.) *Fundamental Themes in Clinical Supervision* (Routledge, chapter 3, pp. 25–46, 2001).

Proctor, Brigid, *Group Supervision: A Guide to Creative Practice; Counselling Supervision Series* (SAGE Publications Ltd; 2nd edition, 2008).

Proctor, Brigid, Training for the Supervision Alliance, Attitude, Skills and Intention. In: John R. Cutcliffe, Hyrkäs Kristiina and Fowler John (eds.) *Routledge Handbook of Clinical Supervision* (Routledge, Handbooks Online, 2010).

Proyer, R. T., Gander, F., Wellenzohn, S. and Ruch, W., Strengths-Based Positive Psychology Interventions: A Randomized Placebo-Controlled Online Trial on Long-Term Effects for a Signature Strengths- vs. A Lesser Strengths-Intervention (*Frontiers in Psychology*, 6, p. 456, April 2015).

Purdie, Jeni, *Life Coaching for Dummies* (For Dummies; 1st edition, 2010).

RCSLT, *Supervision Summary: Information for Speech and Language Therapists* (2017) RCSLT Website https://www.rcslt.org.

RCSLT, Sparkes, Cathy and Sam, Simpson (Lead Authors), *Supervision Guidance* (2019). RCSLT Website: https://www.rcslt.org.

RCSLT, *Telehealth Guidance* (2020). RCSLT Website: https://www.rcslt.org.

RCSLT, *Delegation Guidance and Delegation Learning*. RCSLT Website https://www.rcslt.org.

RCSLT, Website https://www.rcslt.org.

RCSLT, *CPD for Newly-Qualified Practitioners (NQPs) The NQP Framework is a Collection of 24 Goals that are All Linked to the RCSLT's Core Capabilities – The Five Key Areas of Particular Strength for the SLT Profession*. RCLST Website: https://www.rcslt.org.

RCSLT, Williamson, Kathleen, *Competencies Project: Support Practitioner Framework* (August 2002a) RCSLT Website https://www.rcslt.org.

RCSLT, Williamson, Kathleen, *The Model of Professional Practice* (September 2002b).

RCSLT, Howes, Ruth (Lead Author), *Assistant Practitioners Professional Framework APPF.; Covering Competencies, Learning and Development* (In draft/ consultation version, 2022) RCSLT Website https://www.rcslt.org.

Richards, Kelly, Self-care and Well-being in Mental Health Professionals: The Mediating Effects of Self-Awareness and Mindfulness (*Journal of Mental Health Counseling*, 32(3), pp. 247–264, July 2010).

Rolfe, G., Freshwater, D. and Jasper, M., *Critical Reflection in Nursing and the Helping Professions: A User's Guide* (Palgrave Macmillan, 2001).

Rothwell, Charlotte, Kehoe, Amanda, Farhene, Farook and Illing, Jan, Enablers and Barriers to Effective Clinical Supervision in the Workplace: A Rapid Evidence Review (*BMJ Open*, 11, p. 9, September 28, 2021).

Rothwell, Charlotte, Kehoe, Amelia, Farook, Sophia and Illing, Jan, *The Characteristics of Effective Clinical and Peer Supervision in the Workplace: A Rapid Evidence Review HCPC Commissioning with Newcastle University* (Final Report, November 2019).

Saab, Mohamad, Kilty, Caroline, Meehan, Elaine and Goodwin, John et al., Peer Group Clinical Supervision: Qualitative Perspectives from Nurse Supervisees, Managers, and Supervisors (*Collegian Journal of the Royal College of Nursing Australia*, 28, p. 4, 2020).

Scaife, Joyce, *Supervising the Reflective Practitioner: An Essential Guide to Theory and Practice* (Routledge; 1st edition, 2010).

Scaife, Joyce, *Supervision in Clinical Practice: A Practitioner's Guide* (Routledge; 3rd edition, 2019).

Schön, D. A., *The Reflective Practitioner: How Professionals Think in Action* (Basic Books, 1983).

Schön, Donald A., *The Reflective Practitioner: How Professionals Think in Action* (Routledge, 1984 & 1991).

Schuck, Caroline and Wood, Jane, *Inspiring Creative Supervision* (Jessica Kingsley Publishers; Illustrated edition, 2011).

Schultz, Joshua, *Gestalt Therapy Explained: History, Definition and Examples* (Positive Psychology.com, 2021).

Schwartz, Tony, McCarthy, Catherine and Gomes, Jean, *The Way We're Working Isn't Working* (Simon & Schuster UK; Reissue edition, 2016).

Seligman, M. E. P. and Csikszentmihalyi, M., Positive Psychology: An Introduction (*American Psychologist*, 55, pp. 5–14, 2000).

Seligman, M. E. P., Steen, T. A., Park, N. and Peterson, C., Positive Psychology Progress: Empirical Validation of Interventions (*American Psychologist*, 60(5), pp. 410–421, 2005).

Seligman, Martin, *Flourish: A New Understanding of Happiness and Well-Being - and How to Achieve Them* (Nicholas Brealey Publishing, 2011).

Seligman, Martin, *Authentic Happiness: Using the New Positive Psychology to Realise your Potential for Lasting Fulfilment* (Nicholas Brealey Publishing; Reprint edition, 2017).

Seligman, Martin, *Learned Optimism: How to Change Your Mind and Your Life* (Nicholas Brealey Publishing, 2018).

Sharp, Jennifer E. and Rhinehart, Alessandra J., Infusing Mindfulness and Character Strengths in Supervision to Promote Beginning Supervisee Development (*Journal of Counselor Practice*, 9(1), pp. 64–80, 2018).

Sharry, John and Madden, Brendan et al., *Becoming a Solution Detective: A Strengths-Based Guide to Brief Therapy* (Routledge; 2nd edition, 2012).

Simons, Daniel J. and Chabris, Christopher F., Gorillas in Our Midst: Sustained Inattentional Blindness for Dynamic Events (*Perception*, 28(9), 1999).

Shohet, Robin, *Passionate Supervision* (Jessica Kingsley Publishers; 1st edition, 2007).

Shohet, Robin, *Supervision as Transformation: A Passion for Learning* (Jessica Kingsley Publishers, 2011).

Shohet, Robin and Shohet, Jean, *In Love with Supervision: Creating Transformative Conversations* (PCCS Books, 2020).

Sloan, Graham, Good Characteristics of a Clinical Supervisor: A Community Mental Health Nurse Perspective (*Journal of Advanced Nursing*, 30(3), pp. 713–722, 1999).

Sloan, Graham, Clinical Supervision: Beginning the Supervisory Relationship. Implementing Effective, Best Practice for Clinical Supervision (*British Journal of Nursing, Mark Allen Publishing*, 14(17), pp. 918–923, September 2005).

Stewart, Trudy and Birdsall, Mark, A Review of the Contribution of Personal Construct Psychology to Stammering Therapy (*Journal of Constructivist Psychology*, 14(3), pp. 215–225, 2001).

Stoltenberg, C. D. and Delworth, U., *Supervising Counselors and Therapists* (Jossey-Bass, 1987).

Stone, Douglas, Patten, Bruce, Heen, Sheila and Fisher, Roger, *Difficult Conversations: How to Discuss What Matters Most* (Penguin; 1st edition, 2000a, re-issue edition, 2011).

Stone, Douglas, Patton, Bruce, Heen, Sheila and Fisher, Roger, *Difficult Conversations: How to Discuss What Matters Most* (Penguin Books; Anniversary, 2000b, Updated edition, 2010).

Tang, Robert L., *Evaluation of Theory and Research* (Oxford University Press, 2005).

Taylor, Beverley J., *Reflective Practice for Healthcare Professionals: A Practical Guide* (Open University Press; 3rd edition, 2010).

Taylor, S. N. and Bright, D. S., Open-Mindedness and Defensiveness in Multisource Feedback Processes: A Conceptual Framework (*The Journal of Applied Behavioural Science*, 47(4), pp. 432–460, 2011).

Thomas, Frank N., Solution-Focused Supervision: The Coaxing of Expertise (*The Family Journal*, 2(1), pp. 11–18, January 1994).

Trammell, Duane, McGee-Cooper, Ann, Looper, Gary and Lowe, Jack (Foreword) *Being the Change: Profiles from Our Servant Leadership Learning Community* (Ann McGee-Cooper and Associates, 2012).

Tripp, David, *Critical Incidents in Teaching: Developing Professional Judgement* (Psychology Press, 1993).

Tuckman, Bruce W., Developmental Sequence in Small Groups (*Psychological Bulletin*, 63, pp. 384–399, 1965).

Turner, James B. and Hill, Alison, Implementing Clinical Supervision (Part 1): A Review of the Literature (*Mental Health Nursing*, 3(3), pp. 8–12, 2011a).

Turner, James B. and Hill, Alison, Implementing Clinical Supervision, Part 2: Using Proctor's Model to Structure the Implementation of Clinical Supervision in a Ward Setting (*Mental Health Nursing*, 31(4), pp. 14–19, 2011b).

Turner, James B. and Hill, Alison, Implementing Clinical Supervision Part 3: An Evaluation of a Clinical Supervisor's Recovery-Based Resource and Support Package (*Mental Health Nursing*, 31(5), pp. 14–18, 2011c).

VIA Institute on Character Strengths. Website: https://www.viacharacter.org.

VIA Values in Action, Centre for Positive Psychology (Penn State https://www.authentichappiness.sas.upenn.edu).

Villeneuve, L., *L'encadrement du stage supervisé* (Éditions Saint-Martin, pp. 86–92, 1994).

Wallbank, Sonya, Effectiveness of Individual Clinical Supervision for Midwives and Doctors in Stress Reduction: Findings from a Pilot Study (*Evidence-Based Midwifery*, 11(8), pp. 28–34, 2010).

Wallbank, Sonya, Maintaining Professional Resilience Through Group Restorative Supervision (*Community Practice*, 86(8), pp. 26–28, 2013).

Wallbank, Sonya, *Restorative Resilience Through Supervision: An Organisational Training Manual for Health and Social Care Professionals* (Pavilion Publishing and Media Ltd, 2015).

Wallbank, Sonya, *The Restorative Resilience Model of Supervision: A Reader Exploring Resilience to Workplace Stress in Health and Social Care Professionals* (Pavilion Publishing, 2016).

Wallbank, Sonya and Hatton, S., Evaluation of Clinical Supervision delivered to Health Visitors and School Nurses (*Community Practitioner*, 84(7), pp. 21–25, 2011).

Wallbank, Sonya and Wonnacott, J., The Integrated Model of Restorative Supervision for Use Within Safeguarding (*Community Practice*, 88(5), pp. 41–45, 2015).

Webb, Caroline, *How to Have a Good Day: The Essential Toolkit for a Productive Day at Work and Beyond* (Pan; Main Market edition, 2017).

Weitzman, Elaine, *It Takes Two to Talk: A Practical Guide for Parents of Children with Language Delays* (Hanen Centre; 5th edition, 2017).

West, Michael A., *Compassionate Leadership: Sustaining Wisdom, Humanity and Presence in Health and Social Care* (The Swirling Leaf Press, 2021).

Wheeler, John, *Solution-Focused Supervision; Handbook of Solution-Focused Brief Therapy* (Routledge, pp. 357–384, 2012).

White-Davis, T., Stein, E. and Karasz, A., The Elephant in the Room: Dialogues about Race Within Cross-Cultural Supervisory Relationships (*International Journal of Psychiatry in Medicine*, 51, p. 347, 2016).

Wicks, Robert J. and Maynard, Elizabeth A. (eds.) *Clinician's Guide to Self-Renewal: Essential Advice from the Field* (Wiley, 2014).

Williamson, Kathleen, *The Model of Professional Practice* (RCSLT, 2001).

Williamson, Kathleen, *Competencies Project: Support Practitioner Framework* (RCSLT, 2002).

Wilmot, Joan, *Chapter 5, The Supervisory Relationship, A Lifelong Calling In: Shohet Robin, Passionate Supervision* (Jessica Kingsley Publishers; 1st edition, 2007).

Winstanley, J. and White, E., The MCSS-26: Revision of the Manchester Clinical Supervision Scale using the Rasch Measurement Model (*Journal of Nursing Measurement*, 19(3), pp. 160–178, 2011).

Winter, David, Personal Construct Psychology as a Way of Life (*Journal of Constructivist Psychology*, Special Section: The Life and Work of Fay Fransella, 26(1), pp. 3–8, 2013).

Winterbourne View Hospital: Department of Health Review and Response, *Final Report into the Events at Winterbourne View Hospital and a Programme of Action to Transform Services* (Department of Health and Social Care, December, 2012).

Woods, Susan, Patricia, Rockman, Patricia, Diane (Authors) Reibel, Diane (Foreword) Kabat-Zinn, Jon (Afterword) *Mindfulness-Based Stress Reduction: Protocol, Practice, and Teaching Skills* (New Harbinger, 2021).

Woolcomb Rachel, O. T., *Associate, Talking Mats; Using Talking Mats to provide a reflective thinking space within clinical supervision* (TMOT Resource 3 November, Talking Mats, 2019).

Wosket, Val and Page, Steve, *Supervising the Counsellor: A Cyclical Model* (Routledge; 2nd edition, 2001).

Woskett, Carole, Solution Focused Supervision, Healthcare Counselling and Psychotherapy Journal (*HCPJ*, 6(1), 2006). British Association for Counselling and Psychotherapy.

Wright, Jeannie and Griffiths, Frances, Reflective Practice at a Distance: Using Technology in Counselling Supervision (*Reflective Practice*, 11(5), pp. 693–703, November 2010).

Index

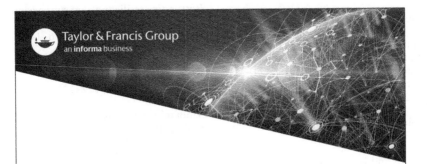

For Product Safety Concerns and Information please contact our EU
representative GPSR@taylorandfrancis.com Taylor & Francis Verlag GmbH,
Kaufingerstraße 24, 80331 München, Germany

Printed and bound by CPI Group (UK) Ltd, Croydon, CR0 4YY
08/06/2025
01897000-0014